*I was so pleased to hear this new book is being printed. It's predecessor, Making Every Day Count, was recommended to me some years ago as a way I could put something into the hands of people who were struggling to find their way into the Bible or looking for an anchor in their morning prayer. It became a much-loved bridge which really helped people to grow in their prayer life and come closer to the Lord and it is a joy to be able to pass on **Every Day Matters** to another new reader, knowing it will do just that.*

Toni Pomfret | Goodnews Books

• • • • • • • • • • • • • • • •

As part of my daily prayer time I always read a Bible reflection, and over the years I have appreciated the spiritual insights of a variety of well-known writers.

Recently "Making Every Day Count" by John Ryeland has become my daily favourite, so I am delighted that he has now produced this new edition with fresh reflections.

John has a real gift for bringing the Scriptures alive, making them relevant to everyday life, and so I have no hesitation in strongly recommending this excellent new book. I know it will be a great blessing to all who read it.

Charles Whitehead
Past President of The International Catholic Charismatic Renewal Council

• • • • • • • • • • • • • • • •

I find the daily devotions that John has written to be most uplifting. Uplifting, because they draw me to the heart of Jesus, my essential lifeline for daily living. I can be concerned about various things in my life but these writings bring me back to be filled up with the love of God and to love Him more.

Not only that, I find these writings a perfect springboard for the meditations I am presenting for a women's prison group and Teen Challenge group. These are women who desperately need to know how much God loves them and how He can transform them, bringing them hope for their life ahead. The illustrations, based on scripture, are a simple, yet deep way to share God's unconditional love. They are truly refreshing and bring a truth that we can ponder on throughout the day that helps us to abide in Jesus.

Annie McRae | Malibu, USA

EVERY DAY MATTERS

Daily reflections on living as a child of God

by

John Ryeland

Introduction

John Ryeland

Some years ago, I was on a retreat and went for a long walk. I wasn't particularly aware of my surroundings until I was suddenly brought up short by an extremely pungent aroma. Looking round, I soon discovered the source: a field of pigs who were blissfully rolling on the ground, releasing their unique odour! As I stood and watched them, a thought dropped into my mind, 'John, you are just like a pig! You smell of what you roll in!'

I don't remember much about my walk back to the retreat house as I was mulling over the various things I 'roll in' and what smell they might produce! It occurred to me that if I roll in negativity and condemnation, the result is bound to be an extremely unpleasant smell, whereas wallowing in the wonder of God's love is certain to release a beautiful fragrance.

This book is an opportunity for us all to roll in something wonderful – God's love – and to benefit from its effect on us and the people around us.

My first book of daily thoughts was entitled **Making Every Day Count** and I have been very touched by the numerous letters, emails and comments about what it means to so many people and how God has used it to change lives. When the final copy was sold, rather than reprint the original I decided to produce a new book, and I find myself amazed to be writing an introduction to this second collection of my daily thoughts.

At this point, having referred to the book as a collection of 'my daily thoughts', a confession is called for! Although it bears my name, this book is the result of many hours of collaboration from several people. I am amazed at the difference between my original writing and the polished script that appears before you now! For this I must thank two people, Gillian (my wife) and Susannah Steel (a brilliant editor and valued friend of CHM), both of whom have encouraged, amended and given an effective re-spray to a rather tatty first draft.

Liz Nicoll, CHM's wonderfully gifted artistic designer, also deserves a special mention. In addition to designing this attractive book, she has spent hours searching for just the right colour photograph to enhance each entry and I am extremely grateful to her. My final vote of thanks is to Sarah Swift, for being a wonderful colleague and for proof reading the manuscript.

I offer you this book of daily readings as a means of turning your thoughts to God, especially his immense love for you. 'Roll' in him, make every day count and live every day with God because every day matters.

Starting again

'... for his compassions never fail. They are new every morning'

Lamentations 3.22-23

A New Year provides us with a real sense of being able to start again. I wonder what part of your life you would love to start afresh? Perhaps you feel that the best option would be to erase parts of last year entirely and start with a completely clean sheet? We cannot, of course, alter the facts of what has happened by undoing the actual events in our lives, but we can change their effects upon us; to change the guilt and hurt that so often blights our memories of past events. This begins with starting each day afresh, just as this verse suggests.

All too often, when we begin to pray, we rush straight into a list of what we want God to do for us, or else we begin with a confession of all we have done wrong. It is far better to start with a renewed sense of God's love for us.

Begin your time with God today by recalling that he loves you and he does not wish you were anyone else! He loves you to the extent that he gave Jesus for you so that you might have wonderful access to him and know that you are forgiven. This is a great way to begin every day of this year – with your focus firmly on God and his love.

Take a moment to do this right now. God has expressed the depth of his love for you by giving Jesus, so acknowledge that you are uniquely loved by him. What a perfect way of starting this New Year!

God reigns

'The Lord reigns'

Psalm 97.1

These words are so easy to say when things are going well, but at times when events are confusing or going badly it is tempting to think that God has been distracted or is uncaring. However, the truth is that whatever is happening – good or bad – these three words ring out: 'The Lord reigns'!

This is where faith really kicks in – the ability to speak these words with conviction even when circumstances are shouting the opposite. It is faith that is able to trust that God's reigning hand is still present, even when it cannot be seen.

One means of growing in this is simply to proclaim it. If there is an area in your life that is causing you bewilderment, focus on it and proclaim these three words over that situation, 'The Lord reigns'. This is not a prayer that God will start reigning over it and bring change, but rather an acknowledgement that he is already reigning over it – and it may be that your proclamation of his reign opens the door for change or enables you to see his hand at work when previously you could only see darkness.

'The Lord reigns' over the things in your life, so start proclaiming this now and see what difference it makes to the year ahead.

2

God has seen it all!

'... you are from all eternity.'

Psalm 93.2

If God is from all eternity, then he really must have seen it all: every struggle that has beset each person in the world, the frustration and the doubts, as well as their every prayer and cry. This does put things into perspective! You are not the only person who has ever lived or struggled with the issues that you face today. Throughout all ages, people have lifted up the very same situations to God and have found him to be faithful, compassionate and loving.

This is one of the reasons the Bible is such a gift to us. Not only is it a revelation of God's love revealed through Jesus, but it is also the story of human struggles in life. There are accounts of temptation, doubt, failure, repentance and restoration – stories of ordinary people dealing with life against the backdrop of the wonder, love and faithfulness of God. It is about individuals reaching up to find the reality of God's love and the change it makes to them.

This is your story too – or at least it could be if you want it to be. This thread of God's love and compassion continues to run through each day, including today, and his invitation is for you to reach up and take hold of it. Spend a moment right now grasping the truth that God has been there for all eternity – so he will certainly be there for you today!

Making connections

'. . . they had not understood about the loaves; their hearts were hardened.'

Mark 6.52

I wonder how many things God does for us that we simply overlook, ignore or fail to recognise their significance? This is exactly what happened to the disciples. They had just witnessed an amazing miracle – the feeding of the 5,000 but failed to recognise its significance and the fact that it had implications for other aspects of their lives.

It wasn't that they were doing anything wrong, but rather that they were not making the right connections, and 'their hearts were hardened' so that what they had just experienced didn't touch them. Clearly this was not good! Similarly, we need to learn to make connections, to recognise what God is doing in our lives and learn from it.

As you look back over the past 24 hours, call to mind one thing that was undeniably the touch of God. Give him thanks for it and then think about the implications of what he did? In other words, what does God's action say to you about his love, how you can trust him and what you can expect of him today?

God saves

'Lord, you are the God who saves me; day and night I cry out to you.'

Psalm 88.1

At the very heart of our faith is the notion that God saves us – indeed the very name 'Jesus' means 'God saves'. The word 'salvation' refers to our eternal destiny, but also to the rescue God can bring to us in this life.

This is probably not a new concept for those of us who put our faith in God, but it is amazing how many other things we look to for help and rescue. There may be nothing wrong in this since it is often through some of these that God brings his help and rescue to us, but it is all too easy to forget that he is behind the varied ways in which we may receive help.

Many of us look to our family and friends to sustain and support us, but it is so easy to forget that they are his kind provision for us. We should certainly not stop receiving love from those around us, but God invites us to see beyond their love and recognise him as the ultimate source of love.

Take a moment to ponder the past day and the ways in which you received care and help from others. Give God thanks for those moments, for the people involved, and for the way in which his heart was revealed by them.

Complex planning (Epiphany)

"We saw his star when it rose and have come to worship him."

Matthew 2.2

Today is the feast of the Epiphany when we are encouraged to reflect on the visit of the wise men to the infant Jesus. Sometimes this can seem a bit odd, like going back to Christmas when the decorations have all come down, but there is something special about this festival.

As we read in the story, a star led the wise men to Jesus. Presumably this involved some planning on God's part! Was this star specially created and if so, when? The light from the star may have taken some considerable time to reach the earth. It also needed to guide men across many miles to a specific village. We are not told of anyone else benefiting from this event – so was it all laid on so that those wise men could find Jesus?

Actually, this is the effort God has gone to for each of us. In Acts 17.27 we read that Paul was preaching in Athens and told the people that God had decreed the times and places where we would live so that we "would seek him and perhaps reach out for him and find him".

In other words, God has gone to immense trouble for you. Think back over your life and recognise the people and events that God has used to bring you to a deeper knowledge of himself. Why all the effort? The answer is quite simply because it matters so much to him that you enjoy a relationship with him; he wants you so much that he has gone to great lengths to lay markers in your life so that you might find him. It's all because you are worth it.

You may like to take a moment to make this personal – look at a cross and say to yourself: "I am worth the death of Jesus."

6

Using our gifts

'All these are the work of one and the same Spirit, and he distributes them to each one, just as he determines.'

1 Corinthians 12.11

Admitting that we have a gift from God can sound very boastful! We tend to shrug it off and think that we are nothing special. Yet it really is OK to recognise that we have a gift – after all, we haven't earned it. It is something God has chosen to give to us just because he wants to, and has nothing to do with whether or not we are good enough. If you think about it like this, it is quite humbling to admit to having a gift from God because it means we could not achieve what we do without it.

So once we have admitted to having a gift, we have the potential of using it for God's glory. It's easy to spend a long time quibbling about whether we have a particular gift from God or if it is simply something that we would do naturally, but however we feel about this, what we have should be a blessing to others. The reason God has given us gifts is not for us to admire his handiwork in us, but for the benefit of others.

You may like to use this simple prayer: "Father, thank you for making me who I am. Let me be a blessing to the people I come across today."

Learning to worship

'Blessed are those who have learned to acclaim you'

Psalm 89.15

There are times when worship comes easily to us – and other times when it is harder. However, this verse is interesting because it suggests that we can learn to acclaim – or worship – God. We feel that worshipping God ought to be totally natural for us, and yet so often it isn't.

Maybe we all need to learn how to worship better. This isn't so much about studying or being taught, but more about practising. As with practising anything, it can seem unnatural to begin with but over the course of time it becomes more familiar. Here are a few suggestions about how you might like to practise worshipping:

- Look back at recent events and worship God for the moments when you can recognise him at work.

- Set your alarm so that you remember to speak a sentence of worship to God every hour.

- Take one of the many titles given to Jesus – Lord, Saviour, Light of the World, Prince of Peace – and use it as the basis for two or three minutes of worship at the beginning of your prayer time.

- Go for a walk and worship God for his creation around you.

- Look out of the window at the passers-by and worship God for making every one of us unique.

Choose one of these and begin to practise worshipping now.

8

You matter

'Now if the foot should say, "Because I am not a hand, I do not belong to the body," it would not for that reason stop being part of the body.'

1 Corinthians 12.15

You matter – even if you do not think you do! The reason most of us doubt our self-worth is because we spend time looking at other people and appreciating their obvious gifts, and because our focus is on them we fail to pay attention to our own gifts.

This is why Paul's analogy of all of us being part of a body is so helpful – we are different from one another. Other people may well be able to do things we cannot do, but rather than rejoice in this, we tend to regard ourselves as inadequate and often useless.

If you find yourself thinking like this, sit down and make a list of the things that you can do well, the ways you are a blessing to others. When you read through your list, you will probably conclude that everyone else also does these things, but if you are honest you will admit that this isn't true. Not everyone does them, nor do they have the inclination or the heart to do so – but you do! This is how God has made you. You are a gift to others, and you matter.

You have crossed over

"Very truly I tell you, whoever hears my word and believes him who sent me has eternal life and will not be judged but has crossed over from death to life."

John 5.24

Crossing over from death to life sounds dramatic! When we hear people sharing their experiences of God and note the faith that seems to flow from them, it can be easy to conclude that they live a different life now. They have truly passed from death to life. However, is this true of you? What if you have never had a similar experience?

The criterion for crossing from "death to life" has nothing to do with any experiences, but rather is this: have you heard Jesus speaking to you and do you believe he was sent by the Father for you? Your answer is probably 'Yes . . . but!' Most of us do believe, but we also waver from time to time and it is easy to think that because we waver we may not qualify for eternal life.

It is interesting to note the language Jesus used: we have 'crossed over'. It is not that we are straddling a borderline wavering between two possibilities, but we have actually crossed over; the change has been made.

This implies that when you face anxious situations or are uncertain of God's presence within you – in other words, when your feelings are attacking your faith – you can come back to the truth with these words: 'I have crossed from death to life'. They are a reminder of who is there for you and what resources are available.

10

Faith and signs

'The Pharisees came and began to question Jesus. To test him, they asked him for a sign from heaven.'

Mark 8.11

In one sense, the Pharisees' request was not unreasonable. They wanted to know if Jesus was really who he said he was, and a clear sign from heaven would certainly allay their doubts. The problem, however, is that it was unlikely that any sign would have satisfied them. We read that their conversation with Jesus occurred immediately after the feeding of the 4,000 – an amazing event that was clearly out of the ordinary. Word of this would no doubt have spread far and wide, including reaching the ears of the Pharisees, and yet they still wanted more proof.

We often hear of people saying how much they want a sign from God, and maybe you have made a similar request yourself. It might have been phrased differently, maybe along the lines of: "How do I know that you love me?" It is still asking God for proof. In the end a decision to believe is needed, whether or not there is any proof.

Such a step of faith is highly valued by Jesus. After the resurrection, he met with Thomas and said, ". . . blessed are those who have not seen and yet have believed." (John 20.29). Ultimately, our choice to have faith is far more important than seeking for signs.

In John 11.27, Martha makes a stunning confession of faith: "I believe that you are the Messiah, the Son of God, who is to come into the world." Make her words your own and use them as a statement of worship.

Bringing things into the light

'You have set our iniquities before you, our secret sins in the light of your presence.'

Psalm 90.8

The power of forgiveness is awesome; it is almost unbelievable that the things we have done wrong can be totally and permanently removed from our record – but there is a catch! We have to bring our sins to God.

It's possible that we don't take our sin as seriously as God does. We try to hide it away, pretend things never happened or take the view that other people's failings are worse than our own. Yet God's desire is that we bring our sin to him. If we make a conscious decision to do this, the power of his forgiveness flows and our sin is removed from us.

However, if we pretend that it doesn't exist and keep it hidden, God can still see it clearly. It may even be that he doesn't judge sin by its severity, but according to whether or not it has been brought into the light of his presence.

Take a moment to ask the Holy Spirit to help you bring to God anything that is hidden. Ask him to show you if you are hiding something and ask for the grace to bring it into the wonder of his glorious light.

Blessing our work

'May the favour of the Lord our God rest on us; establish the work of our hands for us — yes, establish the work of our hands.'

Psalm 90.17

The author of this psalm is asking God to lay his hand on the things we have done and turn our actions into fruitful blessings.

Much of the time we are not aware of what we are doing for God. We go through life making an effort to lead decent lives and be a help and blessing to other people where we can, but often we are unsure if it's making any real difference. The prayer in this psalm is a real encouragement to us: '. . . establish the work of our hands'; or as another translation puts it, 'make our endeavours successful' (NET Bible).

Think back over the past 24 hours and call to mind the things you did for others – large or small. Invite God to touch your activities and bring them to fruition, so that something of him will be in them and your activities will actually have been his actions.

Dwelling and resting

'Whoever dwells in the shelter of the Most High will rest in the shadow of the Almighty.'

Psalm 91.1

In this verse, the concepts of 'dwelling' and 'resting' are wonderfully linked. If you **dwell** in the presence of God, then you will **rest** in his shadow. There is something about the word 'resting' that is so appealing; it implies an ability to find a completely different way of living within the normal stresses and strains of life. Strain may still be present, but it shouldn't dominate everything else. The way to find God's rest is to dwell in him, but how can we do this?

It is worth noting another key word in today's verse – 'whoever'. This assurance is for everyone, not just for one or two chosen people who have learned the secret of union with God. It really is possible for us to dwell in him. God's presence is your home and every time you want to come back to this reality, you can. It is simply a matter of calling to mind the awesome fact that Jesus is always with you because you dwell so closely with him.

Whispering his name at any point of the day or night is a means of returning to the truth that you and Jesus dwell together. Try doing this right now and rest in the wonderful truth that he is with you.

14

God our refuge

'I will say of the Lord, "He is my refuge and my fortress, my God, in whom I trust."'

Psalm 91.2

We would all love to have this sort of walk with God, and be able to say with confidence that he is our refuge and fortress. The truth is that we can! The author of this verse is not laying out some distant dream for the future, but is stating what is present and real right now: the Lord is our refuge and our fortress.

This means that you have immediate access to God as your refuge. Whenever you feel in need you can approach him, knowing that he will not turn you away. It is simply a matter of consciously turning to God for help. It sounds so easy, but turning away from our need and formulating a conscious prayer can be something we forget to do rather more than we would like to admit!

"Father, help me!" is not just a prayer, but also a recognition that the Lord is your refuge, and you are indeed turning to him. Let these words become yours now.

Try doing this. . .

'. . . proclaiming your love in the morning and your faithfulness at night'

Psalm 92.2

These words set out a beautiful and simple pattern for prayer, one that builds faith and thanksgiving, as well as increasing an awareness of the presence of God.

At the beginning of the day, focus afresh on the wonder of God's love for us. His love is always present, but if we spend time proclaiming it – despite how we might be feeling – then it gives us solid ground on which to stand firm in the day ahead.

Then, at the end of the day, look back and try to pinpoint those moments when you can see God has been at work. The truth is that he has been at work constantly in every part of our lives, but to recognise his hand in specific areas is to begin to open our eyes to seeing him at work everywhere.

This pattern of prayer might seem obvious, but there is a discipline in actually taking hold of these two great truths and sowing them more deeply into our lives. Whatever time of day it is with you now, pause to proclaim to yourself either God's love or his faithfulness – or both!

16

Thinking like God

'Then he called the crowd to him along with his disciples and said: "Whoever wants to be my disciple must deny themselves and take up their cross and follow me."'

Mark 8.34

This call to discipleship is deeply challenging: it is a call to live totally for Jesus and not for ourselves. Our actions play a large part in following him, but so too does our thinking. As followers of Jesus, we are to deny thinking about ourselves in ways that differ from how Jesus thinks of us.

Every time we allow ourselves to consider the possibility that we are unloved, or that somehow the promises of God do not apply to us, we are filling our minds with thoughts that are not

of God. We are called to follow him and this includes accepting his thinking.

So what are God's thoughts about us? Psalm 139.17 says, 'How amazing are your thoughts concerning me, God! How vast is the sum of them!'

God's thoughts about each of us are numerous and precious, and to follow him is to accept that we are 'fearfully and wonderfully made' and loved beyond measure. Capture this thought for yourself now.

Knowing forgiveness

'He forgave us all our sins'

Colossians 2.13

As Christians, forgiveness is a familiar concept and features in so many talks, songs and services. What is less familiar for us is the ability to apply it to ourselves. Paul states the truth very bluntly when he says: 'He forgave us all our sins.' In other words, Jesus took from us every sin we ever committed and he paid the price for it forever, so that never again can any of our thoughts, actions or attitudes be held against us or appear on our record.

This is quite something to get our heads around! So many people suspect that God still sees them through the veil of their sins, so that whenever he looks at them he also sees their sins. Paul states that this is simply not true. When we bring our sins to God, it is like opening the door of a dark room so that the light can shine into it; when the light shines, the darkness is gone. This is how we are encouraged to see our lives.

It is us who are so frequently aware of our sins. Then we often get into the habit of looking at others and noting their sins, even though God does not see them at all. Forgiveness is total, eternal, wonderful and promised by God – so let's stand in the light of it.

Keeping alive our vision of God

'... the Lord is robed in majesty and armed with strength'

Psalm 93.1

What is your vision of God for today? Is it like this description – 'robed in majesty'?

You may have been praying for someone for quite a while and nothing seems to be changing, or perhaps there are situations in your life where you really cannot see God working at all. If so, the temptation is to allow these disappointments to affect your vision of God so that you begin to think of him as somewhat ineffectual rather than 'armed with strength'.

Throughout the Bible there are visions of God, varying from descriptions of the throne of God (Revelation 4 and Isaiah 6) to visions such as in today's verse – 'robed in majesty and armed with strength'. These visions are given precisely because we need them! They are not provided as a reminder of how wonderful it is when things are going well, but to encourage us when times are hard.

So if you find yourself questioning just how much strength God really has, try turning to the Bible and reading one of these visions. As you focus on him seated on his throne above all things, rediscover the truth of God's power and majesty as you begin to pray.

Letting God change your heart

'As Saul turned to leave Samuel, God changed Saul's heart'

1 Samuel 10.9

The context of this verse was that Samuel had just told Saul that he would become king. Naturally, there was some reticence on the part of Saul – this was not in the least what he was expecting, nor had he any natural qualification to undertake the role. It would be perfectly possible to see how the story might have ended right here with Saul 'running a mile' to get away from what was being offered to him. However, at this point God intervened and touched Saul's heart so that he felt able to step into the new role to which God was calling him.

This message is also relevant for us. We are unlikely to be called to the high level of leadership to which Saul was called, but we are all called to believe in what may seem unbelievable: that the Lord God of heaven and earth loves us personally, chose us before the very foundation of the world and has called us to live in close fellowship with him. On a human level these things are hard to grasp and believe, but it may be that we need to take the simple step of asking God to change our hearts; to touch us with his supernatural power so that we are able to believe the unbelievable and walk an amazing path with him.

Take this prayer and repeat it a few times so that it settles deep within you: "Father, open my heart to the depth of your love for me."

Compassion and comfort | 1

'Praise be to the God and Father of our Lord Jesus Christ, the Father of compassion and the God of all comfort'

2 Corinthians 1.3

What an amazing description! This verse really does set out what we can expect of God whenever we approach him, and it warrants taking a few minutes to really grasp this description of him.

The words, 'Father of compassion and the God of all comfort', are enough to dispel any doubts we might have about whether God is really there for us and we need to take them seriously. They make an effective prayer for us to repeat throughout the day whenever we need his help. He is the source of compassion and comfort to the world and longs to bring these to us, no matter what we are facing.

At times you might feel anxious about drawing close to God, but these words are such an encouragement. Turn to him and using these words, ask him to bring to you what is actually his very character – compassion and comfort.

Comforting others | 2

'... who comforts us in all our troubles, so that we can comfort those in any trouble with the comfort we ourselves receive from God.'

2 Corinthians 1.4

At times we might wonder if we are really of much use as we seem to go through life without helping others much. What have we possibly got to give to other people? This powerful verse assures us that every one of us can bring to others what God has given to us.

Take a moment to consider how God has given you comfort or brought help to you. You might be able to remember specific instances of his provision or his healing hand upon you. Perhaps his comfort seemed more like a guiding hand through a storm than relief from the elements, or maybe it was the presence of a friend simply being with

you when there didn't seem to be much light or comfort. This is what God has done for you – and this is what you can pass on to others. Your presence alongside a person in need may make all the difference as they walk through a difficult time, or your story, told with conviction and gentleness, may be exactly what they need to hear to encourage them.

What God has given you is a real gift, so allow it to be a gift to others as well. Think about the day ahead of you; what can you offer to the people you will encounter over these coming hours?

Taking God's presence seriously

'... there was Dagon, fallen on his face on the ground before the ark of the Lord! His head and hands had been broken off and were lying on the threshold'

1 Samuel 5.4

The Philistines had captured the ark of the Lord – a holy symbol of God's presence. They placed it in their own temple and the next morning were greeted by the sight of the statue of their god, Dagon, broken in pieces and lying before the ark. This picture is a reminder of the sheer power of the presence of the Lord and how seriously we should take it.

We have no ark nowadays, but we do have something equally awesome – ourselves. The Bible speaks about us being living temples of the Holy Spirit (1 Corinthians 6.19). We are now the living places where the presence of God dwells. When the Philistines carried the ark into their temple, presumably they felt nothing of its awesome power or else they would not have been able to touch it. Only later were they made aware of this. Similarly, the fact that you may not 'feel' the Lord's presence does not negate his awesome power within you.

Spend a few moments reflecting on the phrase, 'I am a temple of the Holy Spirit.' Let the truth of this sink in so that you can find a new awareness of the nearness and wonder of the majesty of God.

Growing our faith

'For no matter how many promises God has made, they are "Yes" in Christ.'

2 Corinthians 1.20

The Bible is full of promises – and so many of them seem too good to be true! They offer things that are often beyond our experience and, if we are honest, beyond our dreams. So this message from Paul is extraordinary. He was stating that although the promises of God may seem unbelievable and out of reach, the life, death and resurrection of Jesus has changed all of this. Jesus has made all the promises real.

How does this work? This is the bit Paul doesn't explain, perhaps on purpose to encourage us to engage with it ourselves! Why not start with your own needs? If you are sick or in some other need, begin by identifying some of God's promises that seem to be applicable to your situation, and maybe write them down.

Then consider how the life, death and resurrection of Jesus illustrate how these promises apply to your need. You might, for example, want to consider some of the accounts of Jesus healing the sick and think about how these stories speak to you in your need. How would you want to shape your prayers in the light of these stories?

It is so easy to blame ourselves for a lack of faith. However, perhaps by pausing, pondering and applying the ministry of Jesus to our own situations, we can catch the heart of the man who said to Jesus in Mark 9.24, "I do believe; help me overcome my unbelief!" Let his words become your words too.

24

Changing attitudes

'Jesus looked at them and said, "With man this is impossible, but not with God; all things are possible with God."'

Mark 10.27

Jesus was talking about how hard it is for us to change our attitudes. The context of this verse is the story of a rich man who came to Jesus and, after talking to him, realised there was a tension between his attitudes and the call of Jesus. A sense of sadness is tangible in the story. The disciples, quite naturally, asked a question along the lines of, "What hope is there for anyone then?" Jesus' reply was far reaching and gentle: ". . . all things are possible with God."

As we think about life, it is tempting to think that we ought to do more repenting, surrendering and giving. However, such thinking is actually putting much of the focus upon ourselves.

Jesus says it is not about us and what we can hope to achieve, but it is all about the transforming activity of God.

There may be aspects of our lives that we wish we could change, but try as we might we can't achieve this on our own. Change really begins when we come before the one who utterly loves us and admit that we cannot change ourselves and that we need him to bring that transformation. This is when God's grace begins to work in us – and change happens.

What would you like to bring to God right now? Place it in his hands and ask him to bring transformation.

Being rewarded

"Truly I tell you," Jesus replied, *"no one who has left home or brothers or sisters or mother or father or children or fields for me and the gospel will fail to receive a hundred times as much in this present age: homes, brothers, sisters, mothers, children and fields – along with persecutions – and in the age to come eternal life.*

Mark 10.29-30

Jesus said that suffering for our faith would occur. This can happen in a variety of ways: outright hostility, misunderstanding, snide jokes, temptations or a struggle to turn away from something we know does not bless the Lord. Whatever form our suffering takes, this verse reassures us that God sees it. What's more, every time we take a stand for him something good is stored up for us. The way Jesus puts it is in terms of reward; that what we give up, we get back.

This is an amazing concept. Every time we choose not to bite back at something someone says, or choose to forgive, we might feel very little but the truth is that something wonderful is put into us, so that the kingdom of God grows within and around us.

You may sometimes be tempted to think of God watching your every move, just waiting for you to trip up and do wrong. Instead, the reality is that he is watching you, looking at every good thing that flows from you, and rejoicing over you. Remember this as you go about your day.

Carrying Christ everywhere | 1

'But thanks be to God, who always leads us as captives in Christ's triumphal procession and uses us to spread the aroma of the knowledge of him everywhere.'

2 Corinthians 2.14

Perhaps the most surprising word in this extraordinary verse is the word 'everywhere'. We have no problem believing that some people carry the aroma of knowing Jesus – those who seem to be 'model' Christians. However, Paul was not just talking about 'other Christians'; he was talking about all Christians, and this means that he was talking about us.

Since Jesus is in us, it follows that wherever we go we carry something of him with us. This is a fundamental truth of our faith. We do not pick and choose when to carry Jesus and the aroma that comes from knowing him – he is with us all the time, so everywhere we go he goes too.

Becoming conscious of this can make all the difference. Imagine if there were times when we felt the presence of God coursing through our veins, or something like a hum of electricity buzzing through us. At these moments it would be natural to wonder what we might bring to the situations in which we find ourselves. Yet the truth is that whether or not we feel the 'hum', we still carry Jesus with us everywhere.

Take a moment to think about the situations you face today, and decide what touches of Jesus you will bring to them.

Pungent or perfume? | 2

'For we are to God the pleasing aroma of Christ'

2 Corinthians 2.15

We have already looked at how we carry the aroma of the knowledge of Jesus to the world, and this verse takes it a step further by saying that we carry it to the Father as well.

Smell is a very evocative sense, taking us right back to a distant memory or even alerting us to danger regardless of whether any risk is visible. This verse says that God smells us! What's more, we smell pleasing to him because we give off the scent of Jesus.

We might have a problem with this! Don't we sometimes smell a bit rotten to God? The Bible says that God remembers our sins no more (Hebrews 8.12); when Jesus took them away he utterly removed the smell of them from us. So when God draws close and breathes the air around us, he simply smells the beautiful aroma of Jesus.

As you draw close to God now, focus on this incredible truth: he does not see your sins, but looks at you with wonder and joy as he catches the scent of Jesus. Hold on to this picture of Father God for a few moments – picture it literally if you can – and enjoy his pleasure in you.

The perfect weapon

'The weapons we fight with are not the weapons of the world.'

2 Corinthians 10.4

We so easily forget what is clearly stated here: we have at our disposal far more resources than people with no Christian faith. Our challenge is to use them.

Often, we find ourselves trying to overcome temptation and difficulties by sheer willpower, attempting to adopt a mental attitude we hope will bring about change. Paul is not saying this is wrong, but that there is so much more for us, something totally other-worldly: it is the presence of the risen Christ within us. How can we access his presence, this 'weapon'?

As with all weaponry, we must practise using it before there is a real need. A trained soldier does not fire a gun for the first time in conflict; he spends many hours practising before he begins to fight. Similarly, we need to 'practise' the presence of Jesus with us before we find ourselves in challenging situations.

Make a point of whispering the name 'Jesus' every day. You are not speaking to someone far off, but rather to Jesus, who is always so close to you. Practise the truth of his presence, starting now, and you will find it easier to recall his closeness when you need him through the day.

Praying and loving through Jesus

'For God did not appoint us to suffer wrath but to receive salvation through our Lord Jesus Christ.'

1 Thessalonians 5.9

We might be tempted to gloss over the last five words of this verse, but they are actually the key to so much in our Christian lives: 'through our Lord Jesus Christ.'

It's easy to focus on all the effort we put into co-operating with what God is doing, such as prayer or showing practical love to others, but it makes a massive difference if we can stop regarding these as activities that we do to find favour with God and instead engage with them because God loves us. If the motive behind our prayers is a suspicion that God will not bless us unless we spend time with him, then our prayer times are likely to be far from joyful. Instead, if our prayer begins with a fresh look at the one who loves us so much, it will hopefully be far more enjoyable and enriching.

This is one aspect of what it means to pray 'through our Lord Jesus Christ'. We choose to pray because of what Jesus has done and what he has freely given to us. Similarly, if we seek to bless and love others out of duty, we will soon be resentful of the demands made upon us, but if every act of kindness is undertaken as a reflection of the enormous love God has for us, then we will respond with different motives and different hearts.

Through his life and death Jesus has given us everything – and he is not going to take it back! Reflect on this and allow it to bring you peace.

New every morning

'Sing to the Lord a new song, for he has done marvellous things'

Psalm 98.1

When we pray, it is easy to get into particular habits! This may not be bad in itself as a certain rhythm in prayer can sustain us as we seek to develop a regular pattern and discipline of prayer in our lives. However, the danger is that we fall into a dull and lifeless pattern, simply praying for the same things in the same old way that we have always done.

We find sensible advice in the words of this psalm: 'Sing to the Lord a new song.' In other words, let's not treat prayer like superstition, fearing that if we don't do it in a certain way then our prayers won't be heard. Instead let's come afresh to God each day, doing or saying something different because '. . . his compassions never fail. They are new every morning' (Lamentations 3.22-23). Every day there is a freshness about the love of God, and a new joy in his heart as he sees us turning to him.

As you spend time with God today – and it is a new day, a different day from yesterday – why not try approaching him in a fresh way?

Being served by Jesus

'For even the Son of Man did not come to be served, but to serve, and to give his life as a ransom for many.'

Mark 10.45

How do you understand the phrase that Jesus came to serve? It might bring to mind something like the image of Jesus washing his disciples' feet. However, it goes deeper than this.

Jesus' service spans the whole of his ministry among us. The very next story after these words from Mark were spoken is about Jesus restoring the sight of blind Bartimaeus – this was Jesus' service to him. We often think that the point of Jesus' ministry is either to reveal his divinity or to offer acts of love to broken people, yet it is also about his acts of service to us.

It might seem hard to ask Jesus to serve you by meeting your needs, but you can be encouraged that graceful service is what he came to do. You may not deserve his kindness or service, but you can still stand before him with your arms open wide in gratitude for who he is, and in the expectation that his mission has not changed.

As you come to Jesus today, what will you bring to him? How will you let him serve you and how does this feel?

The friendship of Jesus

"Zacchaeus, come down immediately. I must stay at your house today."

Luke 19.5

The story of Zacchaeus is one of the most dramatic stories of transformation in the Bible. It is never listed as one of the healing stories, but perhaps it should be since it is a beautiful story of a man's heart being transformed into something wonderful for God.

We all know the story of the short man who climbed up a tree to see Jesus. He was a detested tax-collector, yet by the end of the story we see a man paying back those he had treated unfairly and his former meanness replaced by abundant generosity. Perhaps the most amazing thing about this story is that Jesus did not say one word of reproach to him. Instead he offered him love and fellowship; Jesus wanted to be with him. It is this simple fact that changed Zacchaeus.

There are occasions when we read of Jesus eating with sinners. If all he did was to tell them how sinful they were, I doubt he would have been invited back again. Instead, he simply enjoyed their company. Jesus also wants to enjoy your company today. In fact he wants to be with you right now, and not only when you have improved a little – or a lot! He loves you now for who you are and does not wish you were anyone else. His longing is for you to spend time with him.

Being glad before the Lord

'Worship the Lord with gladness; come before him with joyful songs.'

Psalm 100.2

Who is this verse addressing? Perhaps it's not those who feel full of peace, happiness and wellbeing, as they would hardly need guidance on how to worship with gladness and joy! Perhaps the people the psalmist is really addressing are those who feel very little in the way of gladness and who would rather sing a dirge than a song of joy!

Obedience becomes much harder when we are called to do something we really don't feel like doing – and joyful worship is often like this. At such times, God gives us a gift – joyful songs. When you feel less than joyful, choose a joyful song and sing it to yourself, and allow it to impact you. Catch what it says, recognise the truths that have inspired the song and let them touch your heart.

Try it now! Call to mind a song or hymn of joy and let it move you from where you are to where God wants you to be.

34

Coming into God's presence

'Enter his gates with thanksgiving and his courts with praise; give thanks to him and praise his name.'

Psalm 100.4

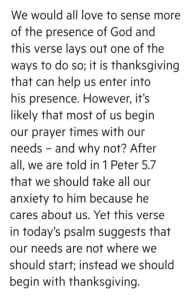

We would all love to sense more of the presence of God and this verse lays out one of the ways to do so; it is thanksgiving that can help us enter into his presence. However, it's likely that most of us begin our prayer times with our needs – and why not? After all, we are told in 1 Peter 5.7 that we should take all our anxiety to him because he cares about us. Yet this verse in today's psalm suggests that our needs are not where we should start; instead we should begin with thanksgiving.

As the verse goes on we learn more about this thanksgiving – it involves praising God's name. Praising the name of God is about giving honour to all that the Bible reveals about him. He is our 'Abba, Father', the God of all comfort, gracious and compassionate and the revelation of God in Jesus. Dwelling upon these truths is a good place for prayer to begin.

If you begin your prayers by simply bringing your needs to him, then they will be the focus of your prayer time. However, if you begin by looking at God, your vision of him will grow and you will step into the presence of the God you are praising and proclaiming. So consciously take your eyes off your concerns and spend a few moments focusing on God – your Provider, Shepherd and Healer.

Keeping grace alive | 1

'As God's fellow-workers we urge you not to receive God's grace in vain.'

2 Corinthians 6.1

Paul's plea here is desperate. He speaks as a fellow-worker of God, implying that he is not speaking on his own behalf but is sharing something that is on God's heart as well. He is urging us to take God's grace seriously – the undeserved love and power of God that we can never earn.

The New Living Translation puts it like this: 'We beg you not to accept this marvellous gift of God's kindness and then ignore it.' Yet so often we do just this. We give our lives to Christ with a real awareness of the enormity of what he has done for us, and then quite quickly slip into a sense that we have to earn his love and work for his continued favour.

Today, God longs to pour out upon you his undeserved love and power. Hebrews 4.16 gives us a glorious sense of us standing before the throne of grace, from where grace and mercy flow.

A prayer I have come to value is this: "Lord Jesus Christ, your grace and mercy flow." Try repeating these words for a couple of minutes now, and in doing so let them sink deeper within you so that you can recall them at every point of your day.

What's significant about today? | 2

'For he says, "In the time of my favour I heard you, and in the day of salvation I helped you." I tell you, now is the time of God's favour, now is the day of salvation.'

2 Corinthians 6.2

Paul had just been talking about how important it is not to ignore the grace of God. He underlines this point with a direct challenge to us to take seriously the concept that God's actions are for today.

It can be comforting to know that no matter what happens today, there is always tomorrow, but sometimes this can dampen our expectation of what God might do today. The grace of God – the free, undeserved power worked by God on our behalf – is active today.

We all have things in our lives that we lift up to God, so as we bring them to him now, let us do so with a renewed expectation that today he has heard our prayers, today he is active and today his touch is upon our lives.

Of course, there is always tomorrow – but it is equally true that 'now is the time of God's favour, now is the day of salvation.'

Practising faith

'David said to the Philistine, "You come against me with sword and spear and javelin, but I come against you in the name of the Lord Almighty, the God of the armies of Israel, whom you have defied."'

1 Samuel 17.45

The story of David and Goliath is loved and cherished by everyone; the ultimate story of the 'little man' defeating the 'big man'. It is a wonderful account of faith in action, a story of someone putting into practice what they actually believe.

We can all say that God is more powerful than our enemies, or greater than the things that stand against us, but when David was confronted by a warrior champion in whose presence the courage of others melted away, he actually believed it. He knew that the name of God – God's very presence – was more powerful than anything that could stand against him. If he didn't, he wouldn't have risked his life by stepping out from the crowd.

So how did David reach this conviction? He said himself that he had practised. When the king questioned him about whether he was really up to the job, David explained that he had already seen God do amazing things so had no doubt that God could do this too.

Our challenge is to practise our faith. One place to start is having faith in God's love for us. It can be so tempting to believe that we are abandoned or alone when things go wrong, or when our feelings just aren't there. This is where faith kicks in; the importance of holding on to what the Bible teaches so clearly, that God loves us and will never let us down. Hold on to this truth now and practise coming back to it throughout the day.

Feeling frail and weak

'. . . for he knows how we are formed, he remembers that we are dust.'

Psalm 103.14

God knows how weak and frail we are. This is such good news! It means we don't have to pretend to be something we are not; there is no need to pretend to be super-human to him. In fact Paul took this to a whole new level when he said, ". . . I will boast all the more gladly about my weaknesses, so that Christ's power may rest on me" (2 Corinthians 12.9). The simple truth is this – on our own we are nothing, but with Christ in us we have everything.

Knowing this and holding firm to it makes all the difference. It means that we will not be tempted to do things in our own strength, but rather to draw upon the presence of the one who is within us. In Colossians 1.27, Paul has written these beautiful words: '. . . Christ in you, the hope of glory.' He is saying that because Christ is within us, nothing needs to be the way it seems – this is what hope is. It is more than a vague dream, it is his vision that things can be different.

You may indeed be weak and feel there is so much stacked up against you, but you have Christ within you – and because of this (and not because of your own strength) there is real hope for this day.

As you sit quietly, breathe in and say: "Christ in me. . .", and as you breathe out, say the words: ". . . the hope of glory."

Having the heart of God

'Thanks be to God, who put into the heart of Titus the same concern I have for you.'

2 Corinthians 8.16

This slightly strange verse has much to say to us about the way God works within us. One of the questions we often puzzle over is whether we are sensing God's will or just our own desires. This verse suggests that the two may not always be very different.

It implies that God puts concerns into our hearts, or in other words, our hearts are catching something of his heart. Of course, we cannot all catch God's heart in its entirety so he gives specific concerns to different people. Perhaps it is only when all our concerns are shared that we begin to catch something of the enormous heart of God.

So what concerns are on your heart? What are the things that move you? What situations cause you to feel a sense of injustice? To which group of people are you naturally drawn? In seeking the answers to these questions you will begin to discover something of the concerns God has put within you. Give thanks for them and begin to pray with expectation that he will open the door for you to act upon them.

40

Good meditation

'May my meditation be pleasing to him, as I rejoice in the Lord.'

Psalm 104.34

People understand the word 'meditation' in different ways and there are all sorts of books seeking to help us meditate in the best way possible. This verse contains a lovely gem to help steer us through the many forms of meditation on offer, and it is this phrase: 'as I rejoice in the Lord.' The psalmist explains that our meditation should be done in the context of our relationship with the Lord, and this is the type of meditation that is pleasing to him.

A wonderful place to start is to take one of the names God has used to reveal himself in the Bible, such as the Lord the Provider, the Lord who heals you, the Lord is peace, the Lord is my shepherd etc, and spend time letting this run through your mind. How do you feel about this particular name of God? What has been your experience of it? What more would you like to discover about it?

In doing this you will be bringing pleasure to God, not simply because he likes you thinking about him, but also because he knows that to put your focus upon him is going to be of benefit and blessing to you. Pick one of these names and begin to meditate upon it.

Facing the day with Jesus

"All things have been committed to me by my Father."

Matthew 11.27

In many ways this sounds like a perfectly simple statement, but the truth behind it is quite astounding. Jesus is saying that there is nothing that has not already been handed over to him. Nothing! This includes everything that you will experience or go through today.

From time to time we all have to face things that we don't look forward to, and today might be a difficult day for you. If so, try applying this verse to the things you are facing. Everything in this day has been committed to Jesus by the Father. In other words, God has looked over this day and out

of his love he has handed the events in it to Jesus. Whatever you will go through today is already in the hands of Jesus.

Your attitude to today can change by standing on this truth. Rather than dreading what you have to face, or approaching it with anxiety, face it in the knowledge that it is already in the hands of Jesus.

If you are facing something hard today or in the days ahead, see it now in the hands of Jesus. He is holding it for you and he is there already, because it has been committed to him by the Father.

Blessing others

'And God is able to bless you abundantly, so that in all things at all times, having all that you need, you will abound in every good work.'

2 Corinthians 9.8

There is so much need in our world. Even as you go through your day you will encounter people with needs and it is tempting to wonder what you can do about it. You may well think you don't have the right words to say or the resources to help, but when you think like this you are judging the situation from a human point of view.

Today's verse says that there is an entirely different way of looking at a situation – not from the perspective of what you can do yourself but rather what God can do through you. Paul says that God is able to touch you in ways that are probably beyond your understanding, so that everywhere you go and in whatever situation you find yourself he will be able to flow through you. The language Paul uses is exuberant. It is not just a matter of God touching you in a small way, he will bless you abundantly. Nor is it simply that you have a little something to give to people, but rather that you will abound or overflow in the good you are seeking to do.

Serving others in God's strength comes down to choosing to believe that he will give you what you need, so ask him to do that now – and hold on to the expectation that he will use you to be a living resource to the people and situations you come across today.

Seeking God's presence

'Look to the Lord and his strength; seek his face always.'

Psalm 105.4

There can be a certain mysticism attached to the presence of God – a sense that there is not much we can do about it as either his presence is with us or it's not, depending on whether God decides to grant us his favour. However, this verse suggests that such thinking may not necessarily be true. God's presence is not something that might randomly come to us, but instead is something that we have a responsibility to look for, be attentive to and actively seek.

Certainly there may be times when God's presence seems a little different or has a deeper intensity, but the point is that we are to seek his presence at all times. So how do we do this?

The first step is the most liberating: if we are commanded to do this, then it must be possible! It would be a cruel command if we could never hope to achieve it. The second step is to pause wherever you are, knowing that Jesus promised he would always be with you, and to ask yourself where he is for you right now. Is he beside you, within you or around you? There really is no right or wrong answer. Give thanks for his presence and enjoy it.

Love

"I have made you known to them, and will continue to make you known in order that the love you have for me may be in them and that I myself may be in them."

John 17.26

Valentine's Day is an occasion when we ponder love! Depending on your circumstances, it can be a day of celebration and anticipation, or a day of loneliness or disappointment. However you feel, there is a profound love in which we are all caught up – the love that God the Father has for each of us.

So how much does he really love us? The answer is staggering – he loves you and me just as much as he loves Jesus. This is what lies behind Jesus' words to his father in today's Bible verse. His prayer was that we would become aware of this truth; that people

would look at his ministry and discover the depth of Father God's love for them.

However Valentine's Day makes you feel, there is an amazing truth for you to contemplate – you are uniquely and powerfully loved by the Father of all creation, the Father of the Lord Jesus Christ himself. You may not feel that this love is as 'real' as the human love for which you may crave, but God's love is so real that he gave his Son, Jesus, for you.

Spend a few minutes thanking him for his love, and as you dwell on it, receive his love more deeply.

Bring a smile to God's face

"She has done a beautiful thing to me."

Mark 14.6

Jesus was talking here about Mary anointing him. Others looked on and grumbled about the extravagance of what she was doing, but Jesus loved it! Mary wasn't acting out of obedience, or doing something she had been told to do – she just wanted to do this for Jesus. She wanted to give something from her heart and her action moved him.

This is not an image of an austere Jesus who is only satisfied when people follow him with slavish obedience. Instead, this is a Jesus who can be surprised, touched and moved. We, too, can bring a smile to his face.

So for you, perhaps the obvious question is this: what can you do today to bring a smile to Jesus' face? What can you do that will bring him pleasure? It may be an act of kindness, a bold move to extend the kingdom of God or a spontaneous act of worship. Do it and bring him joy.

46

Overcoming obstacles

"I have given you authority ... to overcome all the power of the enemy"

Luke 10.19

Jesus said that he had come in order that we might have abundant life (John 10.10). It sounds wonderful, but the trouble is that his words did not automatically bring about the abundant life he promised. It is all too evident today that there are many Christians who would not claim to have abundant life, no matter how much they seek it, and it is probably true for most of us that there are obstacles in our way.

It is worth taking a moment to reflect what these obstacles might be. What is it that stops you enjoying the abundant life that Jesus came to bring? As you think about this question, today's Bible verse about Jesus giving us authority to overcome the power of the enemy, can take on a new meaning.

Jesus made his statement about giving us abundant life so that we could catch his vision of what life can be like; a life in direct contrast to the work of the enemy who came to steal, kill and destroy. In recognition of this, Jesus gives us authority to overcome the works of the enemy – to refuse to accept them as our lot from now on. Instead, we have permission to stand against them by bringing them into the glorious light of Jesus, where we can seek his healing, help and deliverance.

Take a moment to learn these words and reflect upon them as you think about your life: "I have been given authority to overcome the power of the enemy."

The generosity of God

"I gave your master's house to you, and your master's wives into your arms. I gave you all Israel and Judah. And if all this had been too little, I would have given you even more."

2 Samuel 12.8

In this passage God recounts how generous he has been to David. It seems such a 'nice' passage, but actually it forms part of God's rebuke to David after his affair with Bathsheba. In essence God was saying, "Why did you go after what you did not have when I was willing to give you everything?"

Perhaps God is revealing that a lack of belief in his extravagant generosity is at the heart of the desires that lead to sin. Rather than go after what we do not have, the answer is to recognise our desires and bring them to God in the faith that he will not ridicule us, but will meet our desires in different ways or show us how he has met them already.

It is not God's desire for us to be miserable, nor that we fulfil our desires in ways that might be hurtful to others. Far better that we bring everything about ourselves to him so that he can touch everything within us. What do you want to bring to him today?

Seeing God's glory

'The Lord is exalted over all the nations, his glory above the heavens.'

Psalm 113.4

When the psalmist wrote these words, the world was probably no better than our experience is today, with the usual tensions, fighting, unrest, suffering and temptations. However, the psalmist was able to lift up his eyes to look at something that was equally present but unseen by many – the wonder and glory of God. How can we change the focus of what we see?

One way is to try to catch an awareness of the presence of Jesus with us. The Bible speaks about the reality of his presence, even though he may be unseen. If we can find a new faith in his presence with us at all times, we will discover more of his glory in our lives – his love, majesty and power.

Finding the presence of Jesus is first and foremost about trusting in his promise that he is with you. Any pain and confusion you may be experiencing are not indicators that Jesus has abandoned you, but are more like sirens calling you back to have confidence in his presence with you.

What are the particular concerns that you have right now? As you reflect on them, also reflect on the truth that Jesus is with you. How does his presence affect how you feel about your needs?

Being a child

'So in Christ Jesus you are all children of God through faith'

Galatians 3.26

Sometimes we hear people speaking about their faith and their amazing experiences, and it is tempting to see them as a different class of Christian! The impression is that they walk very closely with God and appear to be more blessed than most of us. This verse from Paul brings us back to the truth that every one of us is a child of God; there are no distant relatives within his family – all of us are his children.

However, there are two words in this verse that provide an insight into why some people seem to live differently to others – 'through faith'. What makes the difference is how much we choose to believe what is revealed to us. If I believe I am a much-loved child of God it is going to make a positive difference to the way I pray, whereas if I believe he constantly disapproves of me and barely remembers my name, this will negatively affect my prayers.

Before you pray, it is worth spending some time simply focusing on this statement, 'I am a child of God'. Say it out loud, meditate on it and let the truth of it begin to sink in. God doesn't compare you with anyone or wish you were someone else. You are his child, and he loves you with the same love that he has for Jesus (John 17.26).

Freedom

'It is for freedom that Christ has set us free. Stand firm, then, and do not let yourselves be burdened again by a yoke of slavery.'

Galatians 5.1

One of the key messages in this powerful verse is that we are free. Many times we look to the future and believe that if only x, y or z would happen, we would be free. However, in this verse Paul says that freedom is not a future event but is what we have now. So what does he mean?

Originally he was talking about freedom from observing the law. Part of the emphasis on the law was the belief that if every part of it was obeyed, then acceptance by God would follow and his favour would be poured out. Paul puts it so wonderfully – Jesus has paid the price for our sins so when God looks at us he no longer sees them. There is absolutely nothing that stands in the way of us and the goodness that God longs to pour out upon us.

This is how it is for us today; there is nothing that needs to happen for it to be true since it is already a reality. Once you have grasped this, Paul says, walk in it and let nothing drag you back. Focus on these words for a few moments: "Christ has set me free". Let the truth of them sink in.

Look back and reflect

"The Lord is my rock, my fortress and my deliverer; my God is my rock, in whom I take refuge, my shield and the horn of my salvation. He is my stronghold, my refuge and my saviour"

2 Samuel 22.2-3

In this passage, David was reflecting on what he had learned about God. He spoke these words with absolute conviction as they expressed what he knew to be true. He certainly was not saying that his life had been straight-forward with no difficulties – just think of Saul's treatment of him, his own moral failure and his son rebelling against him! Instead, despite all these difficulties and many more besides, he could look back and see the hand of God upon his life, even if it might have been hard to see it at the time.

When David was forced to flee from his own home because his son was leading a revolt against him, he may not have chosen to call God his deliverer, but years later, as he looked back at how things had worked out in the long term, that is exactly the word he used to describe God.

We can be very quick to judge the character and nature of God by how we perceive life to be right now. Instead, we need to learn to be like David and take a different view; to look back over time and prepare to be amazed at how faithful God has been to us.

As you bring your difficulties to God now, think about his faithfulness to you in the past and let that build your faith for the issues facing you today.

God hears

'In my distress I called to the Lord; I called out to my God. From his temple he heard my voice; my cry came to his ears. The earth trembled and quaked, the foundations of the heavens shook; they trembled because he was angry.'

2 Samuel 22.7-8

These verses express something very powerful about the way we perceive prayer. I suspect that at times we have all experienced praying when it seems as if our prayers are hardly reaching the edge of our lips, let alone the throne of God! Consequently, because we feel as if little is happening, we judge that our prayers are not being heard.

Here, David recalls a time when he prayed and God responded. David was probably speaking literally – he was, after all, a poet – and it is doubtful if there really was an earthquake or a shaking of the foundations of heaven, but what is significant is that when he prayed, God heard and acted. This is also true for us.

When Jesus spoke about prayer, he said: "But when you pray, go into your room, close the door and pray to your Father, who is unseen. Then your Father, who sees what is done in secret, will reward you." (Matthew 6.6)

Jesus' point is this: it is not what you feel about prayer that counts, but the truth about what really happens. It may be that heaven shakes when you pray – you simply do not know – but what you can be certain of is that your Father hears your prayers, whether or not you feel anything. Why not pray directly to him now?

How do you see yourself?

"The Lord has rewarded me according to my righteousness, according to my cleanness in his sight."

2 Samuel 22.25

The way we see ourselves is so important. Other people may look at us and see the respectable mask we seek to wear, but deep down, if we see ourselves in a bad light then all the good others say about us will be as nothing, because the negativity we feel within is all-consuming.

This negativity needs bringing into the presence of God's light, in order that we, like David, might discover what it means to experience "cleanness in his sight." Presumably this was a process that David himself had gone through as he released his own feelings about some of the more shameful parts of his life, and began to understand and live in the reality of the depth of God's forgiveness.

Being clean in God's sight is very different from being clean in our own sight, but we will probably never grasp this until we catch the reality of what Jesus did for us on the cross – he took away our sin. He didn't relieve us of it for a while or help us carry it ourselves – he took it from us completely so that when God looks at us we are clean in his sight. For a moment, think about God's vision of you – not what you think, but your value to him.

God is at work

'... according to the plan of him who works out everything in conformity with the purpose of his will'

Ephesians 1.11

When you are going through a hard time – whether it is due to general pressures, sickness or opposition – it is tempting, and pretty universal, to look to God and wonder why he has let this happen to you? Why has he brought about this particular turn of events? Surely it's logical to think this way; if he is God, then presumably he can prevent anything from happening?

This is a question many people have grappled with over the ages and there is certainly no easy answer. In this verse, however, Paul gives us one approach: to surrender to what God is doing through your hard time. Paul is not saying that God has caused your hardships, or that you have to accept them, but that God has a different plan for your life and is actively at work to bring it about, even in the darkest of times when you cannot find him.

The response to this is worship; to honour God's presence, even if you cannot see him, and to trust in his action, even if it is hidden from you for a while. Some of life's problems may seem to have no answer, but to learn to trust in God's presence and activity in the worst of times is what will keep you from despair. No matter what you are facing, begin to sing a song of worship to the one who has everything in his hands and is working in all things for your good.

Delighting in God

'Your statutes are my delight; they are my counsellors.'

Psalm 119.24

Here is a new way of thinking about the Bible. It's all too easy to regard it as a book of rules and regulations which we have little hope of keeping, and if we feel like this we will probably open the pages with dread rather than with delight. It all comes down to perspective.

Do we really believe that God inspired the words of the Bible just to wind us up? He knows our natural inclinations and what we really want, but has he decided to spoil our fun? Surely this can't be the case and he must have had another motive in mind? So much depends on the way we view God. Do you regard him as harsh and vindictive, always out to teach you a lesson; or does he look at

you with love, as he whispers something new to keep you out of danger and harm?

It makes all the difference if we can open the Bible and read it as the words of the one who loves us. There will still be questions and things we do not understand, but once we catch God's heart of love behind it we will be more likely to find the wonder of his delight in us through its words.

Before you read a passage from the Bible, pause and ask the Holy Spirit to help you catch the delight of what you are about to read; then find one gem that you can take into the day ahead.

Trusting in God's mercy

'But because of his great love for us, God, who is rich in mercy . . . '

Ephesians 2.4

These words provide us with such a beautiful description of God – who overflows with an abundance of mercy. Presumably then, since he is rich in mercy, he must delight in being merciful; it is part of his very nature.

This can give us a real confidence to stand before God just as we are. If we have something troubling us and know that we need his help, it can be tempting to try to hide it away because we fear what he might do or say to us. This is where our faith comes in – not the faith to believe in God's existence (we probably have that already), but rather faith in his character. What sort of God do we believe him to be? Do we trust enough in his mercy to bring him all that is within us?

A good question to ask yourself when you are troubled is whether your picture of God has changed because of what you are going through. Of course, he doesn't change, so have the courage and faith to stand before him and bring every part of yourself to him, trusting that he is indeed rich in mercy.

Spotting the light

"While I am in the world, I am the light of the world."

John 9.5

The gospel accounts of Jesus' life illustrate the truth of this statement. As individuals encountered Jesus he brought light into their lives, and his teaching illuminated their understanding of who he was? So what about us today?

Through the power and presence of the Holy Spirit, Jesus is alive and dwelling with us today; he is still the light of the world. His desire is be the light in your life and to bring clarity to whatever situations you face. As you think about your life, where is there anxiety, fear or tension? In other words, where can you identify an absence of Jesus' light?

Hold these circumstances before Jesus. Tell him what you want him to do and trust him to shine his light upon them. He may not shine it in the way that you expect, but he came to be light for you, so wait with expectation for his light to shine.

58

A Saviour for today

"Today in the town of David a Saviour has been born to you; he is the Messiah, the Lord."

Luke 2.11

It's a shame that some Bible passages are only read in certain seasons, because we miss out on the power of their message through the rest of the year. This is one such passage, usually only read at Christmas, but which actually has a daily application for us.

When the angels made this pronouncement to the shepherds, it did not only have a relevance for that particular day, it would change their lives forever. After these words had been spoken, the shepherds would be able to relate to God and to life in a different way; everything changed because Jesus had come.

We need to take this proclamation seriously; today, there is a Saviour standing very close to you. Whatever plans you have for the day ahead that might be causing you anxiety, you are facing them hand in hand with your Saviour. Whatever you may look back on with regret, you do so in the company of your Saviour. Whatever befalls you throughout this day, you will not be alone as your Saviour will be with you.

'Today, Jesus my Saviour, you are with me.'

A choice of two visions

'But by the grace of God I am what I am'

1 Corinthians 15.10

All of us are people of faith: we put our faith in something and live our lives accordingly. This helps to define us and make us the people we are. So the big question is this: in what do you put your faith?

Many people put their faith in how their past affects them and they live accordingly. It is so natural to look at our lives, the mistakes we have made and the things that have gone wrong, and to assume that such events define us. When we go down that road it is easy to see ourselves as weak and ineffective – people who will probably not achieve much at all.

However, there is another option. When God looks at us he sees his own children, members of his family whom he loves passionately, upon whom he has poured out the power of the cross and within whom he dwells by the Holy Spirit. Thanks to all this, he sees us as people through whom all things are possible.

In which of these visions will you choose to put your faith? All too often we adopt an opinion of ourselves that is quite contrary to God's vision of us and the challenge is to put our faith in his vision so that we can say, '. . . by the grace of God I am what I am' – totally loved and forgiven.

Ponder these lovely words now – and believe them.

Catching the big picture

'Rejoice in the Lord always.'

Philippians 4.4

It may be that your circumstances are pretty dire today and you wonder what you have got to rejoice about. However, if you had said this to Paul he would probably have laughed! In this chapter he speaks about his frequent times of hardship and of going without. He even wrote this letter to the people in Philippi when he was in prison. What did he have to rejoice about?

Paul was consumed with the wonder of God. He had a remarkable ability to look beyond his own personal circumstances and see the wonder of his God, whom he knew loved him through and through.

How can we catch this? As you begin to pray, take your eyes off your own circumstances for a while and seek to catch the eternal truths that the Bible reveals to us. Father God calls us his children; so great is his love for us that he gave us his own Son. Jesus revealed to us what God is really like: he was so passionate about us that he died in order that he would carry the punishment for all we have done wrong. The Holy Spirit loves us enough to want to be so close to us that he lives in us. Think about these truths – there must be something here that causes you to rejoice at the wonder of God.

Take one of these truths, or choose another from a creed, hymn or song. Reflect on it and be dazzled by it. 'Rejoice in the Lord always.'

It's all around!

'The earth is filled with your love'

Psalm 119.64

These simple words should really encourage us to seek the love of God for ourselves. All too often we are dull to his love, wondering why we cannot feel it, and whether he loves us at all. Searching for something we believe is real can give hope.

This verse provides two encouragements as we seek God's wonderful love. First, it tells us that his love exists; it is filling the earth and surrounding us. Wherever we go today, his love is as real as we are. The second encouragement is that it is God's love which is all around us, and not some general sense of well being. It is also personal – it is the love Jesus has for each one of us, a love so great that it caused him to die for us. This is the love that is so present, so near.

So repeat these words to yourself a few times: 'The earth is filled with your love.' Reflect on the truth of them and make this message personal for you.

Hope in God's word

'My soul faints with longing for your salvation, but I have put my hope in your word.'

Psalm 119.81

Many people are waiting for God – perhaps for a particular prayer to be answered, for a new sense of his love or even for healing. All these represent a longing for his salvation in some way. It might seem to you that you have been waiting for so long that you almost feel like giving up.

Evidently the author of this psalm understood this feeling, yet he combines two extremes in his writing. He is utterly honest about what he is going through, even admitting that he is fainting with longing, but he also carries with him a profound hope in

God. The way he describes it is putting his hope in God's word. For us this means taking seriously the revelation the Bible gives us about God, particularly that God's character, nature and desires were all revealed by Jesus. It is so easy to begin to look at God through the spectrum of what he has and has not done for us, whereas a better place to begin is by looking at his character and his promise.

As you seek Jesus afresh, hold on to the knowledge of what he came to do for you, and then look for signs – however small – of his work in your life.

It's all about vision

'And Elijah said to Ahab, "Go, eat and drink, for there is the sound of a heavy rain."'

1 Kings 18.41

This is all about vision: as the people looked up into a blue sky, Elijah predicted a great storm. He knew God had spoken so he kept looking for signs of what God was doing, and eventually a small cloud appeared and the storm was soon upon them.

We have a different vision than that of other people because we are Christians. We see a God who loves us and has been revealed by Jesus to be actively present with us at all times. The challenge is what we do with our vision. Elijah provides us with a wonderful example; even when he could see or feel nothing, he held on to his vision and waited patiently for even the smallest sign that what he was hoping

for was coming about. His lesson to us is to look out for small signs of encouragement along the way, even if we do not see much evidence of God's love or activity at the moment. After all, it may be that we have our vision fixed on God doing everything we ask at once so we miss the small encouragements he gives us as we wait.

As you take a moment to reflect on the past day, what small signs of God's love and action can you see that you might have missed if you march straight into the day ahead? Look back, find his encouragements, and see how God's work in your life grows as a result.

Everything serves God | 1

'... all things serve you.'

Psalm 119.91

These four short, simple words could change your perception of all that happens to you. The message behind them is that God can use everything to his glory, even though he isn't the direct cause of all that happens.

We would all like God to take away the bad things from our lives, and there are many times when we are aware of him doing just that, but God also has another way of working which may not be quite so comfortable. Sometimes he takes the things we are going through and works in and through them, so that when we look back later we can recognise that God was able to do something through them that he may not have been able to do in any other way.

You might find this odd! Surely if God is God, then he can

find a more comfortable way of working things out? An extreme example is the death of Jesus. In itself, this event gave God no pleasure, but he was glorified through what it achieved. If there had been another way in which he could have achieved the same results then surely he would have done it?

You may be facing your own trials, but none of the things you are going through are an end in themselves. They are all events through which God can work. The choice you face is whether you will trust him to bring good out of them: 'Father, I worship you and trust you with all that is going on in my life because I know that all things serve you.'

No closed doors for God | 2

'... all things serve you.'

Psalm 119.91

Yesterday, we looked at the way in which God may, at times, work through our difficulties to bring about his glory rather than taking them away. The reassuring aspect of this is that there is no event or circumstance in which he is unable to work; there are no closed doors to God! Yet how are we meant to know whether our current anxiety is something God wants to take away, or work through?

Our starting point needs to be the revelation of Jesus in the Gospels. We need to take account of the fact that the Bible reveals Jesus healing sickness whenever he came across it on every recorded occasion. Certainly there are times when Jesus paused to do something else first, as in the case of the man lowered down through the roof whose sins were forgiven before he was able to walk. Generally, however, Jesus' desire seemed to be to heal. This does not mean that life will be free from difficulties, but that even in tough times there is always an assurance of help and the presence of Jesus.

In every circumstance and in everything that happens in your life, nothing is a closed door for God. All things serve him and his glory.

Don't you know?

'But the angel of the Lord said to Elijah . . ., "Go up and meet the messengers of the king of Samaria and ask them, 'Is it because there is no God in Israel that you are going off to consult Baal-Zebub, the god of Ekron?'"'

2 Kings 1.3

The context of this passage is that the king had injured himself by falling through a roof, and in his pain he sought the help of other gods. The lesson is quite clear: when we are in trouble, the first place to go is to the God who loves us and is deeply concerned about us.

It is certainly not wrong to turn to other people for help, as one of the greatest ways that God brings help to us is through others, both trained professionals and loving friends, but what King Ahaziah (the man who fell through the roof) did wrong was to deliberately choose to bypass the God of Israel.

We hope we would never do this, but it is worth looking back over the past few days and weeks and reminding yourself of the occasions when you needed help. What was your reaction in these situations? Did you turn to God first, or was he the last resort when things went wrong? It is at times like this that the extent of our relationship with him is really revealed, and the more we feed it the more we turn to God first when we are in need.

When Elijah confronted the king the message was simple: didn't you know that God was always there for you? Perhaps this is a question for us all.

Permission to serve

'He has made us competent as ministers of a new covenant'

2 Corinthians 3.6

Many of us do not regard ourselves as sufficiently competent to be doing God's work. We feel that we don't know enough, read our Bibles enough or pray enough! In some ways this might all be true and there is probably more that we can do to grow in these areas, but that is not the point about Christian service. We serve because Christ served, and because he bids us to serve others – not because we feel competent to do it.

There will be plenty of opportunities to serve others today in both big and small ways. However, we can easily find ourselves wondering if we really ought to get involved. Is it up to me? Have I really got the time? Would someone else do it better? Have I the right to do this? It is the example of Jesus, and the presence of his Holy Spirit living within you, that gives you the right to help others and to serve them in whatever way you can.

Look out for ways to be a servant today. It may be that no one will even notice what you have done to help them, but do it in the knowledge that God knows and approves.

The armour of God | 1

'... put on the full armour of God'

Ephesians 6.13

I remember someone asking a group of people to put their hands up if they had put on the armour of God that morning. Most hands went up. The next question was, "Why did you ever take it off?"

In this passage, Paul shares six truths that could transform our lives if we are aware of them. The imagery he uses is that of armour: perhaps he was looking at one of the soldiers guarding him and it struck him that the armour he wore had parallels for Christians. We will look at these six truths over the days ahead.

The starting point is this: God has armour for each of us. Deep down, we may feel very frail, powerless and weak. It may be that the soldier who caught Paul's attention felt this way, but with his armour on he became a different person – someone with whom we certainly wouldn't mess! We may feel weak, but it doesn't mean we are destined to feel like this for ever. God has given us gifts that can transform us if we take them seriously.

God knows what you are like, your weaknesses and failings, yet he does not dismiss you because of them. Instead, knowing these weaknesses, he clothes you with what you need. Take a moment to have the courage to come before him just as you are, trusting that he will not brush you aside, but will gently clothe and equip you to be strong.

The armour of God: wearing the belt of truth | 2

'Stand firm then, with the belt of truth buckled round your waist'

Ephesians 6.14

It is so easy to live according to feelings, which can be very at odds with the truth of God. To live your life dependant on your feelings is to allow yourself to be blown and buffeted by anything that comes your way, so every negative thought or painful memory is likely to drag you down. However, there is another way to live where you are not bound by your feelings. God has given you a 'belt of truth' to put around you – another way to live.

All that God has revealed about himself and humankind in the Bible is the truth. It is the revelation that he loves us with a love so strong that it caused him to give the most precious thing he had for us – Jesus; that we are his beloved children, who are in a daily relationship with him; and that he is as close to us as the air we breathe and will never move away.

Take a moment to focus on each of these points in turn, and put on this belt of truth before you do anything else.

70

The armour of God: wearing righteousness | 3

'Stand firm then . . . with the breastplate of righteousness in place'

Ephesians 6.14

We are spending a few days looking at the armour of God, and in this phrase Paul encourages us to put on 'the breastplate of righteousness'. The key here is not to analyse whether or not we feel we deserve this, but to recognise that it has been given to us individually as a gift.

We are righteous because Jesus died to take away our sins – and not because we try hard to do righteous things. To put on the breastplate of righteousness is to accept what Jesus has done for us and not try to do it for ourselves. This begins by admitting to ourselves that we have failed, and although we might still be utterly loved by God, without the work of Jesus we would be pretty hopeless!

However, this is not the end of the story. We are invited to put on righteousness – the knowledge that our sins are forgiven. This awareness comes from gazing upon the crucified Jesus and letting our hearts declare that he died for us personally. He took away the sins of the whole world – which includes you! Jesus took away all your sins so that you are now righteous.

The armour of God: being ready to go | 4

'Stand firm then . . . with your feet fitted with the readiness that comes from the gospel of peace.'

Ephesians 6.15

Having our 'feet fitted with the readiness that comes from the gospel of peace' implies that we are already wearing the necessary shoes for whatever lies ahead. In other words, our own lives have already been impacted by the gospel so now we are in a better position to step out and share it with others.

One reason for this is because once we have experienced something first-hand, we know what we are talking about! If we have sensed being forgiven of our sins, then we will be in a position to share this truth with others; if we have experienced Jesus' grace strengthening us in some way, then we will be in a position to testify to this; and if we have experienced God's healing touch, we will be ready to pray with others in need of healing.

It is likely that in some way you have experienced the effect of the gospel of peace in your life, so be ready to take this gospel to others. Look for opportunities today to pass on what you know to be true to someone who needs what you have found.

The armour of God: using your faith | 5

'... take up the shield of faith, with which you can extinguish all the flaming arrows of the evil one.'

Ephesians 6.16

The 'flaming arrows of the evil one' sound like something we would rather not think about! Most of us are simply trying to get through life without thinking about subjects as lofty as 'spiritual warfare'. However, although we may not recognise it as such, all Christians experience these flaming arrows.

Most commonly they come to us as negative thoughts, seeking to distract us from the wonder of our relationship with God. It is interesting that they are called flaming arrows because, like fire, the effect of them can spread rapidly throughout our whole beings. The 'armour' we have been given against these flaming arrows is the shield of faith. This is what we hold up to intercept negative thoughts and stop them spreading. In practical terms there are two key steps to take. First,

it is important to recognise that just because a thought occurs to us doesn't mean that it is true. Rather than allowing our thoughts to dominate our thinking, we need to have the faith to believe that what the Bible says is the truth.

The second practical step is to intercept these thoughts as soon as they appear and refuse to let them take root within us. We may not have much control over what comes into our minds, but we certainly have a lot of say in what we do with them. It is so important to make every effort to stop them taking hold so that we will not have to put out the fire that may follow in the days ahead.

Take a moment to identify if any negative thoughts are filling your mind. What will you do, with God's help, to stop them taking hold in your life?

The armour of God: knowing who you are | 6

'Take the helmet of salvation'

Ephesians 6.17

Salvation means that because of what God has done, we have been changed and will never be the same again. Once we accept that we are totally forgiven, God's presence dwells within us and he promises to give us hope. To 'take the helmet of salvation' is to accept these truths and live our lives in the knowledge of them.

God's salvation is meant to impact every area of our lives, but all too often 'the helmet of salvation' is placed on a shelf where it can be admired, but has little impact because it is seldom actually worn.

Consider the simple but profound truths of our faith:

- we are loved by our Father God

- Jesus died to take away our sins, he rose again and is with us now

- we have the power of the Holy Spirit within us.

Repeat these words slowly for a few minutes until they sink in, and then ask yourself: if these truths are true, what difference do they make to me today?

The armour of God: the sword of the Spirit | 7

'Take . . . the sword of the Spirit, which is the word of God.'

Ephesians 6.17

John 15.14-15
Ephesians 1.4
Romans 8.35-39
Psalm 139.1-4
Isaiah 43.4
1 PETER 2.9
2 Corinthians 1.3-4
John 3.16
Psalm 27.5-6 John 1.12-13
1 Timothy 1.14 Psalm 66.9
PSALM 18.19
Zephaniah 3.17
Matthew 10.29-31

Much of what has been said about the armour of God is about defence against negativity, but the sword we have been given also has the capacity for attack. We have the authority to stand against negative thoughts and to stop them hurting us. If we take this sword (the word of God) seriously, we have the authority to bring radical change to the situations in which we find ourselves, rather than just reacting to what is thrown at us.

We carry the presence of God within us, which means that there is a unique manifestation of God's presence wherever we go. If we take this seriously it can make an amazing difference to every situation we face. This is also a means of attacking what may seem to be negative influences around us in the world, since we stand as people of light, hope and peace in situations that are crying out for these qualities. The world desperately needs Jesus – and it has him, in us!

It is not so much that God has given you a sword, but that you are his sword in every situation in which you find yourself. Let your mind think through what you will be doing today, and 'see' yourself as a source of light, hope and peace to others.

The armour of God: the weapon of prayer | 8

'And pray in the Spirit on all occasions with all kinds of prayers and requests.'
Ephesians 6.18

If God dwells within us and we take him into every situation in which we find ourselves, a logical next step is to pay attention to whatever he chooses to bring to our attention.

We may go to places today where people are all around us. So many of them will be in need in ways that we will never know. However, we can still make a difference! Take a moment to ask God to bring a particular need or person to the forefront of your mind. Then, as you pause for a moment, you can quietly and unobtrusively pray for whatever you sense.

You will never fully know the power and effect of your prayers, but to open yourself to prayer in this way is to let yourself be used by God to bring something of his kingdom to the situations and people around you, which might not be possible by any other means.

Prayer and the heart of God

'It is time for you to act, Lord; your law is being broken.'

Psalm 119.126

This verse encourages us in prayer. In our world we are surrounded by so much that is wrong, and when people suffer and hurt God shares in our pain. When the psalmist wrote that God's law was being broken, it was not just a case of people being disobedient, but rather that God's plans for how he desired this world to look had been marred. The same is true of today; people are not following God's ways and they are in pain – not just people we don't know, but friends and family too. Along with the author of these words, we too can say to God, 'It is time for you to act.' This is not just our opinion or us telling God what to do, but an echo of what has been revealed to us: God desires change.

An amazing aspect of prayer is the realisation that when we pray, we are not just articulating what we would like to happen, but rather we are reflecting the will and the heart of God. So as you pray for those whose plight touches your heart, do so with a renewed confidence that God feels the pain of what you see in the world, and that Jesus came as our Saviour.

Wherever you are – so is Jesus

'One day Jesus was teaching, and Pharisees and teachers of the law were sitting there. They had come from every village of Galilee and from Judea and Jerusalem. And the power of the Lord was with Jesus to heal those who were ill.'

Luke 5.17

This verse gives us an insight into the background of this particular story. Jesus was visible, along with many people – including some religious leaders and teachers – who were listening to him. As the story unfolds we discover that there was also at least one sick person being carried there by friends.

We are made aware of other aspects of this scenario, things unseen. It becomes apparent that the religious leaders bore a certain hostility to Jesus and were watching him. Added to this mix, we also read that the power of the Lord was present.

Today, you will encounter situations where much is obvious, but there will also be other influences you cannot see. Sometimes you might even pick up unseen tensions or anxieties around you. Whatever is going on, it is always worth remembering that one factor never changes – Jesus is there with you, along with all his love, wisdom and power.

A lovely habit worth adopting is to whisper his name in tune with your breathing, to remind yourself of his presence in every situation in which you find yourself. Jesus is always there!

You can't escape from God

'Where can I go from your Spirit? Where can I flee from your presence?'

Psalm 139.7

These words give us so much encouragement. Deep down we really want to get it right with God; we want to do his will and there is always the worry that if we do wander away from him, we will lose him. However, this verse reminds us that his presence will never leave us.

The question asked by the psalmist is this – where can I flee from you? The word 'fleeing' has the connotation of deliberately running away; of us making the choice to escape the presence of God. The following verse in the psalm reveals the answer – there is nowhere that God is not present. He is in the heavens, in the depths and at the farthermost parts of

the world. Wherever you may try to flee, his 'right hand will hold me fast' (verse 10).

The point is this: if we cannot intentionally find a place outside God's presence, surely it must be impossible to inadvertently wander from him, especially if our hearts are inclined towards him? We might make mistakes and fail to give him the attention we should, but the truth for us today is that wherever we are and whatever we feel, the right hand of God holds us fast. Take a few minutes to memorise this phrase from Psalm 139.10, 'your right hand will hold me fast', and come back to it throughout the day.

Following Jesus

'For everyone looks out for their own interests, not those of Jesus Christ.'

Philippians 2.21

Looking out for the interests of Jesus means that you need to be concerned about the things that concern Jesus. So what are some of these?

Our transformation is a key issue. Jesus wants to see his healing touch experienced and our lives reflecting him more and more. When we only look out for our own interests, it is often to do with self-preservation and keeping hold of what we have – but Jesus has other desires.

Another concern on his agenda may well be unity. He loves his church, and whereas we might think we are not involved in complex matters of church unity, we still have a responsibility to guard our hearts and not speak badly or harbour ill thoughts about others,

especially other Christians. Unity begins in our hearts.

Jesus is also interested in love. We need to be constantly open to the truth of God's love, revisiting the wonder of it afresh every day, and then passing it on to others – looking for opportunities to be a blessing to people whether they know it or not.

There is often a cost to looking out for Jesus' interests. You might not want to be transformed in some areas of your life – perhaps secretly you enjoy having a little moan about others! Showing love can be costly. Yet this is the path along which Jesus travels, and if you want to be his follower you need to be travelling in the same direction as him. Where might that path lead you today?

Choosing where to walk

'May your hand be ready to help me, for I have chosen your precepts.'

Psalm 119.173

The author of this verse has chosen to follow in God's ways, so feels certain that God's hand will be there to help him in whatever way is needed. A logical approach!

The trouble is that God does not operate like a slot machine, automatically doing what we want if we make the right choices. After all, there may well be other things he wants to do first. Yet what is certain is that if we walk the path Jesus walks, we will have a closer relationship with him and be in a better position to hear his whisper, find his wisdom and catch the breath of his Spirit. Our lives will be better because of this, whether or not Jesus heals us or answers our prayers in the way we hope.

It all comes down to choice. It is up to you to choose how closely you want to walk with Jesus. You are the only one able to choose how seriously you will take the Bible, how much time you will spend in prayer and how much you will turn to God throughout the day. It is very easy to call out to him and ask where he is when you need him, but perhaps sometimes it is God who calls out, "Where are you?" Try to become aware of his presence with you right now and enjoy his closeness.

The kindness of God | 1

"But love your enemies, do good to them, and lend to them without expecting to get anything back. Then your reward will be great, and you will be children of the Most High, because he is kind to the ungrateful and wicked."

Luke 6.35

There is a wonderfully unexpected message in this verse. We might expect God to be kind only to those who obey him and do exactly as he wants, but here Jesus reveals that God is kind to all, whether or not they deserve it.

This is not a license for us to go out and be as mean as possible, knowing that God will still be kind and gracious to us! Instead, it is an open door to the heart of God, assuring us that when we fail and let him down we are not banished from his love and care, but are welcomed back and invited once again to enjoy relationship with him.

The kindness of God means there is always an open door between you and him. You may see your failure, but he bursts with love for you. This love is not just a vague abstract feeling; it is real and it is kind. Take a moment to sit in the presence of God now, aware that his kindness is surrounding you and that he wants to bless you.

82

Reflecting God | 2

"But love your enemies, do good to them, and lend to them without expecting to get anything back. Then your reward will be great, and you will be children of the Most High, because he is kind to the ungrateful and wicked."

Luke 6.35

It is easy to resent God's command to be kind and loving to others, especially when we feel that some people deserve very different treatment! However, when we show love to others because we know that we are loved by God, something changes and we become living parables of God's love to us.

Whenever we feel the desire to judge or to speak against someone because they deserve it, could it be a reflection of how we expect God to act towards us – we get what we deserve. Conversely, when we show grace to someone beyond what they deserve, we are reflecting the way God treats us. When we show genuine compassion and love for the person in addition to grace, then we really begin to understand something of God's feelings and heart for us.

It starts with action. Over the course of this day, there may be opportunities to treat people as they deserve – perhaps using unkind words or passing on gossip. In these moments recall instead how God acts towards you and try to reflect his heart; be to others as God is to you.

Keeping faith in God

'You have put me in the lowest pit, in the darkest depths.'

Psalm 88.6

At first sight there doesn't seem to be much hope in these words. The writer is obviously in a terrible place of suffering, everything appears bleak, and there seems no reason to assume that God is not behind it. However, there is also something in these words that I think must have brought great pleasure to God: in all the suffering the psalmist is going through, he cannot give up on God and refuses to turn his back on him and walk away.

If we are asked to call to mind people with great faith, we would probably think of those who have triumphed in adversity, or achieved great things for God despite fierce opposition. However, perhaps people with the greatest faith are those who hang on in desperate situations, with no idea what the future holds but still refusing to turn their back on God.

Maybe you are going through a hard time – and it may even seem to you as if God is punishing you for something. The call is still to have faith and maintain a relationship with God, talking to him and trusting that somehow, in all of this, he loves you.

84

God's love in dark times | 1

'For I received from the Lord what I also passed on to you: the Lord Jesus, on the night he was betrayed, took bread'

1 Corinthians 11.23

These powerful words were spoken at a time that must have been surrounded by confusion and darkness, when Jesus knew that one of his close followers whom he himself had chosen was going to betray him. Rather than run away to a safe place or plead with his disciple to change his mind, Jesus went ahead with one of the most symbolically sacrificial acts of all time – the giving of himself, in what has become for us 'Holy Communion'. The sheer wonder of Jesus is clearly revealed when the end began to close in and yet he still chose to give himself fully for us.

We all have moments when we might question the reality of God's love, and wonder whether it really is for us personally. At these times, pondering the way Jesus gave himself fully for us is a powerful reminder of the depth and extent of his love. As Paul put it in Romans 8.32, if Jesus did this, then is there really anything he would hold back from us?

Whether your life is calm or troubled at the moment, allow this amazing sacrifice by Jesus to shape the way you pray today.

Thankfulness | 2

'... and when he had given thanks, he broke it and said, "This is my body, which is for you; do this in remembrance of me."'

1 Corinthians 11.24

What is your attitude when things turn dark? We learn from this verse that Jesus' immediate response was to give thanks. If he did this in a moment of darkness, presumably it was so natural that it must have been second nature to him.

However, for something to become second nature we have to develop and practise it now. How do we do this? It is not about giving thanks for things we are not the slightest bit grateful for, but it is about beginning to turn our minds

to what we truly appreciate – people or occasions that bring wonder and delight into our life. It is one thing to appreciate them, but even better to recognise them as God's specific and individual gifts to us, and to be thankful for them.

Being able to see people, blessings and circumstances as touches of God's personal love for you keeps thanksgiving real. Why not begin to give thanks for what he has done for you?

86

Waiting

'I wait for the Lord more than watchmen wait for the morning.'

Psalm 130.6

The way that this verse puts together two concepts of waiting for the Lord and waiting for the morning says something very powerful and encouraging to us. It speaks about the certainty of the Lord coming to us.

The idea is of a guard on the city wall, waiting for daylight to appear so that the sleeping town can be woken. His duty would entail waiting for the first signs of light to herald the beginning of the dawn – an event that he knew for certain would take place.

The encouragement for us is to wait for God in a similar way. If you are seeking God's help or deliverance in whatever form, then the encouragement is to wait with expectation for the first signs of his touch.

The difference, of course, is that when a watchman waits for the morning he knows exactly when and where the sun will appear. With God we are promised his presence and help, but he is a living God and frequently chooses to surprise us in the way in which his help comes to us. In fact, we often miss his touch if it comes in ways we are not expecting (or indeed wanting). Yet, like the watchman, if we can train ourselves to be expectant and look for the first signs of his touch upon whatever we bring to him, we are more likely to see his unfolding hand upon our lives.

'I wait for the Lord more than watchmen wait for the morning.' Wait for God's touch, which will come with the certainty of the rising sun.

Taking Jesus seriously

"'But I want you to know that the Son of Man has authority on earth to forgive sins." So he said to the paralysed man, "I tell you, get up, take your mat and go home." Immediately he stood up in front of them, took what he had been lying on and went home praising God.'

Luke 5.24-25

This is such a dramatic healing story! A man is lowered through the roof by his friends because they could not get him through the crowded room to Jesus. Imagine the room full of dust from the broken ceiling, with people looking at the paralysed man hanging mid-air, supported only by the ropes being held by his friends! How did he feel? We actually know very little about the man himself, but he does seem to be a man of faith who was prepared to believe what Jesus said.

Just before this verse, we are told that the first thing Jesus said to him was that his sins had been forgiven – perhaps this had to happen before his legs could be healed? Presumably the man believed what Jesus said and accepted his forgiveness, which then opened the door for Jesus to do more. It is interesting that when he told the man to take his mat and go home, the man obeyed and got up immediately. We have no idea whether or not he felt God's power surge through him, but he certainly was quick to believe what Jesus said and to act upon it.

Many people long for healing – to hear Jesus tell them to pick up their mat and walk. This may well describe your situation. Until it happens, be quick to listen to what Jesus is saying to you in the Bible: that your sins are forgiven and God's love has been poured into your heart. Take a few minutes to rehearse these two glorious truths and ask yourself what difference they will make to you today.

Slow growth

"Still other seed fell on good soil."

Mark 4.8

We are all products of the instant age; we expect things to be done immediately – and we certainly want God to do things instantly. When we pray, we hope that God will work according to our time frame and when we sow the things of God into our lives we hope to be instant disciples, immediately and dramatically changed into the likeness of Jesus. However, this is not how it tends to happen.

In 2 Corinthians, Paul talks about us being 'transformed into his (the Lord's) image with ever-increasing glory' (2 Corinthians 3.18). In other words, we are being transformed at a steady and gradual pace. Likewise, when Jesus talked about us being good seed, we are just that – seeds; definitely not instant plants! As such, much of our growth takes place without us even realising that we are growing. The uncomfortable truth is that our greatest moments of growth probably occur in times of difficulty.

Take a moment to ponder what may be difficult in your life at the moment. Whatever the situation, how do you think God wants you to be and what does he want others to see in you? Let him work his growth in you.

What is abundant life? |1

". . . I have come that they may have life, and have it to the full."

John 10.10

As we spend the next few days looking at this verse, it is worth asking a key question: what is this fullness of life to which Jesus refers?

There are two contexts in which we need to see this passage and they both concern healing. The first is that these words of Jesus took place soon after a blind man received his sight. After the miracle, the man was thrown out of the synagogue and Jesus went to find him to talk. Their conversation was overheard by some Pharisees, and it is during this exchange that these words appear. The man who had just been healed from blindness was probably still standing there, and news of what Jesus had just done was no doubt very much in everyone's mind. So when Jesus spoke about the fullness of life that he came to bring, this image of the healing of a blind man is likely to have been in their minds. Fullness of life is restoring anything that we sense has been robbed from us.

The other context for these words is that of sheep! Jesus had been talking about shepherds, gates and sheep. It is likely that he was referring back to the good and bad shepherds of Ezekiel 34, where we are told that good shepherds healed the sick and bound up the injured. Abundant life – healing – is what the good shepherd came to bring to his sheep.

As you approach the one who came to bring abundant life, it is tempting to ask him to give you a sense of peace in the midst of life's storms – and at times he does – but let us not lose sight of the context of this story. Sometimes his abundant life is to directly intervene in the storm, still it, bring healing and touch us beyond our wildest dreams.

90

It's for you! | 2

"... I have come that they may have life, and have it to the full."

John 10.10

Who is this abundant life for? Deep down do you ever wonder if God has favourites? Are there some who go the extra mile for him, give more to him and who live holier lives so are more highly favoured than the rest of us? Surely he wants to give them abundant life more than the rest of us?

Such thinking is actually to totally miss the point of who Jesus is and why he came. The Bible speaks of him coming as a Saviour – not as a 'Rewarder'. He specifically says in John 12.47, "For I did not come to judge the world, but to save the world." He is not looking around to see who deserves his touch, but rather who needs it.

Imagine the scene as Jesus spoke about coming to bring abundant life. Was he looking at one or two really holy individuals as he spoke, or did he sweep his hand over the entire crowd – the good as well as the not so good, the deeply religious as well as the not so deeply religious? If he came as a Saviour and helper, then he came looking for those who really needed his help and salvation, not those who could manage all by themselves.

Jesus came for you. He sees your life and knows the things you lack – and he wants to bring you abundant life. Why not talk to him about it right now?

God wants to use you

"This is what the Sovereign Lord says: it is not for your sake, people of Israel, that I am going to do these things, but for the sake of my holy name"

Ezekiel 36.22

We would all love to be used more by God, but at times it is tempting to ask why he might want to use us. Are we holy or important enough? The problem with thinking like this is that we centre everything on ourselves – 'Why would God use me?'

These words from Ezekiel give us a new perspective on being used by God; it is not about us, but about him. God is desperate for the world to know him and for people to receive his love and mercy, and for this reason he will use us. It is all about him. As you go about your daily routine and come into contact with others, recognise that God has a yearning to touch them. It is not about you wondering if you are good enough for him to use, but rather about how desperate he is to touch his world.

Every one of us can be used today to bring something of God's love to others. Let's be open to this and look for opportunities to be a blessing.

Disappointment and hope

"Lord," Martha said to Jesus, "if you had been here, my brother would not have died. But I know that even now God will give you whatever you ask."

John 11.21-22

We can identify with so much in the account of the raising of Lazarus. It is a story full of hope as well as being relevant for those who sense disappointment with God, and both those emotions are revealed in today's words from Martha. She expresses her disappointment that Jesus did not do what she longed for him to do, and yet hope still remained like an open door for her.

Many people can relate to her sense of disappointment. There are times when we are baffled by the works of God, or the seeming lack of them, and when many of the things for which we pray remain inexplicably unanswered. It would be so easy to shut the door on God, but something keeps drawing us back.

The truth is that there is tension: God is not at our beck and call, waiting for us to click our fingers and watch him jump at our every command and desire, and yet he longs for us to bring our needs and concerns to him. In moments when you feel this tension keenly, you might like to copy Martha and share the cry of her heart: 'I am disappointed but I still trust in you.'

Take a moment to be honest and tell Jesus how you are feeling right now; but also remember to come back to your faith and declare to him your belief that he has not turned his back on you.

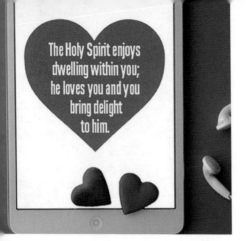

The Holy Spirit enjoys dwelling within you; he loves you and you bring delight to him.

You and the Holy Spirit

'I urge you, brothers and sisters, by our Lord Jesus Christ and by the love of the Spirit, to join me in my struggle by praying to God for me.'

Romans 15.30

We are used to the phrase, 'the power of the Spirit'. It opens us up to the sheer wonder of what he is able to do in any circumstance, despite our powerlessness. In the verse above, Paul uses another equally powerful phrase to describe the work of the Holy Spirit – the 'love of the Spirit'.

The Father's love is often mentioned, and the love of Jesus is demonstrated by his dying for us on the cross, but perhaps we are not so used to pondering the love of the Holy Spirit? The one who works and dwells within us to transform us, actually loves us.

It is all too easy to think of the Holy Spirit dwelling within us with a look of disapproval upon his face, frowning at what we are doing and thinking, whereas the truth is so different. He is within us – loving us, comfortable with his surroundings and enjoying the place he has made as his home.

Take a few moments to find an awareness of the presence of the Holy Spirit within you. Let your mind dwell on the truth of his love for you. He enjoys being within you and you bring delight to him.

94

It's a struggle!

'... I strenuously contend with all the energy Christ so powerfully works in me.'

Colossians 1.29

In these words, Paul was honest about his own situation as well as challenging us about our own attitudes. The first thing he spoke about was the reality of the struggle in which he was involved. Judging by the accounts in the book of Acts, being called to a task by God did not mean it would be plain sailing! Paul endured many hardships and much persecution along the way and if anyone had told him that life was meant to be a bed of roses he would have laughed!

The second thing Paul expressed was the heart of his struggle, as he described the energy of God working so powerfully within him. The very fact that he struggled is encouraging because it implies two opposing factors coming together. If there had been none of God's energy within him, he would not have struggled and would have been defeated quickly.

In your own life, spiritual struggle is when the Holy Spirit within you comes up against something seeking to weigh you down. Even when life seems to be a struggle, you can rejoice because it means that there is an effective power, the Holy Spirit, at work in you. The more you acknowledge the Spirit within, the more you will feel his strength in your life.

What are your struggles? How much of the strength you are using to face them is coming from you and how much from Christ?

Something has to change

'In Christ you have been brought to fullness. He is the head over every power and authority.'

Colossians 2.10

This is an amazing statement! In whatever situation or struggle we find ourselves, there is a whole new perspective to it that is easily missed: Christ is above everything. This doesn't mean that Jesus will automatically change all the difficulties in our lives; he may change us!

There are probably a number of occasions when we all face struggles, and not only is God seeking to change those situations but also to change us; to teach us something, strengthen us in some way or to challenge an attitude or perception we might have.

This is not out of a sense of punishment, but because the transformation God is seeking to bring about in us is all about fullness. His heart's desire is for us to experience life in a far deeper way than we may do at the moment. Sometimes this means our circumstances must yield to his power and authority, and at other times it is us who must change.

Think about the transformation that God is bringing to your life at the moment. What do you sense he is wanting to do?

96

Finding the right clothes

'Therefore, as God's chosen people, holy and dearly loved, clothe yourselves with compassion, kindness, humility, gentleness and patience.'

Colossians 3.12

This verse highlights some beautiful qualities of character and likens them to clothing. There is a lovely sense that we already have this clothing and are simply called to put it on. It is well within our grasp because we have the person of Jesus, who so clearly demonstrates and exemplifies these qualities, living within us. If he dwells within us, then so do these qualities; all we have to do is take them and put them on.

To do this we need to recognise that we need him, in the same way that we might naturally reach for a coat when it is cold.

There may be moments today when you might feel lacking in compassion or kindness, or when your patience is wearing a bit thin. At such times, call upon Jesus – who is closer than the air that you breathe – and ask him to give you what you need. Jesus is the personification of these qualities, and if he is in you then you can receive them from him.

As you look ahead at the day before you, what 'clothing' do you sense you need? Ask for it now.

Making connections | 1

'. . . Simon's mother-in-law was in bed with a fever, and they immediately told Jesus about her. So he went to her, took her hand and helped her up. The fever left her and she began to wait on them.'

Mark 1.29-31

We are going to spend a few days looking at this lovely, simple healing story to see what can be drawn out of it.

The first thing to note is that this story occurs right after Jesus and his disciples had left the synagogue where something interesting had happened. A service had just been interrupted by a man who was severely affected by an evil spirit and Jesus had immediately brought peace to him, much to everyone's amazement. It is at this point that the group went home and discovered that Simon's mother-in-law was sick, so they told Jesus about her.

It seems that they made a connection between what they had just seen in the synagogue and the illness confronting them at home: if Jesus could bring healing to one person, then why not to the other?

The healing stories in the gospels invite us to make the connection with our own situations. If Jesus could heal then, why shouldn't he heal you today? As you read this story again, make the connection! It is the same Jesus, reflecting the same Father, so why not you?

The compassion of Jesus | 2

'. . . Simon's mother-in-law was in bed with a fever, and they immediately told Jesus about her. So he went to her, took her hand and helped her up. The fever left her and she began to wait on them.'

Mark 1.29-31

One of the loveliest features of this story is the naturalness of Jesus' response to Simon and Andrew's request. There seemed to be no debate about whether or not he would bring healing, and his natural response seemed to stem from the compassion that flowed from him.

In Revelation 2.4, there is a verse that says, 'You have forsaken the love you had at first.' This is not simply a reference to us forsaking our love for God, but is also about us forgetting the depth of his love for us. If we forget his love, we forsake it and wander away from it.

When you are in need, instead of jumping straight into prayer, pause to recognise God's compassion for you; take time to feel secure in his love and see what flows from this.

The gentleness of Jesus | 3

'... Simon's mother-in-law was in bed with a fever, and they immediately told Jesus about her. So he went to her, took her hand and helped her up. The fever left her and she began to wait on them.'

Mark 1.29-31

This story demonstrates the amazing gentleness of Jesus as he goes over to Simon's mother-in-law, takes her hand and helps her up.

There can be a fear about the ministry of healing. What will we be asked about or expected to do? However, the healing ministry of Jesus was surrounded with gentleness and respect for the people in need. In this story, neither Simon, Andrew nor Simon's mother-in-law were questioned about their beliefs, moral standing, whether or not they had been particularly holy that week or if they had refrained from sin. Neither were they made to promise anything. All we are told is that Jesus gently went to her, took her by the hand and restored her.

This is the Jesus we would all love to encounter – who comes to us when we are laid low, for whatever reason, and with tender gentleness lifts us up. This is the Jesus revealed in the Gospels and who stands with you now. Take a moment to notice his gentle presence with you and then tell him about your needs.

You have God's attention

'Lord, hear my voice. Let your ears be attentive to my cry for mercy.'

Psalm 130.2

This prayer is very personal. In fact it brings prayer back to its very core – the individual and God. It's about us bringing the things that we are concerned about to him.

It can be very easy to lose this focus on relationship and be casual about prayer, undertaking it as a duty – something we ought to do. However, there was nothing dutiful about the way this psalmist was praying. It was about him calling out and seeking God's attention.

The sheer wonder of our relationship with God is reflected in this verse.

The Lord God, creator of heaven and earth, who has been ruling and reigning throughout history, hears your voice and is attentive to everything you say to him.

As you settle down to pray, you have God's attention! You may or may not have a sense of his presence, but he certainly knows exactly where you are and hears every word you say. Be still before him now and express your heart to him.

Surrounded by love

'But I have calmed and quietened myself, I am like a weaned child with its mother; like a weaned child I am content.'

Psalm 131.2

This tender verse enlarges our sense of God's amazing love for us. We are familiar with describing God as our 'Abba, Father', but this verse gives us a different glimpse of him – as a mother. This beautiful picture of a mother with a contented child sums up the love and care that God has for us, and is something we need to hold on to as we begin to pray.

Right now you are surrounded by the love of God. In a healthy parent-child relationship no baby has to earn their mother's love, it is there all the time. Similarly, when you sit before God you are surrounded by his love, no matter what you have done or are going to do. This is why you can calm and quieten yourself, and from this position of love you can begin to pray.

Hold this picture in your mind right now, of yourself in a position of total trust and dependence on God.

Finding God's love everywhere

'Give thanks to the God of heaven. His love endures forever.'

Psalm 136.26

The rhythm of this particular psalm is worth noting. Each verse makes a statement that is followed by this refrain, 'His love endures forever'. The psalmist is seeking to convey a sense that behind every action of God is his love.

If you read the whole psalm, you will notice that the author even finds the love of God in people's destruction! This seems very hard to us, as if he is revelling in the misfortune of others, but perhaps this isn't the case. He may simply be revealing that he has found the love of God in absolutely everything, good and bad.

You may be quite good at finding God's love in some things, especially in happier times when it is easy to see God's blessings, but to find his love when things are hard or confusing is another thing entirely. This is why this psalm is so helpful, with its constant refrain reminding us where to start. Rather than wondering how God's love can possibly exist in some situations, let's state along with the psalmist, 'His love endures forever'. God's love is real so let's try not to lose sight of it.

'His love endures forever'; repeat this phrase a few times. You might like to call to mind some of the events coming up in your life and let these words be spoken over each of them.

Your responsibility

'Ezri son of Kelub was in charge of the workers who farmed the land.'

1 Chronicles 27.26

This seems like a mighty strange devotional verse! It actually forms part of a list of the various responsibilities given to certain people, with each being given a task to do and held accountable for it. It raises the question, what have we been given to do for which we are accountable?

We are accountable for our own spirituality. It is hard to blame anyone else for a lack of prayer in our lives. Certainly we can feel inadequate when we start to compare ourselves to other people, but it may well simply be that their particular lifestyle allows for a different expression of prayer. Our lives are as they are, and it is up to us – and no-one else – to find a pattern of prayer.

Of course, we could all pray more, but actually God has not called most of us to a life of solitary prayer. We need to work out how to keep our relationship with him alive in the midst of everything else that we do. What's your pattern? Does it feed you? Do you want to change the way you pray?

You are a child of God | 1

'He said to me, "Solomon your son is the one who will build my house and my courts, for I have chosen him to be my son, and I will be his father."'

1 Chronicles 28.6

King David proclaimed to all the officials of Israel that God had chosen Solomon to be his son, and that God would be his father. I wonder what Solomon thought as he listened? It must have given him so much confidence to know that he had been chosen by God himself for the challenging job he was about to undertake.

The truth is that we are not so very different, and we too can have this same confidence in the situations in which God has put us. Paul wrote that we are chosen and adopted (Ephesians 1.4-5) and Jesus said that he came so that we might know the love of God just as he knew it (John 17.26). It is as if God says to each of us personally, "You are my beloved child, I take pleasure in you." (See Mark 1.11)

Take a moment to hear these words spoken over you. It is not wishful thinking because the Bible reveals it to be true: "I am his beloved child and he takes pleasure in me."

You are chosen | 2

'Consider now, for the Lord has chosen you to build a house as the sanctuary. Be strong and do the work.'

1 Chronicles 28.10

Yesterday we looked at what the Bible says about us – that we are chosen and adopted by God. So what are you going to do with this information?

Towards the end of 1 Chronicles, David gave some advice to Solomon, his son, who had been chosen to succeed him as king; he told him to 'consider'. In other words, to think about and ponder just what it meant to be chosen by God. What does it mean for you?

Consider this: the Lord God of heaven and earth chose you. It really does put other feelings of rejection in their place! Whatever others may think of you, God himself chose you and wants you to be a member of his family in order that he can pour out his love upon you. However, there is more to it than this. In order to 'consider' this message it needs to move beyond words; the truth expressed by these written words needs to sink into our hearts, and become truth within us. This is the truth that will set us free.

Take a moment to 'consider' these words – 'I am chosen by God.' Repeat them now and in the days ahead so they become real for you, and let this truth change you.

The God of Jesus is with you | 3

'David also said to Solomon his son, "Be strong and courageous, and do the work. Do not be afraid or discouraged, for the Lord God, my God, is with you. He will not fail you or forsake you until all the work for the service of the temple of the Lord is finished."'

1 Chronicles 28.20

Solomon no doubt felt somewhat daunted by the task ahead of him – following in David's footsteps. To encourage him, David spoke these powerful words which are also a great encouragement to us. He stressed that his God – who had been with him through his life, including guiding him as he fought Goliath and offering him forgiveness after the events concerning Bathsheba and Uriah – would also be with Solomon.

The truth is that this same God is also with each of us, but Jesus put it in an even more amazing way. In John 20.17, he told Mary Magdalene that he was about to go to "my Father and your Father, to my God and your God". In other words, it is not just the God of David who is with us, but the God and Father of our Lord Jesus.

This is why you need not be afraid or discouraged, because you are not alone. The God and Father of Jesus is with you. As you think through the day ahead, keep this firmly in mind.

The enormity of God's power | 4

"Yours, Lord, is the greatness and the power and the glory and the majesty and the splendour, for everything in heaven and earth is yours. Yours, Lord, is the kingdom; you are exalted as head over all."

1 Chronicles 29.11

We have been reading about King David's proclamation to the whole assembly of Israel, which included a time of worship to the Lord. The glorious words of praise in today's verse form part of this.

It is natural to pray when we face a situation that causes us anxiety. At such times, our prayer can take the form of a desperate plea for God's help or for rescue from a certain situation. However, although such prayers are honest and important, they can lack relationship and worship.

Relationship matters because it brings us back to the person of our God to whom we pray, rather than making a desperate plea to someone out there somewhere. Worshipping him matters because it puts our situations into perspective; it brings home the enormity of who God is compared to the size of our difficulty or anxiety.

This verse is an inspiring passage to memorise. It reminds us of just who it is that we come to in prayer and the power that flows from him. Take a moment to read it again, try to memorise it and begin your times of prayer today with these words. See what difference it makes.

Having integrity | 5

"I know, my God, that you test the heart and are pleased with integrity."

1 Chronicles 29.17

These words, spoken by King David, give us this insight: integrity brings pleasure to God.

Integrity is to do with consistency – being the same on the inside as we are on the outside – and it is interesting that God tests our hearts to see whether we have integrity. Throughout this day, there will probably be several occasions when the temptation is to react to something. It could be anything; something said to us or the way that somebody behaves. The way we react to these things depends on the state of our hearts, and it may well be that somehow God even puts these events in our path to reveal our hearts and test our integrity.

These incidents may seem trivial in comparison to great tests faced by some people, but it is probably the case that those who endure great tests and shine through them with integrity have been through smaller tests first and were not found wanting.

One key is to let the Holy Spirit touch your heart, and for you to carry an awareness of him within you through the day. Then when testing moments arise, you will react according to the power of God's Spirit within you, rather than out of impatience and frustration.

Focus now on the truth that you are a temple of the Holy Spirit, and then you will be more likely to recall it when you need to over the course of the day.

Trusted by God

'. . . we speak as those approved by God to be entrusted with the gospel.'

1 Thessalonians 2.4

It is an amazing thought that God trusts us with the gospel. Of course he goes before us, stands with us and even follows after us to patch up our mistakes – but it seems that he doesn't go instead of us. We have been entrusted with the message that Jesus came to save the world, and came to save us. The question is, what are we doing with this message, both for ourselves and for others?

Each of us has a personal responsibility to foster, feed and maintain our relationship with Jesus; seeking his glory, hiding nothing, bringing our needs to him and letting him bring his transformation to our lives. Our responsibility to the world is to shine with Jesus; to let others see the person of Jesus in us, to reflect his compassion and to be willing to take a stand for him.

God chose you before the foundation of the world so that you would be a bearer of his gospel. He has chosen you for this even though you might not feel up to the task. He knows you through and through and has given you the treasure of the good news of Jesus, both for your benefit and as a blessing for all those with whom you come into contact.

'I am chosen and trusted with the gospel.' How does this make you feel?

Worship anyway!

'How can we sing the songs of the Lord while in a foreign land?'

Psalm 137.4

This verse is so honest. The Israelites had been taken from their land and were finding it hard to sing their familiar songs of worship when things were going so badly. Their change in circumstances was adversely affecting their relationship with God.

There are many times when we might be tempted to echo their sentiment. It's one thing to worship when things are going well – when there are definite answers to prayer and an awareness of God's presence – but quite another to worship in the midst of confusion and when blessings seem a distant memory. However, worship in these difficult times touches God deeply. We will never know the reason why there is sometimes suffering in our lives despite having a God who promises to care for us, and there are many things over which we have no control. Yet we do have control over our decision to worship God in all circumstances.

You can make a choice to 'sing the songs of the Lord while in a foreign land'. Whatever you are going through, focus your attention on him and worship him.

Your response

"Woe to you, Chorazin! Woe to you, Bethsaida! For if the miracles that were performed in you had been performed in Tyre and Sidon, they would have repented long ago, sitting in sackcloth and ashes."

Luke 10.13

How do we respond to God's goodness? Could it be that, like the people of Chorazin and Bethsaida, we sometimes fail to respond at all? There is something in today's verse that alludes to our responsibility to the goodness of God.

All of us ask God for many things, and if we were to record every request and then revisit our list at some future point we would probably be amazed at how many of them had been answered. The challenge that Jesus seems to be posing in this verse is what are we going to do in response to his goodness?

The touches of God upon our lives can be transitory or they can be life-changing – perhaps it is us who determine which by deciding how seriously we take his love and goodness towards us? A natural step is to look back over the past few days and consider how God has touched you, then ask yourself what you have done about it. How seriously have you responded to his touch?

Do it anyway!

'I pray that you may be active in sharing your faith, so that you will have a full understanding of every good thing we have in Christ.'

Philemon 6

So often what puts us off getting more involved in church life or causes us to shy away from being a little bolder in our faith is that we do not feel confident enough. It may be that we do not feel that we have enough of God with us or that we do not know enough about Jesus to share confidently.

If you ever feel like this then this verse is fascinating. It is trying to convey to us that we get it the wrong way around! It is not a matter of waiting until we are confident or know enough – when will that ever be? Rather, it is as we take the plunge and step out that our understanding grows.

This is what makes faith come alive. Sometimes we do recognise our own abilities to speak out or undertake a particular task, but much of the time we feel quite inadequate. The reason for doing something in the name of Jesus is because we hold on to the belief that somehow his Spirit is dwelling within us and that as we step out in his name, something of his presence will flow naturally.

If we knew for certain what would happen when we step out, we would all probably do far more for God. However, this verse tells us: do it anyway, and then you will begin to see God at work.

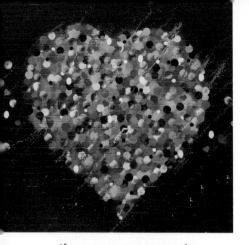

God's unfailing love

'You have searched me, Lord, and you know me.'

Psalm 139.1

If someone was to say that they had searched us and knew us, panic might begin to set in! Exactly how much do they know about us, what about all those things we would rather folk not know about – those things we would love to stay hidden forever?

The sense from this psalm is that God does indeed know everything about us – absolutely everything. He has seen the whole of our lives from our very conception until this present day. So how amazing that this psalm lacks any sort of judgment or condemnation. It simply states the way things are: God sees everything about us and he loves us. He is not horrified by what he sees and remains utterly committed to us.

You are invited to have confidence in this, and to approach Jesus in the knowledge that you are known through and through and are utterly loved. Since he sees everything, you have nothing to hide; and since he loves you unfailingly, you have nothing to fear. How does this make you feel? As you turn to him now, what do you want to say to him?

114

Results and effectiveness

'For what is our hope, our joy, or the crown in which we will glory in the presence of our Lord Jesus when he comes? Is it not you?'

1 Thessalonians 2.19

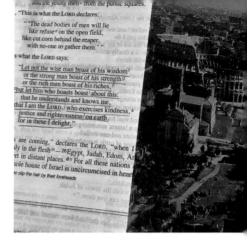

Throughout the letter of 1 Thessalonians, we have glimpses of just how much joy this church brought to Paul. However, it is interesting that when Paul's time in Thessalonica was described in Acts 17, it hardly seemed to be a time of great peace and affection for the city. Most of this account is a description of a riot that took place there! Yet despite the riot and the reception that Paul received, it is amazing to read what God was able to bring about from Paul's short time there – a church was founded and as it grew it proved to be a real blessing.

The point is this: when we look at the outcome of what we do in the name of Jesus, we are probably the worst judges. Unless there are immediate results, we wonder if we have wasted our time. Yet what counts is not what we see but what God does through us whether or not we are aware of it.

Today you may well do different things in the name of Jesus – possibly praying for someone or reaching out to help a needy person. The effectiveness of your actions is not about what happens there and then, but rather is all about what God is able to do and sow through what you have done.

Being great | 1

'Then he said to them, "Whoever welcomes this little child in my name welcomes me; and whoever welcomes me welcomes the one who sent me. For it is the one who is least among you all who is the greatest."'

Luke 9.48

I don't know if you consider yourself among the 'greats' of this world? Most of us probably have a sense that if God were to rank people, we would come way down his list of favourites! However, this powerful verse completely reverses such thinking about who is great. It says that the one who is the least among us is actually the greatest.

If we were to take this verse at face value, it might well affect the way we view others. We would walk down the street noticing those who appear to be the least in the eyes of the world, but be challenged to realise that they were actually the greatest. I wonder if such a shift in outlook would encourage us to be more available for people and to show more kindness?

This message also means that we can't be too quick to dismiss ourselves. Perhaps it is in your moments of greatest weakness, confusion and doubt that God's heart really reaches out to you, for when you feel you are among 'the least', God sees you as amongst 'the great'.

Heaven's resources | 2

'Then he said to them, "Whoever welcomes this little child in my name welcomes me; and whoever welcomes me welcomes the one who sent me. For it is the one who is least among you all who is the greatest."'

Luke 9.48

Yesterday we looked at the idea of the least being the greatest, but there is also another important truth in this verse: to welcome Jesus is to welcome God who sent him. Welcoming Jesus gives us full access to all the wonder and resources of God in our lives.

When we build a relationship with Jesus, we can indeed find a real, ongoing friendship, but it doesn't stop here – there is more. Enjoying Jesus' presence also means that we are close to everything that is in him – his love, kindness, power and

authority. What's more, this verse stresses that this is for everyone. The way Jesus put it is that if we are involved in what may seem like a small activity such as welcoming a child, we are actually welcoming Jesus himself, and all that is within him.

Never think that the things of God's kingdom can't be a reality in your life because you are not good enough. The full resources of God's heaven are there for you so begin asking him now.

Looking back and moving on

'Remember, Lord, what the Edomites did on the day Jerusalem fell. "Tear it down," they cried, "tear it down to its foundations!"'

Psalm 137.7

We all look back, sometimes with regret at things that went wrong and at other times fondly recalling happy memories. On other occasions, like the author of this psalm, we might look back in anger at what has happened and want to see revenge on those who have hurt us.

The trouble with dwelling on the past is that it robs us of the present; it can prevent us seeing what is in the here and now. Paul seemed to have a different attitude and in Philippians 3.13 he wrote about '. . . forgetting what is behind and straining towards what is ahead . . . ' How can we do this?

Actually, there is a recognised Christian spiritual tradition of reflecting on the past day; giving thanks for blessings, confessing sins and learning from events. This leads to a healthy focus on each new day. If we really believe, for example, that our sins from yesterday have been forgiven, we do not need to bring them up again. We can place them in the faithful arms of Jesus and move on to today.

As Psalm 118.24 says, '. . . let us rejoice today and be glad.' Whatever happened in the past, step into today with joy and confidence.

Being a person of peace

"When you enter a house, first say, 'Peace to this house.'"

Luke 10.5

Jesus gave instructions to his 72 disciples whom he sent out into the towns and villages, one of which was to take a blessing to each of the houses they visited. This entailed more than simply saying hello! Jesus was encouraging his disciples to express God's heart to the people they would meet.

The word the disciples would have used is 'shalom' – a word that expressed God's heartfelt desire for his people. 'Shalom' is the hope of well-being in every area of life. Interestingly, another aspect of their mission to the places they would visit was the instruction to heal the sick –

an expression of God's heart that sickness was not his will for people.

Jesus also said that when the disciples passed on their blessing, the effect of it would depend upon the person to whom it was given. There would be some who wanted to receive his peace and others who would reject it.

Let's choose to be receivers! Begin right now by spending a few moments, with your hands open to receive, asking God to send his peace to fill you afresh.

Where is your focus?

'I will praise you, Lord, with all my heart; before the 'gods' I will sing your praise.'

Psalm 138.1

There is only one God, but there are other things in our lives that can take the place of 'gods' by assuming positions of power over us. Today's verse puts all these in perspective. It acknowledges that although other things in life might have some influence over us, there is a way to deal with them.

Part of the issue is where we put our focus, because whenever we spend time focusing on something its influence is bound to grow. So it follows that if our focus is on Jesus, it is his influence that grows and things then tend to change for the better.

Take a moment to name some of the issues that are troubling you or have a degree of control over you, and then proclaim the lordship of Jesus over each of them in a relevant way. It may be, for example, that sickness is exerting control over you – and may even be dominating your life. Proclaim Jesus as the one who came to take your sickness upon himself and to bring you abundant life. Anxiety is another example. If you tend to struggle with this issue, then worship Jesus who said that he came to bring peace such as the world cannot give.

Where will you choose to put your focus today?

Knowing what matters

". . . I know you. I know that you do not have the love of God in your hearts."

John 5.42

Here Jesus is speaking to the Jewish leaders who want to persecute him, and in this blunt sentence he sees right through them and pinpoints the root of their attitudes and actions – they do not have the love of God within them. They are neither exhibiting his love, nor receiving it.

Knowing and dwelling on God's love is everything for us. Without it we may indeed set out to do marvellous deeds and noble causes may move us, but something will always be missing at the very core of our being. Perhaps because Jesus saw the danger of what happens to people when they move away from God's love, in his final meal with his disciples he urged them to remain in his love (John 15.9); to keep coming back to it and to make it a priority in their lives.

We are no different, and if his disciples were in danger of losing the knowledge of God's love, then so are we! Take some time right now to come back to the Father's love for you. One way of doing this is to take the words of Song of Songs 7.10 and slowly speak them to God: "I belong to my beloved, and his desire is for me."

What do you want?

'That night God appeared to Solomon and said to him, "Ask for whatever you want me to give you."'

2 Chronicles 1.7

What would your request be if God appeared to you and offered to give you whatever you wanted? I'm sure you would be very noble in what you asked for, but it is quite fun thinking of all the options!

Solomon's answer to this question was to ask for the wisdom to lead his people; a response for which he was highly commended, and he received a lot more besides. This story gives us an insight into the way that God loves to give gifts. It is all too easy to regard his gifts as signs of his approval or as rewards for being good, but perhaps many of the gifts God gives us are for the service of others.

Take a moment to list what you think are God's gifts to you. If most of these are intended to be for the service of others, how well are you using them?

You are unique and deeply loved

". . . I live by faith in the Son of God, who loved me and gave himself for me."

Galatians 2.20

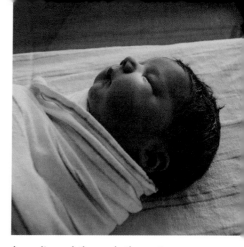

We are all aware that Jesus came to this earth because he loves us, but I wonder if we fully understand the implications of this? When you read that Jesus loves you, it means that he didn't come to earth out of duty, but because he was so captivated by you he was willing to lay aside everything.

When Jesus looks at you he sees something you don't see. You might see your past failures, sins or all the bad things that go through your mind – and if this is your focus you might wonder how anybody could possibly love you. Yet when Jesus looks at you he sees a person who has been uniquely created by Father God. You are not a mistake, someone who has slipped through the net, instead you display God's handiwork all over you.

The challenge is to stop and change the way you think about yourself. If Jesus looks at you with love and was willing to do all he did because of what he sees in you, you have to change the way you see yourself.

You may feel weak and hopeless, yet you are an individual created by the Father, loved by Jesus and in whom the Holy Spirit chooses to dwell. This is something to take seriously. Repeat these wonderful truths to yourself and begin to see yourself in a different light.

All of Jesus for all of you

'Hiram king of Tyre replied by letter to Solomon: "Because the Lord loves his people, he has made you their king."'

2 Chronicles 2.11

As Solomon was preparing to build the temple he asked for help from the king of Tyre who had some of the necessary materials, as well as some of the best skilled workmen. The king of Tyre's reply, provided for us in today's verse, was a graceful recognition that Solomon was God's gift to the people.

In the same way that King Solomon was God's loving gift to his people, so Jesus – our king – is God's gift of love to us. As we think about it, the goodness of God in Jesus is clear: he gives us the gift of salvation through Jesus' work on the cross, the hope of healing through the power of his presence, and comfort from the one who will never leave us. All of Jesus is God's gift to us.

However, there may be occasions when we find Jesus' teachings hard and it is at times like this that we need to remember these are also God's gift to us and are certainly not intended to weigh us down. In his wisdom and love, God knew that the things Jesus said and did would liberate us beyond measure.

Take a moment to focus on Jesus right now – possibly look at a cross or read some of his words in the Bible – and consciously thank Father God that Jesus is available for you and that his actions and words are your Father's generous gift to you.

124

You are God's gift

"As the Father has sent me, I am sending you."

John 20.21

God has sent Jesus as his gift to us, but there is also another challenging strand to these words that Jesus spoke to his disciples after his resurrection. He said, "I am sending you." In other words, just as Jesus was sent by God, so we are sent by Jesus. This means that just as Jesus was God's gift to those to whom he was sent, so we are Jesus' gift to those with whom we interact.

We can often be wary in the company of others, wondering what they think of us or comparing ourselves to them.

What a difference it would make if we could learn to see ourselves as a gift from God to those we meet. So how can we learn to do this? Perhaps a simple step is to ask people how they are and actually listen to what they say! We may not have to say or do much more than this, but we are there for them.

For some of the people you may come across today, you may be the only person who takes the time to listen to them and show an interest. Be a gift to others!

Jesus, you can make me clean | 1

'A man with leprosy came to him and begged him on his knees, "If you are willing, you can make me clean."'

Mark 1.40

We are going to spend five days looking at this lovely story of Jesus healing a man who suffered with leprosy. In many ways the man's attitude reflects our own as we approach God, and many of us would probably echo his words, "If you are willing, you can make me clean." In other words, we know that God has the power to do whatever we ask him, but we are just not sure whether or not this is what he wants to do. Jesus responded to the man without hesitation, confirming that he did indeed want to heal him.

Today, let's concentrate on the words this man put to Jesus. In particular, hold on to the second part of his statement and make it a declaration of faith: ". . . you can make me clean." Repeat this phrase quietly to Jesus.

As you do so, begin by emphasising the word 'you'. Let this become a statement of faith about Jesus – he does indeed have the power and compassion to touch you. After a while switch your emphasis to the word 'me'. You are not excluded from his mission and from receiving his touch – he loves you. Finally, let your emphasis rest on the word 'clean'. Focus on your hopes and dreams of what he can do for you so that bold prayer follows: 'Jesus, you can make me clean.'

You are a personal touch of God's love | 2

"See that you don't tell this to anyone."

Mark 1.44

This seems a strange instruction for Jesus to say to someone who has just had a life-changing experience! One possible reason is that Jesus wanted to carry on with his mission as quickly as possible and the presence of crowds would have impeded him. However, not surprisingly, the healed leper couldn't keep quiet.

There was also something about this statement that was incredibly special for the man himself: the gift of healing was given for him personally. Jesus was not concerned with making statements about it, or using him as a trophy to reveal how in touch with God his own teaching was. Jesus did this act of healing just for him.

We are not notches on the belt of Jesus, but recipients of personal touches of his love. Whatever Jesus has done for you he has done out of love. There may be many more things you would like him to do, in which case the Bible encourages you to come to him and 'Cast all your anxiety on him because he cares for you.' (1 Peter 5.7)

Jesus' love and care for you is personal, so let your gratitude to him be just as personal.

The depth of Jesus' compassion | 3

'A man with leprosy came to him and begged him on his knees, "If you are willing, you can make me clean." Jesus was indignant. He reached out his hand and touched the man. "I am willing," he said. "Be clean!"

Mark 1.40-41

Jesus had just been asked whether he was willing to heal and we are told that his reaction was to be indignant. The word that is translated as 'indignant' is very powerful, but rather than conveying displeasure it expresses the deep sense of injustice Jesus felt for the man and his suffering.

When we are in need and approach God, it is easy to forget that he cares about our situations. In fact, he feels far more strongly than this and is actually moved by the things we are suffering. It was never his plan that

we should live in a broken world where sickness and pain are common. When Jesus took on human form and ministered among us, he encountered the pain and suffering of people first-hand. Pausing to recognise that this man moved him deeply helps us to glimpse something of the Father's heart that led to him giving Jesus' life for us.

Of course God cares about all that you are facing, but it is more than this; he is indignant about your suffering and has a deep compassion for you and your situation.

Jesus takes our healing seriously | 4

'Jesus . . . reached out his hand and touched the man.'

Mark 1.41

At times we read of Jesus touching people to bring healing, but at other times he spoke a word and didn't appear to touch them at all. So perhaps it was significant that when he was healing this leper he deliberately touched him.

Lepers were isolated from their communities because they were regarded as contagious, and to touch them would have been to risk infection. Jesus' touch was a touch of love and compassion; a sign of his commitment and attachment to the man. When was the last time this man had been touched? No matter what the risk, Jesus was going to touch him. It is interesting to note a similar incident in Luke 4.38, when Jesus deliberately bent over a woman with a fever, presumably risking her germ-filled breath right in his face!

Whatever your plight, Jesus has more compassion for you than you can ever imagine. This story about the healing of the leper shows that for Jesus healing was not something to be treated casually or lightly – and he is full of compassion for each of us. Acknowledge his love, find his compassion and begin to rest in the security he gives you.

God's utter commitment to you | 5

"But go, show yourself to the priest and offer the sacrifices that Moses commanded for your cleansing, as a testimony to them."

Mark 1.44

In this story, Jesus healed the man of leprosy but it was only the priest who could formally re-introduce him into society. He may have been healed, but Jesus was determined that he should have fullness of life and until the priest had made his declaration, the man would remain an outcast.

This highlights Jesus' total commitment to us. There may be areas in our lives where we have sensed the touch of God and things have improved, but actually his commitment to us is 100%. Paul wrote in Philippians 1.6, '. . . he who began a good work in you will carry it on to completion until the day of Christ Jesus.' In other words, improvement is not ultimately Jesus' goal! It might encourage us along the way, but his commitment far exceeds merely an improvement in one area of life.

You would probably be thrilled to receive any touch from God, but holding on to the vision that God is utterly, 100% committed to you personally is an amazing thought. Take a moment to sit in his presence, dwell on this truth and begin to worship him.

Being in a relationship

'I called to the Lord'

Psalm 18.3

Many people, whether they count themselves believers or not, would admit to calling out to 'someone up there' in times of need.

What makes the prayers of Christians different is that we are not just talking to anyone; we are calling out to a specific person – a heavenly Father who has been revealed to us by Jesus. This makes a difference. A prayer offered to 'someone-or-something-vaguely-out-there-somewhere' has no assurance of being picked up, since the person offering the prayers cannot even be sure there is anyone out there. Yet we can be absolutely certain that our prayers will be heard by ears that are inclined towards us and from a heart that has proved its love for us.

It's not that God does not listen to the prayers of those outside the body of faith, but we have an assurance that our prayers are taking place within the context of relationship, the relationship that we have with him and he with us.

As you pray, rather than simply making your request, pause to consider the relationship surrounding your prayers. The Father loves you with an everlasting love; he fashioned you in the womb, adopted you as his very own child and gave Jesus for you.

Such is his love for you that of course his ears are attentive to your prayers.

Jesus is not confined to a book

'The number of those who ate was four thousand'

Matthew 15.38

The feeding of the 4,000 is a remarkable story, not least because it occurs only one chapter after Jesus fed 5,000! It can be tempting to think that for some reason Matthew was simply re-recording the same event. However, this second account is really encouraging for us.

When we read a story in the Bible, sometimes we find ourselves longing for that to happen to us too. Similarly, we can read amazing stories of what God does in some people's lives, or we hear testimonies shared in church, and again we can think, 'Well, good for them – but what about me?' The feeding of the 4,000 teaches us that what God has done previously, he can do again.

When we read of Jesus healing sick people in the gospels, the stories are not meant to be accounts of what happened once many years ago, but rather glimpses of what Jesus can do today. Similarly, when someone speaks about what God has done in their life, it is not that they are specifically chosen by God to be healed or touched in some way, but rather an encouragement for us to believe that God is alive and active and could do the same for us.

Jesus is alive! He is not confined to the pages of a book, but is living with you; his arms are open wide and his ears inclined to you.

The light is here

*'. . . even the darkness
will not be dark to you;
the night will shine like
the day, for darkness
is as light to you.'*

Psalm 139.12

Saying that nothing is impossible for God can be something of a cliché in the sense that, while we know it to be true, it doesn't really give us any indication of how we might encounter his presence and power for the things we need. This verse gives us a clue about how we can begin to find faith for our own situations, and it begins with vision.

The concepts of darkness and light can be very powerful, with things weighing upon us feeling like 'darkness' and God's light as the necessary antidote. This dual imagery suggests struggle and fighting – and this is how it often feels. Yet the way the message is put across in today's verse is quite different; it speaks of the darkness being the same as light to God. This isn't an image of a struggle in which we are looking for the Lord's rescue. He is here already, within the darkness, and since his light is also present he is certainly not wringing his hands with anxiety about what he is going to do and how he will cope!

God can't draw any closer to you than he is at the moment, since he is already within you. If you are facing a situation that feels like darkness around you, rest in this truth: the light doesn't have to come because it is already here, with you and within you.

God's compassion | 1

"But a Samaritan, as he travelled, came where the man was; and when he saw him, he took pity on him."

Luke 10.33

The story of the Good Samaritan is one of the most well-known parables taught by Jesus, and today and tomorrow we will look at some different elements within it.

The tale is familiar: a man was in need, but two people failed to help him because the observance of their religious duty prevented them from coming to his aid. However, a third person, a Samaritan – who was ranked low in society – had compassion and helped him.

We are told that the Samaritan 'took pity' on the man in need. The implication of this phrase is to have compassion, a term sometimes used to describe Jesus in his healing ministry. The compassion we may feel at times is a reflection of God's feelings for us in our own moments of hurt and distress. He does not impassively look on as we endure painful struggles, rather his heart is moved.

Far too often, our image of God is of someone who disapproves of many of the things we do and wants our constant repentance, when in reality he is moved by our plight and cares deeply about the things that hurt us. It can be quite hurtful if a child lashes out at their parent with the words, 'You don't care!' I wonder how God feels when we say that to him?

Reflecting God's compassion | 2

"'Which of these three do you think was a neighbour to the man who fell into the hands of robbers?" The expert in the law replied, "The one who had mercy on him." Jesus told him, "Go and do likewise."'

Luke 10.36-37

All of us have one question in common: what does God want of us? It would be really helpful if God gave us our instructions first thing each morning so that we would know beyond any doubt that we were doing his will! These verses challenge what we mean by doing his will.

God's will, expressed here in the command of Jesus, is that we should go and be like the Samaritan – showing help and compassion to those with whom we come into contact today. Did God specifically tell the Samaritan to care for the wounded man? No! Did the Samaritan do God's will when he cared for him? Yes! The instruction is clear: "Go and do likewise." This story is so releasing, as it removes any uncertainty about whether or not we have heard God's voice correctly.

Today, be kind to the people you meet. Show them care and compassion and by doing so you will be fulfilling God's will.

Being certain of God's care

'I know that the Lord secures justice for the poor and upholds the cause of the needy.'

Psalm 140.12

As he looked back over his own life, David knew this verse to be true because it had been his own experience. It is interesting that the word translated as 'poor' carries with it a wider meaning, of being more like those who are pushed down by their circumstances. The ESV translation phrases this verse: 'I know that the Lord will maintain the cause of the afflicted and will execute justice for the needy.'

This was certainly David's experience. Although he had been told he would be the future king, he was hounded by Saul, who attempted to murder him, and at one point his own men openly talked about stoning him to death. His son staged a coup against him and drove him out of the city. David's life was hardly a bed of roses, and yet at the end of his life he could say these words: 'I know that the Lord secures justice for the poor and upholds the cause of the needy.'

When you are going through difficulties or times when you feel pushed down by your circumstances, it can be hard to maintain your trust in God. It is often only when you look back that you can see God's hand supporting and guiding you. If you are facing a tough time now, take these words of David and repeat them to yourself: 'I know that the Lord will maintain the cause of the afflicted.' Emphasise the first two words – 'I know'.

Carrying his presence

"But will God really dwell on earth with humans? The heavens, even the highest heavens, cannot contain you. How much less this temple that I have built!"

2 Chronicles 6.18

These words form part of Solomon's dedication of the temple he had just built. No expense had been spared on this building project because of the enormity of its significance: it was to be the very house of the Lord. Yet even as he was praying over this finished building, Solomon grasped that even the most magnificent of buildings could not, in truth, be a house fit for God, such is his vastness and glory.

The very thought of God living in a specific building is amazing! What would it have been like to stand in the place that was deemed to house the presence of God? This adds renewed significance to Paul's statement in 1 Corinthians 6.19 that we are temples of the Holy Spirit. Our bodies are now the physical places in which the Holy Spirit dwells, and we bear his presence everywhere we go.

Are there events today that are causing you anxiety? If so, remember that you do not face them alone because you have the presence of God within you. With his presence comes his wisdom, strength, patience and kindness. Before you face a tricky situation, think it through and acknowledge that you will not be alone – God's presence is with you.

God sees!

***'Though the Lord
is exalted, he looks
kindly on the lowly'***

Psalm 138.6

It is quite easy to feel lowly! In fact, at times it's tempting to feel like a pawn in the hands of others in the light of world events, or perhaps at our work places. A sense of lowliness may stem from the fact that we feel at the mercy of circumstances, such as sickness or a lack of something in our life. Lowliness can create a sense of powerlessness and loss of control over what is going on.

This verse acknowledges such feelings. It begins by speaking of God in elevated terms as one who is exalted, and whom we might sometimes feel is holding us like pawns in his hands. Yet his 'exaltedness' is different from all the other things that might exert power over us. He sees us, our lowliness and all that goes on in our lives, but the message of the Bible is not just that God sees our plight, he has done something about it. The exalted God came to this lowly world and to every person in it.

The exalted God sees you as you sit in his presence. You may feel like a pawn in the hands of others, but you are a cherished jewel in the hands of God. Hold on to this truth for a few moments.

138

Continual prayer | 1

'May my prayer be set before you like incense'

Psalm 141.2

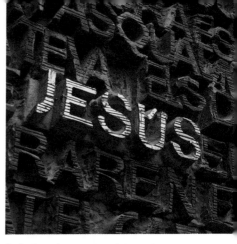

Likening our prayers to incense before God encourages us to think about the way we pray. The point of incense is that it continually rises to God and affects the atmosphere. So it follows that in the same way our prayers should be woven into the atmosphere of our lives and flow naturally from us. This is not just about saying prayers, but about an attentiveness to God in everything we do.

This might seem completely unachievable, but a practice adopted by many is to try to link the phrase, 'Lord Jesus' – or simply the name 'Jesus' – with their breathing pattern. It doesn't really matter how it's done, but doing this is an attempt to bring Jesus into all that we do.

Begin by sitting down and trying it for a few minutes and you may find that it happens spontaneously at other times of the day as well. As you do this, the atmosphere around you will change as your very breathing becomes like incense to God.

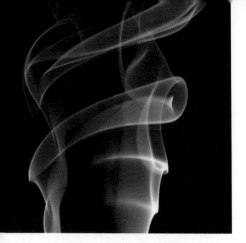

Bringing pleasure to God | 2

'May my prayer be set before you like incense'

Psalm 141.2

We can sometimes feel as if our prayers trickle out of our mouths and achieve nothing! At other times it can feel as if we are trying to push through a brick wall and we wonder why we bother. The concept that our prayers are like incense to God seems a far cry from how we feel!

The image of incense being burnt in the temple signifies something pleasing and attractive to God, and this can be applied to our prayers, which also bring him pleasure. The reason our prayers are attractive to God is because he loves us so deeply; it gives him great delight when our thoughts and hearts turn to him. To believe this, we must begin to accept the joy that we, God's beloved children, bring to him.

Let the words that the Father spoke to Jesus be his words to you – you are my child, whom I love; with you I am well pleased. Hear him speak these same words over you. No wonder your prayers are like incense to him, because he delights in you.

The Fatherhood of God

'He said to them, "When you pray, say: Father . . . "'

Luke 11.2

When Jesus told us to begin our prayers by addressing the Father, he was inviting us to step into the same relationship with God that he himself enjoyed. This is the relationship that the Father has planned for us, and he has no other relationship in mind – there is no such thing as his 'close' children and his 'not-so-close' children. We are all his precious, beloved children and we are invited to recognise this and live accordingly.

Jesus invites us to begin our times of prayer by saying, 'Father', but all too often we rush past this word and onto issues that are uppermost in our mind. Instead, spend longer focusing on your relationship

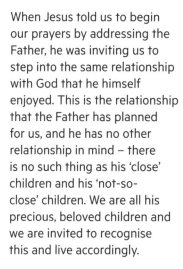

with your heavenly Father and take up Jesus' invitation to speak to God using the same word that he used, and to enjoy the Father's love just as he did.

If you are honest, when you pray you may not feel great closeness or intimacy with God, yet the invitation still remains. Your feelings may be holding you back, but they will never change if you ignore what Jesus says. By responding to his invitation you will be putting yourself firmly into the relationship that the Father has chosen for you. Spend a few moments saying, 'Abba, my dear Father', and as you reflect on these words enjoy a sense of his great love for you.

Persistence

'Then Jesus said to them, "Suppose you have a friend, and you go to him at midnight and say, 'Friend, lend me three loaves of bread'"'

Luke 11.5

This verse is the beginning of what seems to be a strange parable! Some unexpected guests turn up late at night, so the next-door neighbour is asked to help out with some food. Although the groggy neighbour is unimpressed at being woken from his sleep, the persistent request causes him to give in and supply what is needed. The parable then goes on to encourage us to ask.

We might be left wondering if God is this grumpy when we bombard him with our requests, and whether he only gives in because he cannot stand our nagging any more – but of course God is not like this! The parable is not about the nature of God, but rather the value of persistence. If even a grumpy, groggy neighbour can be moved by persistence, how much more is this true of God who loves us to call out to him.

Why do we have to persist? It may be a measure of our commitment to the things we pray about, or perhaps persistence gives us increasing insight into situations. As we persist in prayer, perhaps we also catch something of God's desperation to see his kingdom come. Whatever the reason, it is something God values and we need to take seriously. He wants to see his kingdom grow in the events and circumstances of your life, so offer yourself to him and as you give him your needs ask him to extend his kingdom over them.

Clean in God's eyes | 1

'But now he has reconciled you by Christ's physical body through death to present you holy in his sight, without blemish and free from accusation'

Colossians 1.22

This verse expresses so clearly the heart of God and his vision for us. It also reveals the enormous gap that so often exists between how God sees us and how we view ourselves.

You may regard yourself as weak, struggling and often failing, but this verse says that as far as God is concerned, you are far from this; you are without blemish and free from accusation. This is not because God wears special spectacles that prevent him seeing certain things! It is because the physical death of Jesus took your sin from you so that it is simply not there anymore. So if the sin is not there, how can you be accused of it?

This is so important to grasp as we begin to pray because when God looks at us he does not see what we think he sees. We assume he is thinking that we must have some nerve coming to him considering our past record, whereas the truth is that he is thrilled when we turn to him. He takes such pleasure in us because thanks to what Jesus has done, in his eyes there is nothing to accuse us of.

Have the courage to see yourself through God's eyes: clean, without blemish and free from accusation. How does this make you feel?

Keeping God's vision of you alive | 2

'But now he has reconciled you by Christ's physical body through death to present you holy in his sight, without blemish and free from accusation – if you continue in your faith, established and firm, and do not move from the hope held out in the gospel.'

Colossians 1.22-23

Yesterday we looked at how God sees us; the way in which he does not see our negative traits that we imagine must be so obvious and how he takes such great pleasure in us. However, the verse continues with an 'if' – a condition. This condition is that we stand firm in our faith, not wavering from what we believe.

So what happens if we do waver? Does God see all the bad things? Does he suddenly remember all our sins and cast us out of his

presence? Of course not! If we waver, it doesn't change what God sees, but it does change us! If we believe the truth that we are free from accusation, it will dramatically affect the way we approach God and the way we pray.

Your calling is to keep alive your faith in the way that God sees you, to focus on it every day and to hold before you the wonderful truth that you are clean and without blemish in God's eyes.

The active God

'When my spirit grows faint within me, it is you who watch over my way. In the path where I walk people have hidden a snare for me.'

Psalm 142.3

If each of us was invited to suggest an ideal environment for people to experience the presence of God, we would undoubtedly come up with a range of different ideas. I suspect that many would involve creating a peaceful and comforting atmosphere. However, it is not often that we find ourselves in a perfect environment and this verse assures us that the absence of perfect circumstances is no barrier to God's presence.

We read about God's presence in the most difficult of circumstances – when our spirit grows faint or when we are in a dangerous place. It actually goes further than this and says that God's presence doesn't simply exist, he is actively watching over us on our way through life.

However you feel, and no matter how strong or weak your faith, take a moment to recognise this truth – the living God is watching over you.

Giving thanks

'. . . give thanks in all circumstances; for this is God's will for you in Christ Jesus.'

1 Thessalonians 5.18

We are all probably quite good at thanking God in some circumstances, especially when something lovely has happened, but the command in this verse is that we should give thanks in all circumstances – every single one!

This presents us with quite a challenge, particularly since there are many things for which it seems quite wrong to give thanks. However, giving thanks in *all* circumstances is very different from giving thanks *for* all circumstances. Paul is encouraging us to look at every situation and to try to see something of God's touch and provision in it.

Our difficulty with this is that we are not used to looking at situations in this way. When we look at difficulties and problems we are diverted from the active presence of God. It would be nice if his presence meant that nothing bad could ever happen to us, but sadly this isn't the case. However, it does mean that if we open our eyes to him, we will see little touches of his handiwork all around us.

Is there a situation that is really hard for you at the moment? If so, turn your attention away from the hardship or anxiety and instead focus on the little touches of God and give him thanks.

Sanctification is good!

'May God himself, the God of peace, sanctify you through and through. May your whole spirit, soul and body be kept blameless at the coming of our Lord Jesus Christ.'

1 Thessalonians 5.23

Sanctification sounds like hard work! It suggests a process of great sacrifice that is probably not very enjoyable. However, this verse puts it very differently. It speaks about sanctification as something flowing from the God of peace.

It makes sense that the God of peace would naturally want us to share in his peace, and perhaps this is ultimately what sanctification is about – bringing us all to a place of inner peace where we are no longer struggling with things that draw us away from God.

Sanctification is certainly not about being miserable. Just look at Jesus: he provided wine for a wedding and told many parables containing great touches of humour; he was also deeply at peace and not thrown at all by external circumstances.

He was gloriously holy, perhaps perfectly encapsulating the phrase in Psalm 96.9 – 'worship the Lord in the splendour of his holiness'.

Sanctification is something to be welcomed: it is about you becoming more and more like Jesus. When you picture Jesus, what sort of expression do you see on his face? Try to catch a sense of the laughter and joy that must have been a great part of his life.

It's not how good the prayer is – it's how good God is!

'Lord, hear my prayer, listen to my cry for mercy; in your faithfulness and righteousness come to my relief.'

Psalm 143.1

At times, most of us wonder whether God will answer our prayers, particularly if it is about something dear to our heart. It's easy to think that it depends on the sincerity of our prayers and how God feels about our request.

However, the author of this psalm viewed it differently. He recognised that his request was not judged by the quality of the prayer itself, but rather by the character of the one to whom he was praying. This is the value of beginning every time of prayer by focusing on the presence of God and our relationship with him, rather than simply rushing straight in with our prayers and requests. What is the main issue you want to bring to God today? Take a moment to remember that you are entering the presence of the living God, the one whom the Bible reveals as loving, faithful, gentle, kind and who is also powerful beyond description. When you pray, you are speaking to this living God, and not just 'saying prayers'. Turn to him now, spend time with him, and only then bring your requests to him.

148

Be wide-eyed in wonder and belief!

'Your eye is the lamp of your body. When your eyes are healthy, your whole body also is full of light. But when they are unhealthy, your body also is full of darkness.'

Luke 11.34

Jesus is saying here that what we look at will shape us inside. The Message Bible puts it like this: 'If you live wide-eyed in wonder and belief, your body fills up with light. If you live squinty-eyed in greed and distrust, your body is a dank cellar.'

This is about how we see God and ourselves. If you believe that God is kind, loving, powerful and rich in mercy, this vision will shape the way you approach him and the things you bring to him. Conversely, if you think of him as tough, mean and grudging, this too will shape your approach to him. Similarly, if you know that you are unconditionally loved by God, this will produce a completely different attitude within you than if you view yourself as a person of no consequence, struggling alone. What is your image of God?

The Bible is a beautiful window on to the wonder of God and his love for you. Read about the love it reveals and be 'wide-eyed in wonder and belief', so that your attitude towards God and your perception of yourself might be changed.

Trials can breed faith

'... among God's churches we boast about your perseverance and faith in all the persecutions and trials you are enduring.'

2 Thessalonians 1.4

It is tempting to regard ourselves as failures when things start to go badly. We wonder where we went wrong, whether we have sinned against God and why he seems to have abandoned us? However, when Paul looked at the Thessalonians, rather than shaking his head in despair at all they had done wrong, he boasted about their perseverance and faith.

We are encouraged to be people of faith, and we like to think that we live up to this – yet faith and trials seem to go hand in hand. Trials are not a sign of God's disapproval, nor are they necessarily sent to us by God, but they can be the breeding ground for faith.

Trials may take a variety of forms: opposition to what you stand for, sickness, a particular difficulty you are going through, or perhaps not seeing the fruit of your ministry or prayers. Whatever the trial, the calling is the same – perseverance and faith. Keep going and don't give up! Hold on to a vision of the abundance of God's love for you and give him thanks for touches of his goodness that are still evident when times are hard.

God is with you – that trumps everything!

'God is with us; he is our leader.'

2 Chronicles 13.12

These words, spoken by King Abijah, were not natural words given the circumstances. His army was facing decimation; he had 400,000 soldiers and his rival had twice that number. Yet whatever he lacked in manpower, Abijah made up for in faith. His faith was based on two things: God's promise about the kingship of Israel, and the fact that he knew God was with him. These were what enabled him to stand before his enemy with an impressive confidence.

The enemies facing us, such as an illness, hostility from others or thoughts that condemn us, may not be a literal army, but can be just as destructive and wear us down. Yet we too have the same weapons as Abijah, the promises of God and his presence.

One promise, or revelation, worth keeping in mind is the statement from Ephesians 1.20-22: 'he raised Christ from the dead and seated him at his right hand in the heavenly realms, far above all rule and authority, power and dominion, and every name that is invoked, not only in the present age but also in the one to come. And God placed all things under his feet . . . ' In other words, there is nothing or no-one more powerful than Jesus. The second promise is that he is with us.

What made the difference for Abijah was that he didn't just know these two things, he really believed them. As you face your own difficulties, whatever they are, take these words and repeat them to yourself until they become part of you: 'Jesus, you are above all things, and you are here with me.'

Being complete

'For the eyes of the Lord range throughout the earth to strengthen those whose hearts are fully committed to him.'

2 Chronicles 16.9

This verse has the potential to discourage us! Are we really fully committed to God? If not, does this mean he won't strengthen us? The actual sense of the Hebrew word for 'committed' is more about those who are 'complete' in him and this is probably truer of us than we might think.

Often we think of ourselves as weak and not doing too well in our Christian lives, but the flip side of this is that we are only too aware of our desperate need of God, and know that we can only really be complete in him. If this is the case then it is not just the fully committed that he is looking for, but also those of us who know our need of him.

The other wonderful truth expressed in this verse is that God is actively looking for us; he is searching for those who know their need of him. As you recognise this need and admit that you can only really be complete in him, begin to believe that he is looking out for you to strengthen you.

Loving yourself

'LORD, I love the house where you live, the place where your glory dwells.'

Psalm 26.8

There is something very captivating about this sentence. The psalmist was thinking about the temple and the wonderful sense of God's presence that he often felt there, and he simply described how he loved it and enjoyed being there.

This verse also contains a huge challenge for us – we are now 'the house' where God dwells. In 1 Corinthians 6.19, Paul speaks about us being temples of God's Holy Spirit. The question we need to address is this: how do we feel about the place where God has chosen to dwell?

For many of us the answer is that we do not have a very high regard for ourselves, feeling that we could do a lot better

and suspecting that God is slightly embarrassed by us. In fact, if we are honest we may wonder why he would choose to live within us at all. However, let's take on board a little bit more of today's verse. What if the psalmist was actually catching something of what God thought about his temple? Suppose God loved the house where he dwelt then – and suppose he still loves all the houses where he dwells now, and it is his absolute pleasure and delight to dwell within us?

Hear these words as if it was one member of the Godhead speaking to another about you: 'I love the house where you live.' Dwell on this and believe it.

No fleeting shadow!

'Lord, what are human beings that you care for them, mere mortals that you think of them? They are like a breath; their days are like a fleeting shadow.'

Psalm 144.3-4

How can we be of any significance to God? Before we were born there were countless generations of people, and there will probably be generations after us – so how can we be of any significance to him?

This is not a new question; it was asked by the psalmist thousands of years ago. Yet even as he raised the question, he knew that God did notice him and did care. The very next verses in the psalm go on to speak about God coming down to us and reaching down to pull us out of deep water. In other words,

the fact that our minds may not be able to comprehend the incredible personal nature of God's love doesn't negate it; it doesn't change his heart or desire to reach down and touch us.

Dwell on this wonderful truth so that it strengthens your faith. You could never invent a God who would love you with such a personal love, nor could you invent a God who would become human like you and then die for you. You might think you are too small and insignificant for God to notice – but thankfully he does not agree with you.

You belong to God

'To the people of the church of Thessalonica, who belong to God our Father and the Lord Jesus Christ.'

2 Thessalonians 1.1
(Good News Translation)

There is something special about belonging, and this verse captures so beautifully the truth that we belong to the Father and to Jesus.

This 'belonging' came about when Jesus died for us. The Bible speaks about it in terms of Jesus 'purchasing' us (Revelation 5.9). In other words, this has already happened and was entirely initiated by God. The part we play in the process is to enter into this sense of belonging and to choose to believe that it is true for us in a personal way so that we are able to say with growing confidence, 'I belong to the Father and to Jesus.' If you are wondering where the Holy Spirit is in all of this, Ephesians 1.13 tells us that it is because we belong to the Father and to Jesus that we have been given the Holy Spirit.

To belong to God means that you are his. At times we get very concerned about our failings and wonder if this means we belong at all, when all along it is probably the whisper of the Holy Spirit that is calling us back to the ways of God. To belong to God also means that he will not leave us abandoned in our needs. As it says in Romans 8.32, if God gave us Jesus, surely there is nothing he would hold back from us?

Let your mind catch the wonder of these words: 'I belong to God the Father and the Lord Jesus Christ.'

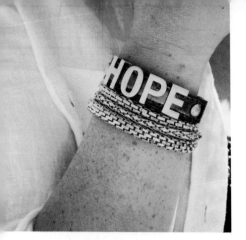

Chosen by God

'Paul, an apostle of Christ Jesus by the command of God our Saviour and of Christ Jesus our hope'

1 Timothy 1.1

If we were all to recall our individual stories of coming to faith, each of us would have a different story to tell. For some it may have been an intellectual struggle or a crisis that brought them to a place of decision, for others a growing awareness of something beyond this life, or for many a personal acceptance of the faith in which they were brought up.

In today's verse, Paul brings us back to the core of all our faith stories; it is God who chose us. It is easy to believe that this applied to the apostle Paul – after all, he did have rather a dramatic conversion experience (see Acts 9) – but it is also true for all of us. Ephesians 1.4 puts it so powerfully: 'For he chose us in him before the creation of the world.' However you think you came to faith, it was actually God who chose you!

There may well be times in your life, possibly even today, when you will experience some form of rejection or a lack of confidence, but whatever you face nothing can change the fact that you have been chosen by God. Take a few moments to focus on this truth: 'I have been chosen and hand-picked by God, and that makes me special.'

The wrong dying son

'King Joash did not remember the kindness Zechariah's father Jehoiada had shown him but killed his son, who said as he lay dying, "May the Lord see this and call you to account."'

2 Chronicles 24.22

One of the most telling aspects of this particular account is the contrast between the son's dying words and those of Jesus. In this story, the dying son asks for the actions of the king to be held against him, whereas when Jesus, the Son of God was dying, he asked that those killing him would be forgiven (Luke 23.34).

As you consider this difference, your perception of God's attitude towards you might be challenged. For some people, the sense of God always being present is not particularly comforting as they suspect he watches their every move, recording their failings and calling them to account for every error. If you tend to think like this you are listening to the wrong dying son! Jesus is present with you at all times, but not as one watching and disapproving. Instead, he enjoys being with you, has totally proved his forgiveness of you and is seeking to empower you for the days ahead.

The presence of Jesus is something in which you can truly rejoice and not fear. Take a moment to make these words your own: 'Jesus, I rejoice in your presence with me now.'

Putting your faith in God

'Blessed are those whose help is the God of Jacob, whose hope is in the Lord their God.'

Psalm 146.5

It may seem strange for us to think that the God of Jacob is our help. Why bring Jacob into it? He isn't even our ancestor!

This psalm is about faithfulness. It is about God's promise to be faithful to us today. Believing in his faithfulness begins with us noticing his faithfulness in the past; for example, his faithfulness to Jacob. If you read the story of Jacob, you may feel God was much more faithful to him than he deserved, since Jacob never really stopped being a deceiver. Despite his faithlessness, God was always faithful and verse 6 goes on to underline this lesson for us – 'he remains faithful for ever.'

It is interesting that as the psalm continues, all the promises are in the present tense: 'He upholds the cause of the oppressed and gives food to the hungry. The Lord sets prisoners free, the Lord gives sight to the blind, the Lord lifts up those who are bowed down' (verses 7-8).

The psalmist was saying that just as God had been faithful to people who may not have deserved it in the past, so he is still faithful to us. God has not changed and we are indeed blessed if we put our hope in such a remarkable God.

You really matter to God

"Are not five sparrows sold for two pennies? Yet not one of them is forgotten by God. Indeed, the very hairs of your head are all numbered. Don't be afraid; you are worth more than many sparrows."

Luke 12.6-7

These words, spoken by Jesus, are almost unbelievable! God sees every bird and not one of them is forgotten by him – and then his message gets better still. If this is true for the birds, how much more so for us. God even knows the number of hairs on our heads. It can be so hard, especially in times of difficulty, for us to believe that we matter to God – yet we do.

The New Testament tells the story of God, in the person of Jesus, coming to this world to live as one of us. It speaks of him being tempted in every way just as we are

– which means just as you are. It speaks of Jesus dying on the cross for the sins of the whole world – which means for your sins. It speaks of Jesus rising from the dead to live in you – not just other people, but you. Every one of us matters. Every person you will come across today matters so much to God that Jesus died for them.

Take a few minutes to let the truth of these words touch you, 'I really matter to God'.

Mighty in power

'He heals the broken-hearted and binds up their wounds. He determines the number of the stars and calls them each by name. Great is our Lord and mighty in power; his understanding has no limit.'
Psalm 147.3-5

At first glance these appear to be random verses strung together! What has healing the broken-hearted got to do with calling the stars by name? Actually there is a lovely link.

If you feel broken-hearted or wounded, your wound may not be one that people see. On the outside you may appear as usual, but inside you might be desperately aware of the pain. When the psalmist says that God sees and recognises every star, he is suggesting that while we might see a mass of stars that look alike, God views each one individually. In

this same way, God sees each of us and notices every part of us, including our wounds and hurts that may well be invisible to others. Such is his power and understanding.

One step on the road to finding healing is to recognise that God understands you completely. Knowing this will encourage you to trust him with the deepest things in your life. If there are parts of you that feel wounded or hurt, bring them to God in the full assurance that he understands and is 'mighty in power'.

160

Bringing pleasure to God

'... the Lord delights in those who fear him, who put their hope in his unfailing love.'

Psalm 147.11

This verse seems to suggest there is a link between fearing God and putting our hope in his love, which might seem strange since we often think of them as opposites. There is a sense that God's love should be taken more seriously than is often the case.

Focusing on his love can seem rather self-indulgent; after all, there are so many other things we should be praying for and working towards. Yet this verse says that to hope in God's love actually brings him pleasure.

How amazing that we have the capacity to delight God! So often we assume that this only applies to people who do outstanding works or sacrifice everything for him, but bringing pleasure to God is something we can all do in a simple way by putting our hope in his love.

So why not take a moment to bring God pleasure now? Remind yourself of God's unfailing love for you and all that he has done to bless you, and then trust in his love for you today.

Remind yourself who God really is | 1

'They spoke about the God of Jerusalem as they did about the gods of the other peoples of the world – the work of human hands.'

2 Chronicles 32.19

This verse is part of the story of King Hezekiah and took place when his enemy, Sennacherib, was laying siege to Jerusalem. Messengers were sent to taunt the people defending Jerusalem and they began by mocking their king, Hezekiah. Eventually they went further and began to mock God, in whom the people trusted, saying that he was little more than a man-made idol. The story continues and it becomes evident just how wrong they were! Both Hezekiah and Isaiah cried out to their God who they knew to be different, and without Hezekiah even going to battle the army of Sennacherib was destroyed.

The challenge for us as we read today's words is to consider how much power we believe God has over the situations facing us? If we are honest, there may be times when we are not sure he has much power at all, and pray with very little expectation that anything is going to happen.

Before you begin to pray about whatever concerns you today, spend some time reminding yourself of the character and power of God. By doing this you will find a new confidence when you come to lift up your concerns to him.

Expect God to work – even if you don't know how | 2

'And the Lord sent an angel, who annihilated all the fighting men and the commanders and officers in the camp of the Assyrian king.'
2 Chronicles 32.21

Yesterday we started to look at the story of King Hezekiah. Jerusalem was under siege, so the King and Isaiah both called out to God for help. It is likely that they didn't really know what they were expecting God to do – but they were desperate. They knew about the power and wonder of God even if they couldn't see exactly how their prayers would be answered.

Your situation may not seem quite as desperate as theirs, but the principle still applies. You, too, can turn to the power and wonder of God, even if you have no idea what he might do about your particular situation. Your lack of vision for how God might act doesn't mean that he doesn't have a plan. It is all too easy to assume that there is little point in praying just because you can't see how God will help.

Prayer begins with you exalting the character of God, and then bringing your concerns to him. Do so in the knowledge that he is faithful and hears your requests, and then wait in expectation to see what he will do.

Keep going!

'. . . you may have had to suffer grief in all kinds of trials. These have come so that your faith – of greater worth than gold, which perishes even though refined by fire – may be proved genuine and may result in praise, glory and honour when Jesus Christ is revealed.'

1 Peter 1.6-7

The opening verses of Peter's first letter speak in such exalted language about what it means to be a Christian that it is hard to recognise ourselves in what he is writing!

The words above are an example of this, as they speak of the tremendous faith we exhibit in our trials and how it will all be for the praise and glory of Jesus. Sometimes we read such words and feel a bit of a fraud. Compared to the persecution and martyrdom of the first Christians, or compared to the suffering that others go through, we may feel that these words don't apply to us. Yet they do!

In Matthew 17.20, Jesus speaks of faith like a mustard seed,

and in chapter 13.32 Matthew tells us that the remarkable thing about mustard seeds is their growth from seed to tree. Whenever you look upwards in your needs, bringing your difficulties and anxieties to Jesus, you are demonstrating faith – your belief that there is more to your life than you are currently experiencing. Every time you do this, your faith grows a little more and you honour Jesus.

You may not think you are up there with the great saints, but the reality is that every time you expose the seeds of your faith to what is going on in your life, in some way glory and honour are given to Jesus. Keep going – you are doing fine!

Hold on!

'Jesus told him, "Don't be afraid; just believe."'

Mark 5.36

These beautiful words can be found in the story of the raising of Jairus' daughter from the dead. Jesus was going with Jairus to bring healing to his daughter, but they were interrupted on their way by the woman who was then healed of bleeding. As a result of the time this took, his daughter died and the news reached Jairus. It is just after this that Jesus spoke these words to Jairus, "Don't be afraid; just believe." What Jesus was saying to Jairus was this: hold on.

Did Jesus really need to say anything? After all, in just a few moments Jairus was going to see an astounding miracle before his very eyes. However, it may be that in some way

Jesus needed Jairus to hold on. He didn't tell Jairus what was going to happen or expect him to believe what might seem unbelievable, but he simply needed him to hold onto the fact that it was not over yet.

Faith is meant to be a gift to us, but all too often we make it like an impossible mountain we have to climb, and if we stumble or fall we go back to the bottom until we learn to get it right. The gift is this – whatever your situation, Jesus is with you. Hold onto this and trust him to still be at work even when you haven't got a clue what is going on.

Our God is greater

'... whom shall I fear?'

Psalm 27.1

Psalm 27 is a beautiful psalm that addresses the whole issue of fear. It recommends overcoming fear by replacing it with a focus on the greatness of God and his presence with us.

The psalm begins by exalting the greatness and wonder of God; there may be an enemy opposing us, maybe even an army, but the reality is that God is stronger. The light and salvation of God are greater than the darkness of any fear we might experience. Then the psalmist moves on to consider how wonderfully safe and secure it would be to continually dwell in God's presence, with him keeping us safe in times of trouble. You may be thinking that this is easier said than done!

It is very hard to focus on God's strength and proximity to us when fear has gripped us and is claiming all our attention. However, this is where practice comes in! In times of calm, practise worshipping God for his greatness, power and majesty, and acknowledge that he is close. Jesus said that he would never leave or forsake you, so get used to living in his presence. By doing this you will become accustomed to turning your thoughts to the wonder and presence of God, so when troubles arise you will do this quite naturally. When fear begins to surface it will not seem as bad, simply because your eyes will naturally be turned in a different direction.

Take time to ponder the wonder and the greatness of God, any way you find helpful, perhaps by singing or listening to a song or reading a great psalm of praise. Do this until your vision is fixed on God and nothing else. Then take a moment to focus on his presence. Ask yourself where he is for you – in front of you, beside you, or within you. It really doesn't matter where you sense him, but consciously take time to enjoy his presence with you.

166

It's not all down to you

"Not by might nor by power, but by my Spirit," says the LORD Almighty.

Zechariah 4.6

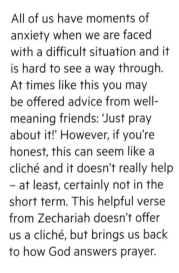

All of us have moments of anxiety when we are faced with a difficult situation and it is hard to see a way through. At times like this you may be offered advice from well-meaning friends: 'Just pray about it!' However, if you're honest, this can seem like a cliché and it doesn't really help – at least, certainly not in the short term. This helpful verse from Zechariah doesn't offer us a cliché, but brings us back to how God answers prayer.

When situations loom large in our lives, we simply cannot see how things can be resolved. We think of all the practical steps we can take and they are still not enough. These powerful words spoken by God bring us back to the reality that prayer is vitally important because our own natural resources are totally insufficient. The help that God brings is not based on our own resources, but on his Spirit. Often the Spirit may choose to work through human resources, but it is still the work of the Spirit who brings it all about.

If you are facing an anxious situation, of course it is right to pray, but first of all call to mind where God's help comes from and the mighty resources he has at his disposal. You may well find that this completely changes the way you pray!

Be honest about your needs

'When I said, "My foot is slipping," your unfailing love, Lord, supported me. When anxiety was great within me, your consolation brought me joy.'

Psalm 94.18-19

There is something about these words that speaks of honesty and truth. The writer is absolutely honest about his situation – at times he felt he was slipping, and sensed anxiety growing within him.

Quite often we hide what we are really going through. It's easy to put on a mask for others, and sometimes even for ourselves, to conceal what we are feeling. However, if we are covering it up we are not bringing it into God's light.

This leads on to the other great truth expressed in this psalm: namely that we have a saviour God who rescues

us. Even in the midst of his own precarious position, the psalmist recognised the unfailing love, support and joy that God brings.

A good question for us as we go through challenging times is this, 'What do I need God to do for me?' It is not about what we can do for ourselves because then we would not need God, but what is it that only he can bring to you or your situation?

As you come before God now, be honest about what you are going through, because he is the one who has the power and love to bring you what you need.

It's for you!

'Then Jesus asked, "What is the kingdom of God like? What shall I compare it to?"'

Luke 13.18

Immediately before Jesus posed this question there was an account of a person being healed. A woman had been sick for 18 years and as soon as Jesus saw her he set her free. The story took place in a synagogue, and rather than the chief official rejoicing in what he had just seen he complained because it had taken place on the Sabbath.

After healing the woman, Jesus asked the question we read in today's verse and went on to compare the kingdom of God to a tree in which birds could build their nests. In other words, the assembled people had all just seen a beautiful demonstration of the kingdom at work in one person's life, and Jesus went on to declare that everyone could make their home within it. He was simply saying that the kingdom of God is for you.

It can be so tempting to think that the wonderful things of God are always for other people. As you turn to God today, believe that his kingdom is for you too. He loves you being with him and has so much to give you.

Being godly to others

'Let love and faithfulness never leave you'

Proverbs 3.3

This beautiful proverb gives us an insight into God's heart for us as we interact with others. So often we question what God wants us to do in a particular situation, but if we remember to act with love and faithfulness, we won't go far wrong.

In 1 Corinthians 13, Paul painted a marvellous practical picture of what love in action looks like. If you can hold fast to this when you are in the company of others – being kind, not boasting and keeping no record of wrongs – you will be doing God's will in these situations. Similarly, we are also called to faithfulness. Perhaps one way of describing this is to grasp God's vision for the person you are with and what he wants for them. If you can hold onto the fact that God wants to bring abundant life to them, you are more likely to try to be God's hands and voice to them.

Turn this proverb into a prayer and keep these words on your lips when you meet and talk with others: 'Let love and faithfulness never leave me.'

An uncomfortable meal!

'One Sabbath, when Jesus went to eat in the house of a prominent Pharisee, he was being carefully watched.'

Luke 14.1

We sometimes think about enjoying close fellowship with Jesus over a meal together around a table. This story records one meal that some people had with Jesus – but it was distinctly uncomfortable! We are told about three separate occurrences during the meal that probably made the assembled diners squirm. The first was when Jesus healed someone, the second when he rebuked the guests for their sense of self-importance, and the third when he challenged his host to be more caring to those in need.

On other occasions, we read of Jesus eating with sinners. Was he equally blunt with them? If so, do we really want to be close to Jesus? Presumably he usually behaved differently or he would not have received many invitations! However, today's verse gives us a clear insight into why Jesus acted as he did on that particular occasion – 'he was being carefully watched.'

It is our attitude to Jesus that sets the scene. In his ministry, he showed such kindness to the people who knew they needed him, yet was so challenging to those who disapproved of him and his actions. What made all the difference was how people regarded him.

As you spend time with Jesus now, have the humility to come to him as you are. If you are hurt, let him know you hurt; if you are joyful, then pour out your joy to him; and if you are confused, share your confusion with him. Be yourself with Jesus so he can be himself with you.

Guard your heart

'Above all else, guard your heart, for everything you do flows from it.'

Proverbs 4.23

It is God who changes our hearts, but it is us who have to guard the change. We can so easily let the wonderful things God does for us slip away; a profound sense of God's love can be quickly replaced by a feeling of being a million miles away from him, or some precious words spoken to us by God can get completely forgotten the very next day. This command to guard our hearts is to resolve to let the things of God stay and deepen within us.

One way of doing this is to keep a journal – just a few lines to record the truths and thoughts that come to you.

Then, as you read back over them you are reminded of them and they become uppermost in your thoughts once more.

The reason we are commanded to guard our hearts is because they affect our behaviour and attitude, both to others and to ourselves. All too often we can be 'up' one day and 'down' the next. Guarding our hearts – holding onto the things God reveals to us – brings a stability and consistency to our lives.

As you reflect over the past few days, what are the truths God has been trying to share with you? Jot them down, hold on to them and guard your heart.

You have authority

'May God, who has caused his Name to dwell there, overthrow any king or people who lifts a hand to change this decree or to destroy this temple in Jerusalem. I Darius have decreed it. Let it be carried out with diligence.'
Ezra 6.12

In the book of Ezra, we read about people returning from exile and beginning to rebuild the temple. Not everyone was keen on this idea and there was opposition and mutterings of "Who said you could do this anyway?"

To settle the matter, an appeal was made to King Darius to ascertain whether or not the people had authority to rebuild the temple. After a search through all the records, a command from the previous king was discovered, stating that the work should be undertaken. Armed with this, the work continued with renewed confidence.

As you read the Bible today, consider what it gives you authority to do. The words of Jesus express the heart of God for us, so when you read his words you are reading the very heart of God.

When Jesus asks you to do something, you have his authority to do it. For example, you have his authority to remain within the love of God, to be kind, to bless others and to see yourself as someone within whom the presence of God dwells. Such things are not just for others, they are for you and for all of us. The King has spoken!

Choose life

'At the time of the banquet he sent his servant to tell those who had been invited, "Come, for everything is now ready." But they all alike began to make excuses. The first said, "I have just bought a field, and I must go and see it. Please excuse me."'

Luke 14.17-18

There are many applications of this parable, such as Jesus throwing the kingdom of God open to those beyond the Jewish faith, but perhaps it is at its most challenging when we apply it to ourselves. Jesus has invited us to partake in the wonders of his abundant life. This sounds so wonderful, but can be hard to receive. Yet he points out that there are always people who miss out because they won't take up his invitation.

It's worth considering what might prevent you from fully embracing the life Jesus offers. Maybe you suspect

he will ask you to give up something or you fear what others might think of you, or it may be you can't take seriously an offer of intimacy with God, struggling to believe it really could be for you. As you read this parable, can you see the amazing offer that people are turning down? Wouldn't it be tragic if other people think this about you as you hold back from what God wants to give you?

God is close to you right now, in all his gentleness and tenderness, so tell him what it is that holds you back from fully embracing the life he offers.

174

How would Jesus serve?

'Those who have served well gain an excellent standing and great assurance in their faith in Christ Jesus.'

1 Timothy 3.13

It is easy to see how serving others gains us a good reputation, especially among those we serve, but Paul is saying more in this passage. He says that service brings us an assurance – or a boldness – in our faith. How does this work?

Paul suggests that when we serve others our faith in Christ increases. The reason for this is because when we serve we are becoming Christ-like, so we naturally begin to see things from Christ's perspective. All too often we tend to think about how other people might benefit us, whereas if we approach them with an attitude of how we can serve them, then we have caught the heart and attitude of Jesus. This gives us insights into his character that we could probably not gain in any other way.

A common question is, "What would Jesus do?" This can sometimes leave us feeling a little inadequate as we face up to the fact that we are unlikely to respond just as he would, but perhaps an alternative question should be, "How would Jesus serve?" The answer might be equally challenging, but in seeking to serve others instead of receiving from them, we begin to see the world from a whole new perspective – his!

Overcoming temptation

'My son, pay attention to my wisdom, turn your ear to my words of insight'

Proverbs 5.1

If there is one fact that unites us all, it is this: we all face temptation. You might think you are the only person facing a particular temptation, but the Bible clearly states some good and releasing news – there is nothing new about the particular temptations you face; they are common to us all (1 Corinthians 10.13).

This theme of avoiding temptation also features in the book of Proverbs, and in today's passage the writer gives us two insights. First, he begins his advice with the words, 'My son'. We may not know why he chose these words, and exactly whom he was addressing, but if we take the Bible as a love letter from Father God to his children, male and female, then these words take on a new significance. God is trying to share his insights and wisdom with us, his much-loved children. We are not dismissed from his loving heart just because

temptation strikes us. When you feel the pull of temptation, this little endearment is a glorious invitation to turn to 'Abba, Father', and enjoy the wonder of relationship.

The second truth is that God has insight. His Holy Spirit lives within us and if we choose to seek him and listen to the voice within, he will whisper to us a way out of our temptation. The wonder of this is that even if we get it wrong and fail, Jesus has opened the way for us to return to the Father's loving heart by receiving the forgiveness his death has released for us.

What is your greatest temptation at this moment? Rejoice that the Father's love for you is greater than your temptation. If you feel you have failed, accept the forgiveness that is available to you. Then listen for the voice of the Spirit within you, guiding you to a different place.

176

Longing for God

'As the deer pants for streams of water, so my soul pants for you, my God. My soul thirsts for God, for the living God.'

Psalm 42.1

These beautiful words express something very deep: a soul longing for God. It strikes me that longing can take many forms – a yearning for a deeper relationship with God, for freedom from a recurring sin or a memory that seems to have a hold over us, or for release from sickness.

The writer of the psalm does something that many of us may well admit to doing – he talks to himself! Although he still has faith in the living God, some fears are beginning to creep in that cause him to question God's goodness. In this psalm, his thoughts are expressed rather like a conversation between these two opposing trains of thought. He is seeking to bring every part of himself back to the wonder of the living God and to deliberately trust in him despite life's difficulties.

You may be going through hard times and starting to doubt whether God will ever do anything to help. If this applies to you, do as the psalmist did and try to find something to help you hold onto God – possibly a Bible verse that you know well, a deep knowledge of the love of God that you cannot deny, or simply the words of Jesus in the Bible, 'I am with you always'. Let this truth speak to every part of you and to the situations you are going through.

What's your attitude?

'Whatever the God of heaven has prescribed, let it be done with diligence for the temple of the God of heaven.'

Ezra 7.23

It is true of so many things in life, and certainly our Christian beliefs, that it is not just what we do that counts but also our attitude. Ezra was told by the king to return to his own people and encourage them in their pursuit of God. To support him in this mission, the king gave him a letter encouraging the people to do what they do 'with diligence'. The word 'diligence' carries with it a sense of zeal, energy, conscientiousness and persistence. This could present some of us with a challenge! We might be able to say that we pray, worship and read our Bibles but the king was encouraging his people to do more than this: to do what they did wholeheartedly.

The effort you put into something is likely to reflect what you get out of it. If you spend time with God simply because you think you ought to pray, there is likely to be a formality that has little to do with relationship. Similarly, if you only worship in church because that is what happens at the beginning of the service, it's possible you won't be doing it with great commitment.

As you pray today, pray as someone who is utterly loved and cherished by God; as you read the Bible, read it with the expectation that God desires to speak to you personally through it, and as you spend time in worship do it with the enthusiasm of one who has been rescued from darkness and brought into the light.

The trustworthiness of God

"In the same way, those of you who do not give up everything you have cannot be my disciples."

Luke 14.33

There are some verses in the Bible that we wish were simply not there! Verses such as this seem to ask too much – if Jesus could have toned down his language a bit it would be so much easier! What was he really saying?

Jesus was talking about trust. A sure sign of the trust we have in God is what we are prepared to trust him with. If we say we trust him, yet don't include him in any of our planning and seek to hold onto everything ourselves, it is hardly trust. Trust is acknowledging that we really do put everything into God's hands and believe that he will work for our ultimate good and the good of others.

The incredible good news, of course, is that God says he is trustworthy. He invites us to trust him because he knows that if we hand control of everything over to him, things will go a lot better.

Is there something in your life at the moment that is causing you anxiety? First, take a moment to focus on the reality of God's presence with you, and then make a deliberate choice to hand your concern over to him. You may find it helpful to envisage it in the palm of your hand and to consciously hand it to him. God is asking for your trust; he loves you so much, and through your trust he can bring about things he could not do any other way.

Bearing God's presence | 1

'His divine power has given us everything we need for a godly life'

2 Peter 1.3

Try making a very subtle change to this verse by inserting 'me' instead of 'us' to read: His divine power has given me everything I need for a godly life.

Over the next week, we are going to look at ways in which we can strengthen our spiritual lives, because the stronger we are, the less likely we will trip up. Set-backs are not just about moral failures, but also about those moments when you find yourself disappointed by your own reactions to events or people, or when you catch yourself thinking far less of yourself than God thinks of you.

This inner strengthening begins with you catching the truth that God has already put

his power within you; it is there already. All you have to do is pause and draw upon it. It comes back to a helpful verse that I have often used: 'I bear your name, Lord God Almighty' (Jeremiah 15.16). In other words, the very presence of God dwells within you. Take a few minutes to mull over this verse right now, perhaps repeating it to yourself, so that the truth it reveals comes to mind when you need it through the day.

You may like to link it in with your breathing. If so, as you breathe in say: 'I bear your name', and as you breathe out: 'Lord God Almighty'. Repeat this a few times and let the truth of it sink in.

Letting Jesus shine through you | 2

'... make every effort to add to your faith goodness'

2 Peter 1.5

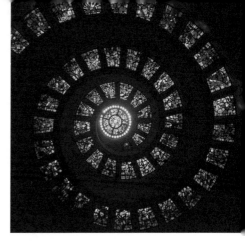

Yesterday we were reminded of God's presence within us, and now Peter talks about how we can allow our faith to make a difference.

In this context, our faith is the belief that wherever we go we have the presence of God within us, bringing the potential to change every situation we face. Think through the day ahead of you. What situations will you face and who will you meet? Peter's encouragement is not to automatically head into the day, but to catch a vision of how you will live it. He urges you to add goodness to your faith.

This word 'goodness' carries with it a sense of moral excellence. If you like, it is the very best that you could possibly be – perhaps how Jesus would be in your situation. This is what you are encouraged to capture as you look ahead. Since the life and presence of Jesus is within you, it really is possible to live like this – but you are more likely to do so if you plan ahead.

Spend a few moments thinking about some of the situations facing you. How would Jesus handle them? Take time to genuinely thank him that he is already within you and will remain there, and head into your day letting his life shine through you.

Knowing Jesus is different to knowing about him | 3

'. . . make every effort to add to your faith goodness; and to goodness, knowledge'

2 Peter 1.5

Knowledge can mean different things; the learning of facts or the search for wisdom for example. It is interesting that in this letter the word 'knowledge' is often used in the context of us knowing Jesus (see verses 3 and 8). Perhaps Peter was reminding us of the truth that there is a difference between actually knowing Jesus and knowing about him.

This is an on-going challenge for us all. It is easy to look back over the past day and realise that our investment in a relationship with Jesus has been quite low; although we may well have gone through the entire day knowing about him, we haven't enjoyed relationship with him. How can we remedy this?

To be constantly aware of your relationship with Jesus means that you have to begin somewhere. Start by taking a few minutes to whisper his name – he is with you right where you are. Even if you don't sense his presence, try to hold on to this truth and believe it. Since he is with you, what do you want to say to him and what is his response?

The power is within | 4

'... make every effort to add to your faith ... self-control'

2 Peter 1.5-6

Self-control applies to so many things – such as breaking the control bad habits have upon us or checking our words before we say something harsh – and just as New Year resolutions seldom last for more than a couple of days, all too often we fail in our attempts at self-control.

Interestingly, the message of the Bible is that laws, whether applied by others or by ourselves, have little power to bring change to what goes on within us. So why does Peter encourage us to add self-control to our faith if it doesn't work? The way this passage is laid out is rather like making a lasagne – it is about adding layers to what is already there! None of these qualities – goodness, knowledge, self-control – is enough in itself, but they are to be seen in relation to each other. We have already noted that a resolve to exercise better self-control has a tendency to fail, but it takes on a new meaning when it is added to our belief that we bear the very presence of God. Rather than us being able to control what is within, we realise that we have another power within us bringing change – the power of Christ.

Take a few minutes to enjoy the presence of Jesus within you, perhaps by gently speaking his name, sensing his breath within you as you breathe, or simply by letting the truth of the words, 'You are here', sink in deeper. When you are next conscious of the need for self-control, remember to come back to this and draw upon the power of Jesus within you.

Keep going | 5

'. . . make every effort to add to your faith . . . perseverance'

2 Peter 1.6

One of the most common excuses for giving up something is: "I tried it once, but it didn't work." This can apply to almost anything in life, including our Christian ministry or our attempts to draw on the power of Christ within us. Perhaps it is for this very reason that Peter added perseverance to his list of ways in which we can strengthen our spiritual lives.

Perseverance means that if we try something new and it is hard, or we discover that things do not turn out as we would like, we carry on anyway in the belief that God values our commitment and our vision.

There are stories of people who prayed for individuals or events for years before they saw the fruit of their prayers. Indeed, Hebrews 11 contains references to those whose heroism was not in their achievements, but in their perseverance.

You carry the presence of God within you, and the fact that you may not see the daily outworking of this does not change this truth. Come back to it – God is in you. Take this into today, and the next day, and the day after. It is your faithfulness to this truth that daily opens the door for God to act through you.

184

Seeing things through God's eyes | 6

'. . . make every effort to add to your faith . . . godliness'

2 Peter 1.6

The word 'godliness' implies being like God – a challenge you may think is one step too far as you struggle with any number of difficulties that seem designed to trip you up in your walk with God! So how are we meant to be like God, because to be truly like him would involve not just what we do but also the words we speak, think and have on our hearts?

Perhaps godliness begins with us trying to see things through God's eyes. If we could glimpse how he views things surely this would help. So how can we take the first steps along this road?

It is about trying to break into that brief moment between something happening and our reaction to it. If we can open the door at this point to ask our Father God how he sees the situation, rather than reacting out of our natural passions, things may well change. We all know only too well that if someone is rude to us, the temptation is to snap back, but God sees what they have been going through. If we could glimpse this, our reaction may be more compassionate.

We can be certain that we will face many opportunities to practise godliness today – many moments when we can choose whether to react in haste or seek to catch God's heart. How much better for us all if we can choose God's path. One way to start is to look back over the past day and recall moments when you could have acted more like him. This is not an exercise to show yourself up, but hopefully a way of recognising those moments when you had a choice and learn from them, ready for the next time they present themselves.

Be kind | 7

'... make every effort to add to your faith ... mutual affection'

2 Peter 1.5-7

In other versions of the Bible, the phrase 'mutual affection' is translated as 'kindness', 'affection' and 'warm friendliness'. If it is not too much of a cliché, it is simply about being nice to people. It is about looking out for the needs of others and doing what you can to help them.

This calling to be nice is part of the Bible passage in which Peter laid down the foundations of our spiritual lives and encouraged us to grow in stature rather than to stumble and fall. Where 'nice-ness' comes in to this is that if we have an attitude of wanting to be kind to others, the focus is taken off us and our own needs. It's not that our own needs are unimportant – they matter; indeed Peter himself said in his letter, 'Cast all your anxiety on him because he cares for you.' (1 Peter 5.7) However, the point is that we may do better if we give our own needs to God and focus on caring for others; by doing this we may find other people drawing alongside us to meet our needs.

Touch God's heart today by looking out for opportunities to be kind and caring to others.

Showing love | 8

*'... make every effort to
add to your faith ... love.'*

2 Peter 1.5-7

The final characteristic
on Peter's list of qualities
we need to cultivate is
probably the one that we have
been expecting – love. How
does love differ from all the
other qualities he mentioned?

The other attributes are all
important, but perhaps the
one missing element that Peter
now wants us to capture is
the nature of sacrificial love,
which he had seen exemplified
in the life of Jesus. He heard
Jesus speak about sacrificial
love, saw Jesus accept the
treatment handed out to him
when he could so easily have
evaded it, and noted the level

of sacrifice Christ was willing
to endure for us. So Peter
encourages us to exhibit love.

If you remember, the aim of
this list of virtues – goodness,
knowledge, self-control,
perseverance, godliness, mutual
affection and love – is to stop
us from stumbling and falling in
our faith. The contribution that
love makes is to ensure that by
being sacrificial in our dealings
with others, we will avoid simply
trying to meet our own needs
or getting what we can out of
people or situations. Jesus laid
down his life and gave himself
totally for you. So what can
you do for others today?

Them and us

"I am too ashamed and disgraced, my God, to lift up my face to you, because our sins are higher than our heads and our guilt has reached to the heavens."

Ezra 9.6

This is not just a 'normal' prayer of confession. Something about the way the people were living had just been brought to Ezra's attention and although it wasn't anything that he had been involved in himself, he was so moved that he lifted up his voice to God and examined his own heart too. Ezra didn't see sin and accuse others of being sinners – he included himself in the sin.

When people fall, or when situations go wrong, it is very easy for us to apportion blame, saying, "They shouldn't have done that" or "If only they had listened . . ." A very honest way of praying for others who may have got themselves into difficulty is to acknowledge that within ourselves are the same human qualities that have caused problems for them. This may involve admitting before God that we too have moments of greed or a tendency to lash out in anger, for example.

Someone once said that Christianity was about one beggar telling another beggar where to find bread, and there is something wonderfully true in this. As you come across people today who may be in difficult situations because of their actions, take a moment to pause and search your own heart. Do you detect these same tendencies within you? God certainly won't punish you for your honesty, but he will respond to the open door of your vulnerability.

What's grace?

'You then, my son, be strong in the grace that is in Christ Jesus.'

2 Timothy 2.1

One of the most striking things about this verse is that it is in the present tense. It is all about 'the grace that is in Christ Jesus' right now, rather than what was in him in the past or will be one day in the future. The grace of God is here and now – so what is it exactly?

The grace of God is what we are unable to produce ourselves – God's life within us. It brings something beyond our own means into the situations facing us. We may need grace to love someone that we struggle to love or the grace to speak boldly when we feel timid.

It is also encouraging that we are told to be 'strong' in this grace; in other words, to draw upon it and not be anxious that we are calling upon it often. It is not that there is a limited quota of grace, God's desire is that we constantly draw upon what he has made available for us so we can live the life he wants us to live. The big question is whether we will remember to do so. Jesus is with us at all times and in all places, and so is his grace. Whatever your need, his grace is there for the asking.

In what area of your life do you sense that you need his grace? Give thanks for what grace you do see – and ask him for more.

You and the power of God

'. . . I am suffering even to the point of being chained like a criminal. But God's word is not chained.'

2 Timothy 2.9

Paul's declaration was more than just fine words. As he looked at the chains binding him, restricting his movement and mobility, he could still declare that though he might be bound, the word of God was not.

You are unlikely to be facing the persecution that Paul faced, but it may well be the case that you face some sort of limitation: perhaps past events have had a negative impact upon you, or you carry emotional wounds and find yourself unduly timid in certain situations. Yet however bound or limited you may feel, be encouraged that God can still work wonderfully through you.

When you act in accordance with the word of God, whether in obeying his command to love or speaking up when you don't feel like it, your words and actions carry a power that is beyond your feelings. You may be chained and hampered, but the word of God that prompts you is not.

You carry within you the very presence of God, which includes his grace to call upon whenever you need it and his word to guide and encourage you. Whatever limitations might weigh you down, the presence of God has a power of its own that is beyond anything you can even imagine.

Your role

'. . . if we are faithless, he remains faithful, for he cannot disown himself.'

2 Timothy 2.13

Many people wonder whether God really uses them to bring about his purposes. If we are honest, we can probably think of many reasons why God might not use us: we don't pray very well, we're not holy enough or we don't live exemplary lives as some other people seem to.

We all know the importance of praying and avoiding sin, but it doesn't affect how God treats us. Paul explains in today's verse that it is all about God's faithfulness and not about our faithlessness.

God has a vision to see his world transformed by people like us. In fact, he only has 'people like us' to bring about his transformation. He is utterly committed to it and will remain faithful to his vision no matter what, so he will certainly use you regardless of how bad you think you are.

Rather than focusing on what you think might separate you from God, spend some time giving thanks to him for his vision for the people you will come across today, and offer yourself for his use.

God's filter

'Do not judge'

Matthew 7.1

This is probably one of the most disobeyed commands in the Bible! Entertaining an accusation is something most of us do without thinking about it. Perhaps the most striking aspect of this command is what it implies about the nature of God.

The aim of the commands in the Bible is to help us become more like God, and it is an amazing thought that he does not entertain accusations or judgments against us. In fact, it is almost unbelievable! How can it be that our perfect God looks at us – who are far from perfect – and does not judge us? He doesn't even 'tut' away to himself at just how bad we are!

The Bible refers to this as the gift of righteousness, achieved when Jesus died for us. It is best explained by a play on words: we are justified – 'just if I' hadn't sinned. So when God looks at you, it's not that he disregards what you consider to be the obvious sin in your life, he looks at you through the cross of what Jesus has already done for you. Through this filter, you are totally clean.

Take a moment to present yourself before God and have the confidence to believe that he really does not even see what has been forgiven.

192

Don't just talk!

'Wisdom has built her house; she has set up its seven pillars. She has prepared her meat and mixed her wine; she has also set her table.'

Proverbs 9.1-2

You have doubtless needed wisdom many times in your life, perhaps when you were facing a situation beyond your control or when someone was causing you distress with their words or actions. Whatever the cause, the problem was that you simply did not know what to do.

This verse assures us that wisdom exists. The book of Proverbs tells us that wisdom is somehow intricately bound to our relationship with God; wisdom is always available to us because God is always there for us. When things get difficult, seeking God's wisdom is more than just praying about something. It involves being in his presence and listening for his voice. We often speak about God's 'voice' which gives the impression that he sounds the same as anyone else speaking to us. Yet God's voice of wisdom can take many forms, such as a random thought or a Bible verse that suddenly comes to you.

If you are worried about something, rather than talking to God about it, try listening for his wisdom on the matter. It is always a good idea to share things with a friend, but when you begin to listen for God's voice it can lead to a deeper relationship with him, where prayer becomes a dialogue and not just a list of concerns.

What have you got?

"Whoever can be trusted with very little can also be trusted with much, and whoever is dishonest with very little will also be dishonest with much."

Luke 16.10

The chances are that all of us want more from God than we currently have – whether it be a greater sphere of influence, a larger ministry or a deeper awareness of his love. We know that our lives would be so much more productive if God gave us them, and that there is no way we can attain them without him.

However, this verse adds a twist to our view. Our focus should not be on what else God can give, but rather on what he has already given us and what we are doing with it.

If, for example, you want a deeper knowledge of God's love, today's verse may challenge you to consider what you are doing with what you already have. The Bible gives many assurances that you are deeply loved, in fact, you are loved to such an extent that God gave Jesus for you. What are you doing with this fact? How grateful are you for it?

It is entirely appropriate to seek wonderful things from God, but don't forget what he has already given you. Before you ask for more, what are you doing with what you already have?

194

Leaving hatred alone

'Hatred stirs up conflict, but love covers over all wrongs.'

Proverbs 10.12

It is amazing how easily we can stir up distressing memories! An episode may have long passed, but it is easy to revisit the painful event and imagine all the things we would like to have said at the time. We really are stirring up something that would far better be left alone.

The opposite of this scenario is love and forgiveness. Love, we are told in the Bible, covers over all wrongs and choosing to forgive means you are no longer imprisoned by the past actions of others.

Forgiving others begins by receiving once again God's love for you. This involves consciously taking time to revel in his profound, personal attentiveness and care for you alone. It is also about accepting that you have been forgiven and recognising how merciful God is to you. Then you will be in a better position to consider those for whom you still feel resentment – can you entrust them into the hands of God? This is not about belittling the wrong someone has done to you, but is about trusting God with the outcome and continuing to do so.

How strong is your faith?

'He said to him, "If they do not listen to Moses and the Prophets, they will not be convinced even if someone rises from the dead."'

Luke 16.31

How strong is your faith? You probably wish it was stronger; how can you strengthen it? If only you had some proof, it would help; if you could see something dramatic happening in front of your very eyes, you would be convinced and your faith would grow.

In this verse Jesus said that for many people it won't be like this. Dramatic experiences can draw us closer to God, but for some people these will never be enough: they will always attempt to explain it away or find some other explanation. Jesus seemed to be saying here that the most effective way of deepening faith is to take seriously what he said in the Bible.

Choose a passage from the New Testament, perhaps one of the stories about Jesus, and as you read it think about what it shows you about God, about his character and his heart. Try to make it personal – what is God saying through this passage about his love and desire for you? Take this into the day ahead and let your faith grow stronger.

The waiting father | 1

"The younger one said to his father, 'Father, give me my share of the estate.' So he divided his property between them."

Luke 15.12

The story of the Prodigal Son is well known and much loved by many people. It is a parable, so was probably told by Jesus with the intention of emphasising one main point. It is risky to read too much into the details, but there are a few things to be glimpsed in this beautiful tale about a father and his two sons.

Since the father would have known exactly what his sons were like, and that one of them tended to be wild and impetuous, it seems likely that the younger son's decision to take his money and leave would not have come as a surprise. The next time we encounter the father in the story is when he saw his son returning from afar. Commentators and writers have often described this as a picture of the waiting father – a father who never gave up hope that one day his son would come home.

When these two pictures, the impetuous son and the waiting father, are put together, they fill us with hope. It really doesn't matter how far we feel from God, because he is there watching, waiting, hoping for us to come back to him and full of joy when we do. There are many times when we turn away from God in big and small ways and it is easy to assume he must be disappointed or fed up with us, but this story assures us this is not the case and he is still there for us.

On another level, this message is about our everyday spirituality. Can we be bothered to pray today? Is it worth reading the Bible? The picture of the waiting Father still stands. He is looking forwards to seeing you and spending time with you because you are so precious to him.

Inexhaustible love | 2

"After he had spent everything, there was a severe famine in that whole country, and he began to be in need."

Luke 15.14

In the story of the Prodigal Son, this wayward boy – who at one time had been so rich – squandered every penny of his inheritance. Yet despite this, the amazing compassion of his father remained undiminished. The son had spent everything and exhausted all his resources, but he could never exhaust his father's love.

You may be rich or poor, triumphing or failing in your Christian life, giving much or little to others, yet the one thing you also possess that can never be exhausted is the deep, personal love and compassion of your Father God for you. You are invited to simply whisper the word 'Father' in complete and utter confidence that when God hears this word on your lips, he knows it comes from his child who he loves deeply.

Whatever this day holds for you, live it in the confidence that you are deeply loved by Father God. Hold on to this and let it be personal for you.

Abundant love | 3

"But the father said to his servants, 'Quick! Bring the best robe and put it on him. Put a ring on his finger and sandals on his feet.'"

Luke 15.22

The reaction of the father to his wayward son in this well-known parable is amazing. He didn't simply welcome him back as a labourer, or with a warning that he had one last chance, but showered him with gifts – far more than his elder brother felt he deserved! He really was left in no doubt that he was honoured and cherished.

It is easy to look at some people and not feel surprised that God would want to shower them with blessings and favour because they appear to be such saintly people or good examples of a godly life. It is quite another matter to think of God wanting to pour out such blessings upon you, with your weaknesses and failings. Perhaps it is all a matter of perception? We can easily become consumed with our own failings and imperfections, and assume that God sees us in the same light. However, this picture of the father's abundant generosity shows his whole vision was focused on, and consumed with, love for his son.

You stand before your Father who loves you with the same love he had for Jesus (John 17.26). Catch the wonder of this truth: your father rejoices over you with singing and if he had a literal robe right now he would wrap it around you.

Your chief weapon

'Those who carried materials did their work with one hand and held a weapon in the other, and each of the builders wore his sword at his side as he worked.'

Nehemiah 4.17-18

Here Nehemiah was speaking about the people being wary and on their guard because of the possibility of a sudden attack. They were constantly aware of such a threat and acted accordingly. In your own life, you may be aware of the way that you can feel quite close to God one minute and then do something daft and feel far from him the next. Our awareness of God's presence can vary and fluctuate in such a short space of time. Like the men who were rebuilding the walls of Jerusalem, we, too, must learn to carry our weapons with us at all times.

In Paul's first chapter of the letter to the Ephesians, our weapons are clearly laid out for us. He wrote that the foundations upon which we should build our lives are to know that we are chosen and adopted by the Father, and forgiven by him.

These are the basic weapons that we are meant to carry with us – the knowledge that at all times, whatever our feelings, the living God has chosen us to be his very own children, upon whom he desires to pour out his love. Whatever attacks befall us and however our feelings may fluctuate, it is this true understanding that we need to come back to.

You belong to God and his loving heart is turned towards you; nothing can change this.

Everyday faith

"Suppose one of you has a servant ploughing or looking after the sheep. Will he say to the servant when he comes in from the field, 'Come along now and sit down to eat'? Won't he rather say, 'Prepare my supper, get yourself ready and wait on me while I eat and drink; after that you may eat and drink'? Will he thank the servant because he did what he was told to do? So you also, when you have done everything you were told to do, should say, 'We are unworthy servants; we have only done our duty.'"

Luke 17.7-10

We all like to be thanked! When we have gone out of our way to help someone, or given something that cost us, a sincere 'thank you' makes everything worthwhile. So given this, these words from Jesus can seem a bit like a slap in the face! He seems to be saying, 'You've only done your duty so why do you expect to be thanked?'

As with every recorded word of Jesus, we have his words but not the expression on his face as he spoke. Did he say the words in today's passage sternly, or was he acting out the story with a smile on his face trying to make a point? The topic just before these verses was to do with forgiveness and faith; the importance of putting our faith into practice. I wonder if Jesus was trying to get across the fact that we should not think of forgiving others and demonstrating faith as a big deal, as actions that deserve God's profuse thanks. Instead, they should be sewn into our normal lifestyle and flow naturally from us.

The challenge for us is whether forgiving others and demonstrating faith do flow naturally? Someone once said that forgiveness should be as natural as breathing and practised with as much frequency. Others have suggested that our lives should be 'naturally supernatural'. It's not as if we are doing God a favour, but rather we are simply living the life to which he has called us.

Take a moment to thank God for his generosity to you and ask for the grace to practise faith and forgiveness today. There will definitely be opportunities to put both into practice!

Don't be embarrassed!

'So do not be ashamed of the testimony about our Lord or of me his prisoner.'

2 Timothy 1.8

Paul was encouraging Timothy not to be ashamed to testify about the Lord. You might think this could never apply to you – how could you possibly be ashamed of God? Yet it might be the case more often than you think.

Every day there may be times when the relevance of your faith strikes you, yet you choose to put it aside. You may be touched by someone's plight and wonder if you should say something about how Jesus could help them, yet you hold back from speaking in case it sounds odd. Perhaps you are facing uncertainty and sense God speaking to you, but again you ignore it – either because you are unsure or you are enjoying a good wallow. At times like this you are choosing to turn away from the path God is laying out before you.

Yet the good news is that if you recognise yourself in these examples, then you also need to recognise that you are in a relationship with God and he is seeking to communicate with you. Of course, there are times when you might get it wrong, but this doesn't mean that God abandons you! Instead, he wants you to see where you went wrong so that you can get it right in the future!

The next time you sense a prompting to bring God into a conversation, or a nudge to point you in a different direction, respond to it! The Lord God of heaven is communicating with you.

202

How can you delight God?

'The Lord detests dishonest scales, but accurate weights find favour with him.'

Proverbs 11.1

This proverb seems so ordinary yet speaks about something very powerful. One translation (ESV) puts the second part of it like this: 'a just weight is his delight'. God loves it when we approach everything with integrity and honesty. It is a simple calling to be honest in all our dealings and not to cheat people in any way.

Of course, we hope that we would never do this, but it is interesting how much dishonesty can creep in. If we want someone to do something for us, it can be so easy to try to manipulate them; and there may be occasions when we are tempted to be less than honest in small ways, thinking that it won't matter.

It isn't that God is storing up every minor misdemeanour in his 'big black book', but rather that it brings real delight to him when he sees us trying to act with honesty and integrity, even in small matters. How amazing that we can bring delight to God! Through this day, seek honesty in even the insignificant things in life and sense his delight in you.

Handling fear

'He had been hired to intimidate me so that I would commit a sin by doing this, and then they would give me a bad name to discredit me.'

Nehemiah 6.13

It certainly wasn't plain sailing when Nehemiah rebuilt the walls of Jerusalem! As he called the people to work, he was constantly bombarded with threats by those who sought to stop the building work. This verse outlines one of the attempts made to intimidate him and make him afraid.

You may have experienced what it is to be afraid, perhaps about a specific situation, person or just a general fear that something bad is going to happen to you. So what did Nehemiah do about his fear? It is interesting that he didn't fight back, nor seek to cast out the fear, but he put it to one side and carried on with what he had been called to do.

This is a wonderful lesson. Fear can paralyse us and stop us taking a step into the future. Nehemiah didn't deny what he was feeling, but he simply walked forwards into the day ahead regardless. What is it that you fear today? Acknowledge this to God, but also acknowledge that you are called by him to be his co-worker. He needs you in the very situation that you fear. How would you act if your fears were not there? Take his hand and walk boldly into the day ahead.

204

Acting by faith | 1

'When he saw them, he said, "Go, show yourselves to the priests." And as they went, they were cleansed.'

Luke 17.14

It is worth noting the chronology of this verse, which is part of the story of Jesus healing the ten lepers. They came to Jesus asking for healing and he told them to go and show themselves to the priest (the only person with the authority to pronounce them clean). What is interesting is that Jesus told them to do this before they were actually healed! It was only as they were on their way to the priest that their healing took place. By being obedient to Jesus, they ran the risk of standing before the priest asking to be pronounced clean while they still had leprosy! It is full credit to them that they set off on their way, trusting that something would happen as they walked.

We, too, are called to share our faith in a comparable way, to believe before we see the results. Just as the ten lepers were told to do something before they saw the evidence with their own eyes, so we are called to show love whether or not we feel loving, to remain in God's love whether or not we feel his love, and to believe in the truth that we carry his presence with us wherever we go, whether or not we have any visible evidence.

All too often we act in response to our feelings, whereas what brings God the greatest pleasure is when we act in response to what he says. Today you carry his presence to every person you meet, so act on this knowledge whether you feel it or not!

Stick with Jesus | 2

'He threw himself at Jesus' feet and thanked him – and he was a Samaritan.'

Luke 17.16

Sometimes it's very easy to feel like an outsider. You may not have had the same experiences as other people – your life may seem different to theirs and your struggles somehow seem unlike the ones they face – and you wonder what God really thinks of you. Does he wish you were a bit more like others?

If you feel like this, the story of the ten lepers is very encouraging. After they had all been healed, one of them came back to thank Jesus. Just one person made the effort to connect with Jesus again, and he was a Samaritan – the one everyone considered to be an outsider. Yet he impressed and moved Jesus that day.

It isn't really about feeling whether you belong or believing the right things, it's all about your personal connection to Jesus. In all the struggles you go through, are you still able to stick close to him? Are you still able to turn to him, no matter how feebly, and acknowledge that somehow you belong with him? If so, you are doing more than ok!

Aim for more | 3

'Then he said to him, "Rise and go; your faith has made you well."'

Luke 17.19

When the Samaritan returned to give thanks for his healing from leprosy, Jesus asked him: "Were not all ten cleansed? Where are the other nine?" They were also healed of leprosy, so didn't their faith also make the other nine well?

It does seem as if the man who returned received more than physical healing. Let's not diminish what the other nine received – it really was a major event to have leprosy healed – but the man who came back was able to experience what it was like to connect with Jesus and to be commended by him.

Many of us are seeking healing, either in body, mind or spirit, but this passage emphasises that healing is not everything. If we make it our sole focus, we become like the nine lepers and are in danger of missing out on so much more – the joy of a living relationship with Jesus.

Take a moment to sit quietly in the presence of Jesus. Don't bring your needs to him immediately, simply remain in his presence and connect with him. Only then begin to express your heart to him and allow him to express his heart to you.

Living your life in God's presence

'When Abram was ninety-nine years old, the Lord appeared to him and said, "I am God Almighty; walk before me faithfully and be blameless."'

Genesis 17.1

This command is full of glorious possibilities! One translation of the phrase 'walk before me' is this: 'Live out your life in my presence'. This sounds very grand, but it gets exciting when we make it more specific.

Living our lives in God's presence means living this very day in his presence, which in turn means living this next hour in his presence – and that starts right now. One way to grasp the significance of this is to consider how the next ten minutes might change if you were aware of Jesus standing by your side. Would you act differently? How would you think differently? What would you say differently?

The chances are that if you took this reality seriously, the next ten minutes would be quite different from how they might be if you had no sense of his presence.

When you have tried thinking in this way about the next ten minutes, do it for another ten . . . and then another ten after that. You have already started to live your life with a new awareness of his presence.

God won't go away

'They refused to listen and failed to remember the miracles you performed among them. They became stiff-necked and in their rebellion appointed a leader in order to return to their slavery. But you are a forgiving God, gracious and compassionate, slow to anger and abounding in love. Therefore you did not desert them'

Nehemiah 9.17

This chapter presents us with an image of people walking away from God, despite his constant presence with them. If only they had stopped to wonder where he was they might have discovered he had never left! It wasn't him who distanced himself, but rather the people themselves who had wandered off. God is portrayed as never changing, always forgiving, gracious and compassionate.

The circumstances of your life may create different challenges from those in the days of Nehemiah, but the same truth still remains: God is always forgiving, gracious and compassionate. If there have been moments in your life when you particularly sensed the love and presence of God, the truth is that he was no more present or loving to you then than he is right now; you simply had a different perception of it. Similarly, at times when God seems absent or uncaring, the reality is that he has not changed and it is simply your perception that is different.

Right now, God is forgiving, gracious and compassionate to you. He has never changed or gone away, so spend a few minutes speaking to him and receiving from him.

Your relationship with Jesus

"But the tax collector stood at a distance. He would not even look up to heaven, but beat his breast and said, 'God, have mercy on me, a sinner.'"

Luke 18.13

What should the ideal relationship with God be like? This is quite a difficult question to answer. You might be tempted to suggest that it should be a life of unbroken intimacy with Jesus; each day marked by your friendship with him.

Jesus told this parable about two men who stood before God. One felt justified by his actions and the way he practised his faith, while the other seemed so in awe of the wonder and nature of God that he was overcome by his own unworthiness. It is the second man, sinful though he is, who seems to bear God's favour.

It is very easy to be aware of our failures, even failures in our Christian life – and there are enough people around who will remind us of them! In this parable, Jesus suggests that we don't have to look at our successes or failures because what counts is turning to him in honesty and humility, trusting in his mercy towards us.

If you can come to God, trusting in his goodness rather than in your own actions, then this is one of the most precious relationships you can have – and also the one that he most wants to have with you. Come to him right now, just as you are without any pretence. He is longing for your company.

Pursue what is good | 1

'... pursue righteousness, godliness, faith, love, endurance and gentleness.'

1 Timothy 6.11

In his letter to Timothy, Paul encouraged his follower and friend to pursue the six different qualities we will look at over the next few days. However, the first point to notice is the command itself. We are told to pursue – or to chase, or go after – such qualities. In other words, each of the qualities that Paul mentioned is fully attainable and we simply need to commit to going after them.

We often suspect that God's longings for us are completely unattainable and that we are bound to fail; we don't think we have a hope of doing what he wants. In this verse Paul tells us to think differently. We may never be fully righteous, but righteousness is still something to be pursued, and by pursuing it we will have done well.

Throughout each day we are subject to emotions and feelings, some positive and others negative, and it is tempting to dwell on them and allow them to influence us. Do we have to follow them? Let's commit to pursuing what is good. Think about the day ahead and plan something good that you can bring to it.

Righteousness – what's that? | 2

'. . . pursue righteousness, godliness, faith, love, endurance and gentleness.'

1 Timothy 6.11

We tend to think of righteousness in terms of how upright and moral we are and whether or not we sin, trying to turn away from the things that grieve God and pursue what brings him pleasure. However, the pursuit of righteousness is not just about our actions. It is also about understanding how God sees us and how we perceive ourselves.

If it is true that God loves us so much that he adopted us as his own children, and sent Jesus to die for us so that our sins might be forgiven, how do you think God sees you? The familiar phrase, 'The love of God', is a concept that we are called to take seriously. God's love is not simply a nice phrase or a comforting thought, it is real – so real that Jesus suffered greatly for us.

Pursuing righteousness involves earnestly seeking to capture a sense of God's love and passion for us, and deliberately shutting the door to any feelings that cause us to doubt this. The death of Jesus reveals the incredible extent God went to in order to forgive our sins and bring us back to him. You are personally loved by God, your sins were paid for by Jesus and God looks at you with love, tenderness and care. Pursue this reality!

212

Godly – me? | 3

'... pursue righteousness, godliness, faith, love, endurance and gentleness.'

1 Timothy 6.11

Godliness can sound a bit boring! It often carries with it the connotation of giving up everything that might be pleasurable. A better definition of godliness is being like God, as Jesus revealed him. Whatever else you say about Jesus, his life certainly was not boring! He went to parties with people many of us would disapprove of, courted controversy and saw the amazing power of God at work.

There is a well-known phrase, 'What would Jesus do?' In so many situations in which we find ourselves it is a wonderful question. We often tend to react according to our emotion, whether it be love, anger, fear or something else entirely. Yet as we read the stories of Jesus we see someone who not just reacted according to his feelings, but who sought to bring the purposes of God to those he met.

Yesterday we looked at the notion that to pursue one path often necessitates turning your back on another. Pursuing godliness – acting like Jesus did – may well mean ignoring what we might instinctively do or say, so that we bring his will, words and actions to a situation or person. Without wanting to pile on undue pressure, today you may be the only person who is able to bring the heart of Jesus to the people you come across.

The reason for pursuing godliness is for the benefit of everyone you meet today and in the days ahead.

Growing faith | 4

'... pursue righteousness, godliness, faith, love, endurance and gentleness.'

1 Timothy 6.11

Many times each day we have opportunities to pursue faith. This involves choosing to believe what we cannot see or feel; without it we are at the mercy of our feelings and emotions.

The Bible invites us to see ourselves as precious children of the living God, loved by him to the extent that he gave Jesus for us, and trusted by him to carry his presence with us wherever we go. Believing this invitation takes faith.

We must turn our backs on any feelings of inadequacy and doubt and carry God's presence with us every minute of the day, whether we feel it or not – and whether others notice it or not.

Ultimately it all comes down to a matter of choice. Choose to believe that you carry something of God's presence with you; choose to believe that at any point in the day his love and passion for you is far stronger than you could ever conceive and choose to pursue faith and not be a slave to your feelings.

Receive love . . . give love | 5

'. . . pursue righteousness, godliness, faith, love, endurance and gentleness.'

1 Timothy 6.11

There are two aspects to pursuing love: seeking God's love for us, and longing to show his love to other people. Actually, they are linked. When we have a deeper knowledge of the unconditional, self-sacrificing, all-consuming love of God for us, it is bound to affect how we interact with others.

It can be very easy to do things for other people but with a sense of resentment; our actions may seem loving, but our hearts are not. One of the best ways to change this is to really take on board God's love for us; spending time pondering the truths of

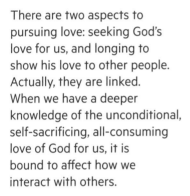

what the Bible says and making them real and personal. Then it is only a short step towards applying these truths to the people we meet today. What is God's heart for them? How much does he love them?

Perhaps one of Jesus' most challenging commands is in John 15.12: "Love each other as I have loved you." This command is based on a profound appreciation of his love for us. Try taking this love seriously and applying even a little of it to those who will cross your path today. In this way you will bring joy to the heart of God.

Endurance is Christ-like | 6

'. . . pursue righteousness, godliness, faith, love, endurance and gentleness.'

1 Timothy 6.11

If we are honest, the thought of pursuing endurance is not particularly attractive, as it implies keeping going with something for a long time before we see a result. Most of us like to see things happen pretty instantly, whether it is prayers answered, minds changed or weight lost! We can manage to endure a little, but to pursue endurance implies choosing to do it for a sustained period.

At the heart of Christian endurance is a sense of keeping a vision before us, even if we cannot see it fulfilled yet. It is a calling to be like Jesus. When we read about his life, it often seems as though his prayers were answered immediately – in fact, the word 'immediately' occurs frequently in the healing stories of Jesus – but he also knew about endurance. Hebrews 12.2 says: 'For the joy that was set before him he endured the cross'. He held on to a vision

that helped him to endure the horrors of the crucifixion.

What's more, Jesus is still enduring. In John 17.20, Jesus prayed for us in these words, "I pray also for those who will believe in me through their message, that all of them may be one." When we think about the divisions within the church today we can see that this prayer of Jesus has still not been answered and he is pursuing endurance about this particular desire.

Are there issues that you struggle with? Are there things you wish God would hurry up and do? Keep alive the vision of what he has promised and keep going. To endure is to experience something of what Jesus experiences every day as he looks at his broken church. He certainly knows what you are going through.

216

Being gentle | 7

'. . . pursue righteousness, godliness, faith, love, endurance and gentleness.'

1 Timothy 6.11

It is sometimes easier to define a word by mulling over what it doesn't mean, or by considering the opposites! Gentleness is the opposite of forcing our views on others; it is not shouting at people or manipulating them in any way. There is something about gentleness that respects other people and treats them in the way we would like to be treated ourselves. This is what we are told to pursue.

This is, of course, a picture of how Jesus interacts with us. We are probably all too aware of the things we think Jesus might say to us.

However, this is a long way from the truth. In Matthew 11.28, Jesus says to all of us: "Come to me . . . for I am gentle." He does not invite us to come to him so that he can make us feel worse than we do already, but rather so that he can embrace us with the love of God, and love us into the place where he wants us to be.

Take a moment to sit and reflect on the fact that you are deeply and uniquely loved by God. As you do this, relax in his presence and sense his gentleness towards you.

Jesus, friend of sinners

'Now the tax collectors and sinners were all gathering round to hear Jesus.'

Luke 15.1

Even sinners gathered round to listen to Jesus. I wonder why they came to listen to him? Presumably it wasn't because he kept telling them they were sinners and needed to repent – after all, so many other people told them that. They wouldn't have flocked to Jesus to hear the same message yet again! There must have been something in his words that was life-giving and not condemning.

There are challenges in this account for us. The first is how we judge others. It is so easy to look at people and judge what we regard as sin in their lives. As far as we are concerned, this is obvious – but it is not what God sees when he looks at them. A challenging prayer is that God will open our eyes to see people through his eyes of love, rather than our critical perspective.

The second challenge is about how we see ourselves. If we are prone to judging others, it is likely we are equally harsh on ourselves, assuming that God wants to address our sin. Perhaps he doesn't though! Perhaps he longs to meet with us to encourage us and lift us out of the pits we may be in.

Jesus is with you now, so spend some time allowing him to draw closer. As you listen to his voice, either through the Bible or by being still before him, expect his words to be full of love, not judgment.

What's happening?

'When the kings joined forces, when they advanced together, they saw her and were astounded; they fled in terror.'

Psalm 48. 4-5

This verse describes what happened when the kings advanced on Jerusalem to attack it. They saw something of God that caused fear to rise within them. I wonder what the people living in Jerusalem saw? Perhaps nothing at all!

The Bible describes us as 'temples of the Holy Spirit' (1 Corinthians 6.19). We carry something of the presence of God within us, and yet so often we are unaware of this glorious truth because we don't feel it. One way to recognise his presence is to try to grasp the change and transformation he is bringing about within us.

You may find it hard to ask other people if they are noticing any change in you, but it might be helpful to sit down and try to reflect on this yourself:

- What has God been doing in your life?

- What difference has his presence made to you?

- Where can you see touches of transformation occurring?

When you hear people giving testimony to the great things God is doing in their lives, it can sometimes be discouraging if you feel that not much is happening to you. Yet the reality is that wonderful things may well be occurring in your life, though perhaps more slowly or over a longer period of time. Discover what God is doing within you – and be encouraged!

Taking God seriously

'For I am not ashamed of the gospel, because it is the power of God that brings salvation to everyone who believes: first to the Jew, then to the Gentile.'

Romans 1.16

Most of us wouldn't say that we are ashamed of the gospel, but perhaps we are in danger of changing it a bit here and there! In its simplest form, the gospel is this: out of his love, God gave Jesus for us, so that by believing in him we might be saved. So simple, but actually so hard to put into practice!

First, it requires that we believe in God's free, undeserved and unearned love. How many times do we have the idea that God will love us a bit more if we ... pray more, give more, love more, sin less, or any number of other things we think might encourage God to love us more?

The gospel also requires a response from us – to believe, to put our trust in God. It is tempting to think that we have already done this, but it is probably quite salutary to recognise how many times each day our faith in Jesus dips and we find anxiety and fear creeping in.

It also requires us to accept that God's gift to us is the person of Jesus. It is easy to start regarding prayer as a duty, or our Bible reading as something to get through, rather than enjoying the personal nature of the relationship with Jesus that God offers us.

The gospel is amazing! You need never be ashamed of it or doubt it, but can trust in its love and simplicity for each new day of your life, including today.

Do good

'... be ready to do whatever is good'

Titus 3.1

Do you ever feel that you have failed God because you do not match up to the worthy achievements of some of the people you know? If so, remember that God does not ask you to do what you cannot manage.

Three times in this chapter (verses 1, 8 and 14) Paul stresses that a central calling upon us is to do good; to be on the lookout for acts of kindness we can do for others. This might include any range of things: thanking people for the things they do for you (even if it's their job), encouraging others in their work, lending a helping hand or speaking to someone as you pass them in the street. The very phrase 'do-gooders' has become a term that we apply to others almost as an insult, whereas it is actually a calling, and one that every single one of us can fulfil.

We do not practise goodness so that we can find recognition, or so that others will notice we are being good – indeed, our very acts of goodness may be misunderstood or ignored by others. We do good because it reflects the kindness of Jesus. What good can you do as you go about your day?

Are you up for an adventure?

'Jesus answered, "Very truly I tell you, you are looking for me, not because you saw the signs I performed but because you ate the loaves and had your fill."'

John 6.26

If you were to take a minute to make a list of all that God has done for you, I suspect that you would be surprised at how many things come to mind. The reality is that if you could see it from God's perspective, the list would be never-ending! So what is your reaction to what God has given you?

In this verse, Jesus seems to be saying that there are different ways we can look at his actions. On the one hand we can accept his gifts and enjoy them, or on the other hand we can take them a bit further and ask, 'What does this show me about him?'

Suppose, for example, you are facing an anxious moment in the day ahead and after prayer you find a level of peace you were not expecting. What do you do? Certainly you can thank God for it, but also ask what this tells you about God: what does his gift teach you about him and how does it affect the way you approach him about other things?

Our life with God is a daily adventure and his desire is that we grow in our relationship with him, so that as we discover more about him our faith and love for him grow.

Take a moment to reflect on one or two things that you recognise as God's touch upon your life recently, and consider what difference they have made to you and what they have taught you about God?

222

Letting the Bible read you

'And we also thank God continually because, when you received the word of God, which you heard from us, you accepted it not as a human word, but as it actually is, the word of God, which is indeed at work in you who believe.'
1 Thessalonians 2.13

How wonderful that the word of God is at work in us who believe. There is no mention of us necessarily being aware of it or feeling it, yet it is active. How does this happen?

One key way is through reading the Bible. It has been said that it is not so much how we read the Bible, but rather how we let the Bible read us. Reading the Bible is not just about understanding the words on the page but letting them touch us. We read a passage to learn more about the nature and character of God and to discover what he says about us, but we also read it to find its specific application for us. A good question to bear in mind is this: 'How does this passage speak to my current situation?'

If you are going through challenging circumstances, take time to read carefully a passage of the Bible, and ask how it speaks to you in your current situation.

Working for God

'For we are God's handiwork, created in Christ Jesus to do good works, which God prepared in advance for us to do.'

Ephesians 2.10

As we look forward to the day ahead, we often naturally ask God to bless it in order that things might go well for us. Another way of asking for his blessing is to catch the truth of this verse that today (and every day) we have been created to do the things the Father has prepared for us. However the day looks, whatever is in the diary, God has already gone before us to prepare work for us to do.

At this point it can be tempting to panic! What if we miss the things he has prepared? Should we spend time praying to find out what these good works are? However, God is unlikely to go to the trouble of preparing things for us if there is a strong likelihood that we will miss them! Our calling is to enjoy the day ahead, to do what we have planned to do, and in every situation we find ourselves, seek to do good and encourage others.

If this is our attitude about the hours ahead, it will be an amazing opportunity for God to do all sorts of things, seen and unseen by us. He is perfectly able to prompt us with specific nudges, so let's live today in the knowledge that we are doing God's work.

224

Being loved

'Let him lead me to the banquet hall, and let his banner over me be love.'

Song of Songs 2.4

These words don't simply express a dream or a fanciful thought, but a reality. God has led you to a place where so much is available to you, and he has expressed his deep love for you, not because of what you have done but because of who you are – someone in whom he delights.

So many people take the attitude that God will love them when something changes – perhaps if they do more for him, spend longer in prayer or give sacrificially. However, this verse says that God has poured out his love and made everything available to you already – before you ever did anything.

This is important if you want to approach God with a need that you cannot meet yourself. Why would he choose to listen to you? What have you done to deserve his help? The fact is that you can approach him for help with confidence because it is not about what you have done, but rather what he has done.

Take a few minutes to think about the wonderful love for you that is expressed in these words: 'Let him lead me to the banquet hall, and let his banner over me be love.' Hold on to the amazing love God has for you; it is not just a love for the whole world, it is personal for you.

Your Father

'But you are our Father'

Isaiah 63.16

When Isaiah spoke these words they were not really spoken in a spirit of worship, but rather out of a sense of desperation; things were not going well. God seemed to be a long way off, and while Isaiah could remember the good things of God, they seemed a distant memory. So as he spoke these words, perhaps as a reminder to himself or even as a reminder to God, he was recollecting that this was not how it was meant to be – that there was more.

As you think about life, what state are you in? You too might be going through a hard time, with the good things of God seeming like a distant memory. If you feel like this, come back to these beautiful words: 'You are our Father'.

This is the relationship God planned for you. It is not wishful thinking, it is God's revelation to you. He is the father who has called you to him, who longs for relationship with you so much that he gave Jesus to open the door, and is waiting and longing for your friendship.

226

Keep going

"I only know that in every city the Holy Spirit warns me that prison and hardships are facing me."

Acts 20.23

We live in an environment where achievement is highly valued: we are encouraged to set goals, review them and strive for higher things. However, this statement by Paul challenges such an attitude. He reveals that the Holy Spirit has shown him what his life will look like: prison and hardship. These are definitely not the sort of goals we would choose to set ourselves!

Paul goes on to reveal what he believes is the true nature of achievement: to persevere in the work that Christ has given us, whether or not we see worldly success. We all appreciate a sense of achievement when our efforts bear fruit, but Paul assures us that in God's eyes achievement is to hold fast to what we believe despite what goes on around us.

There is an encouraging saying that we are called to be faithful, not successful, so don't be tempted to focus on your achievements. Instead look at your calling – what is it God has asked you to do? Then keep doing it well, regardless of whether or not other people see success.

Freely receive, freely give

'Be kind and compassionate to one another, forgiving each other, just as in Christ God forgave you. Follow God's example, therefore, as dearly loved children'

Ephesians 4.32–5.1

Following God's example sounds like a real challenge! How can we possibly be like him? This verse provides a clue: it is about being kind, compassionate and forgiving.

Before you start thinking that this is too much to remember and perhaps fail at, it is worth spending a moment reflecting that these qualities are how God chooses to behave towards you. At every point of this day, God chooses to be kind, compassionate and forgiving to you.

If you are called to follow God's example in your dealings with others, you need to recognise

these lovely qualities so you are in a better position to exhibit them yourself as you interact with people. They are not simply actions for you to try to remember, they should flow naturally from your heart in the same way as they come pouring out of God's heart.

Today, God plans to be kind to you; he wants to show you compassion and his heart's desire is to forgive you. Receive these beautiful truths and let them change your heart.

228

Being directed

'This is what the Lord says – your Redeemer, the Holy One of Israel: "I am the Lord your God, who teaches you what is best for you, who directs you in the way you should go."'

Isaiah 48.17

There is something very powerful about these words as they set the context for the way in which God speaks to us.

The notion of God teaching and directing us comes as no real surprise. After all, we are quite accustomed to the idea of God directing us – we're just not sure we like the idea too much! The thought of someone telling us what to do sounds too controlling. There might also be a sense of God as a bit of a spoilsport, wagging his finger and saying "No" in a stern manner whenever we are having fun.

The most wonderful aspect of this verse is the way it is introduced. God speaks and directs us as our redeemer. He is the one who wants to take our lives and make something wonderful out of them, the one who came to save us and lift us out of the pits in which we find ourselves, and the one whose love for us drove him to give his very self to us. God wants us to experience life in all its fullness.

Enjoy being free

'. . . Christ Jesus, who gave himself as a ransom for all people.'

1 Timothy 2.6

A ransom is when someone pays an agreed price to get something or someone back. In this case it is us held in captivity, and Jesus who gave himself as the price, or the ransom, for our freedom.

You may well be wondering why Jesus would give himself as a ransom for you? Surely it must be because you are worth it. The thought of you being held captive hurt Jesus so much that he was willing to do anything to gain your freedom.

It follows that if Jesus paid the ransom for you, his heartfelt desire must be that you enjoy being free. Take a moment to ask if there is anything that robs you of your freedom. It may be circumstances, illness, a memory or something completely different. Jesus did not come so that you would remain in captivity, but that you might enjoy life to the full. So be honest about your situation and tell him what you are going through right now.

As you share your needs with Jesus, remember to give him thanks for what he has already done for you – he gave himself so that you might be free.

230

What do you need?

'What causes fights and quarrels among you? Don't they come from your desires that battle within you?'

James 4.1

In this simple statement James cuts through to the heart of human strife; it all stems from the desires that battle within. It's likely that we have all witnessed situations where the desires of one person clash with the desires of others, causing untold misery. However, it is harder and more challenging to turn the spotlight on ourselves. What are the desires that battle within you? What effect do they have on both you and others?

James goes on to offer this simple encouragement: if you want something, ask God – but not with selfish motives. Perhaps his encouragement would be to look beyond your actual desires to an underlying need, because that is what should be brought to God. Suppose, for example, you long for more money, but your underlying desire is a need for security. It is this deeper need that God wants you to bring to him, as this is the area of your life he longs to touch.

When God invites you to bring your needs to him, he is not suggesting he is a divine slot machine to give you everything you want. Rather, he is inviting you to trust him with the deepest needs of your life. He wants you to turn to him and find afresh the depth of his love for you. Why not do that right now?

Opening the door

'How abundant are the good things that you have stored up for those who fear you'

Psalm 31.19

Do you ever think of God as being a bit stingy; of carefully counting out his blessings to us, taking care that he doesn't go over our allotted quota? This verse speaks of the abundant generosity of God, and says that God stores up good things for us because there are so many of them. There is nothing stingy or mean about this. In fact, it points to the lavish nature of God's goodness to us.

So if there are abundant good things waiting for us, how do we open the door to receive them? The key is to be open to believing that they really exist. If our basic assumption is that God doesn't think much of us, our expectation of his goodness is low; if we choose to believe he has an abundance of good things he longs to give us, we will begin to look for them and see something of his generous open hand.

Let this verse be a declaration from you to God: how abundant are the good things that you have stored up for me! Say these words to yourself and catch a sense of his heart for you.

232

Winning battles

'. . . the one who is in you is greater than the one who is in the world.'

1 John 4.4

This verse states an amazing truth with great clarity and force: whatever spiritual opposition you may face, the one who lives in you is greater. So what does spiritual opposition mean? What are we talking about?

Such language may conjure up images of battles, but the reality is that the greatest opposition facing most people is in their minds. On that battlefield, the skirmishes tend to be in the realms of temptation, difficulty in accepting God's love and believing in the reality of his presence. This is where our enemy loves to fight his battles because we can be so weak at retaliating.

The promise is that Jesus, who lives in us, is greater than the enemy – but this does not stop the battles taking place. The reason that John shares this truth with us is so we have the foresight to remember that the one living within us is stronger than any other force working against us. Our calling is to recognise moments of battle when they arise and respond appropriately, by recalling this truth.

If you are going through a challenging time in some area of your life, call it to mind now and consciously remind yourself that Jesus, who lives within you, is sovereign and there is nothing too difficult for him. In this way you will find that his strength flows into you and wins the battle. You may like to reflect on these words: 'Jesus in me is greater than the one who is in the world.'

Training for godliness

'... train yourself to be godly.'

1 Timothy 4.7

This is such an encouraging phrase because it makes the point that we are not yet godly! All too often we can beat ourselves up with the memory of our failures, of how we think we ought to be a much better Christian or how poorly we fare in comparison with others. Discouragement and a sense of failure can so easily follow. So Paul's encouragement is to 'train yourself'.

None of us would wander into a gym for the first time, put the running machine onto the fastest setting and feel a failure if we couldn't keep it up for an hour; nor would we select the heaviest weights and walk out in disgust if we couldn't lift them up 100 times!

The sensible approach is to start with an achievable goal and reach a certain level of competence before progressing steadily to new challenges. Just as we train ourselves to be fit, so we are encouraged to train ourselves to be godly.

An excellent way of doing this is to spend a few minutes reflecting on the past day – where did you get things wrong and where did you see God at work? In the light of this, where do you need his grace today so as not to repeat the mistakes of yesterday? This is not just introspection but a process of honestly opening yourself up to the touch of God and letting him change you.

Being in a relationship

'Blessed is the one . . . whose delight is in the law of the Lord'

Psalm 1.1-2

The word 'delight' is not often a word that springs to mind when regarding the law! More commonly we think in terms of obedience – and sometimes even resentment. The difference comes down to relationship.

We all know that we have some sort of relationship with God, but the challenge is maintaining it on a daily basis. When we find ourselves going through the motions of prayer, or regarding God's commands as restrictive, it is worth checking our relationship with God: have we let it slip or not given it much attention? The reassuring fact, of course, is that it is always something to which we can return. It is a matter of focus.

The psalm goes on to speak about our relationship with God in terms of being planted by streams of water. There is a security and stability about this; the water is not suddenly going to reroute itself, nor is the tree able to get up and replant itself somewhere else. Coming back to a relationship with God is not hard, since neither you nor he has really moved.

Refocus on God's love for you, and on his faithfulness and commitment in never leaving you alone even for one minute. Ponder these truths, recognise that he is with you right now, and let the Holy Spirit bring new life to your relationship with him.

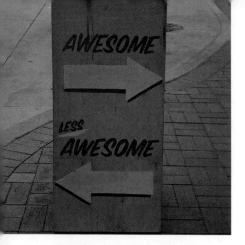

What would Jesus do?

'... grow in the grace and knowledge of our Lord and Saviour Jesus Christ.'

2 Peter 3.18

Sometimes people wear wristbands saying, 'What would Jesus do?' It is a very good question – but what is the answer? There are two things we can do to increase our knowledge of Jesus.

The first is to find the wonder of Jesus in the words of the Bible. You might think you know him quite well, but it is so refreshing to discover Jesus once again in the well-known stories. Choose a narrative from the gospels, and as you read it ask yourself some questions:

- What does this show me about Jesus?

- What was he thinking in this story?

- What were his emotions?

- How would I have reacted to him if I had been there?

The second way of becoming more intimate with Jesus is to try to act, rather than react. By this I mean trying to be increasingly aware of his presence within you so that whatever occurs throughout the day you and Jesus face it together. The more you can do this, the more you will find yourself acting out of his presence, rather than simply reacting to circumstances.

Think ahead to something you are going to do today or tomorrow. Take a moment to see Jesus in that situation rather than yourself. How would he act? What would he do? What difference does this make to you?

236

Who are you?

'I urge you, as foreigners and exiles, to abstain from sinful desires'

1 Peter 2.11

If we want to live pure and holy lives, simply resolving to do so doesn't seem to make much difference. In this verse, Peter suggests that our behaviour will change once we realise who we are.

Before you seek to change your life, Peter urges you to catch a new vision of yourself: that you are a stranger in this world. You do not belong to it in the way that some others do, and because you are different you are not bound to follow its ways.

In Philippians 4.13 we read, 'I can do all this through him who gives me strength.' In other words, your ability to do things does not come from yourself, but from the one who lives within you. However, unless you know the Holy Spirit is living within you, you won't call upon him for the strength you need. Similarly, unless you know that you are a stranger in this world and not bound to follow its pulls and temptations, you will not know that you can stand against them.

You are a temple of the Holy Spirit, created to carry God's presence with you wherever you go, so reflect on this and carry the truth of it through today and into the days ahead.

What makes a difference?

'Get rid of all bitterness, rage and anger, brawling and slander, along with every form of malice.'

Ephesians 4.31

Throughout this chapter of Ephesians, Paul writes at length about the implications of having Christ within us. It can be tempting to regard this as a list of rules and regulations – do this but don't do that! – but Paul's intention is to urge us to take the reality of Jesus within us seriously. His presence is not simply a comfort for us, but is also meant to be a blessing to others.

Paul encourages us to 'get rid of all bitterness . . . ' How can we do this? Bitterness is not a characteristic of Jesus, so when it becomes evident in us, it must be coming from elsewhere. The same is true of all negative emotions. When

we become aware of them, it is time to remember the presence of Jesus within us, and to do our best to ensure that it is his nature that flows out of us.

Take a moment to reflect on the past day. Were there times when you sensed you were reacting negatively to people or situations? As you recall those occasions, how could you have found the presence of Christ within you so that his emotions shone instead of yours? Now look forward to the day ahead; are there particular moments when you will need to draw upon him? Visualise him in those situations, and remember to draw upon his presence in those times.

Come back!

"From this day on I will bless you."

Haggai 2.19

The message of the prophet Haggai was quite simple: a call to rebuild the Temple of God. What was so encouraging for those involved was that God blessed them very quickly – not when they had been obedient and faithful for a long time and eventually finished the work, but right from the outset. Within a very short time-frame, the hand of God was upon them.

Right now you may be feeling that your spiritual life has gone a bit flat, with prayer uttered more out of duty than joy, and that the relationship you once enjoyed with God now a thing of the past. Basically, you may feel that something is missing. If so, what you are sensing is God's heart; perhaps he too is missing the relationship and is calling you back.

The good news about this nudge from God is that his promised blessings can come quickly, just like they did to Haggai and the people of his day. There is no need to wait until you have wrestled in prayer for months! The blessings of relationship begin the moment you step back into the wonder of relationship with Abba Father, with Jesus who stands at the door and knocks, and with the Holy Spirit who lives within you.

If you feel that you have drifted away from God, come back! Begin by simply speaking the name 'Jesus'. He is present and has been waiting for you all this time.

Jesus – the witness | 1

"Even now my witness is in heaven"

Job 16.19

The story of Job is painful as we read of a man's journey through the agony of suffering. Many regard it as a story of gloom, yet within it are beautiful words of hope and passion. Indeed, today's words contain enormous vision.

Suffering impacts us in many ways. Some people speak of the strength and comfort they receive in the midst of hardships, while others speak of crushing despair. Suffering can become a time of insight or a time of blind groping in the dark. The book of Job has elements of both and his words above reveal something of his vision despite his suffering; even in the dark and gloom of his situation, he knew he was not alone and there was one in heaven who saw everything he was going through.

The Bible longs for us to catch this – God has seen our suffering. In the person of Jesus, God came and experienced the reality of human suffering, physical pain and mental anguish, and he is also here with us now – present with us in all we are going through. He really does know and is a true witness to our pain. We are not alone.

You may not think that your hardships equate with those of Job and others may well be going through worse, but your suffering is real for you. The words that Job spoke are equally true for you: Jesus is a witness to your suffering. He has experienced the pain you feel and stands with you.

Jesus – the advocate | 2

"Even now my witness is in heaven; my advocate is on high."

Job 16.19

Job has already spoken of God as a witness to his suffering and he now uses a second word to describe him, advocate. This is wonderful news – we have an advocate!

An advocate stands with us in court to ensure that we are not forgotten or misrepresented. We do not have to push the analogy too far and imagine ourselves in a court of law, but let's hold on to this truth: there is one who does not forget our situation. People forget! It is not malicious on their part and it may well be that some people have poured out their hearts to you, only for you to forget about their plight. Jesus does not forget, he cannot. He has come into your life and stands with you in everything you are going through.

There is even more! Jesus is not simply the one who stands with you, he is an advocate with power – the power to bring change to your circumstances and suffering. The advocate does what you cannot do. This is Jesus – not just a sympathetic bystander but an active saviour by your side. Turn to him as he's with you right now!

What can you offer?

'Peter said, "Silver or gold I do not have, but what I do have I give you."'

Acts 3.6

Peter's confidence was incredible when he was confronted by the crippled man in Acts 3. So too was his approach. He didn't pray about the situation – or even pray for the man! Instead he recognised that within him was the presence of Jesus, and so he simply spoke and acted accordingly.

The challenging question for us is this: was the presence of Jesus within Peter any more powerful than the presence of Jesus within us? The same Jesus who spoke with Peter is alive for us today, and the same Spirit who filled Peter also fills us. What marked Peter out is his confidence; he knew with absolute certainty that God was alive in him in a powerful way. So our challenge is to seek to capture this same confidence.

Paul uses the phrase, 'Christ in you, the hope of glory' (Colossians 1.27). Try taking this to heart by personalising it: 'Christ in me, the hope of glory.' Another helpful verse is Jeremiah 15.16, 'I bear your name, Lord God Almighty.' Choose one of these and spend a few minutes repeating it to yourself. By doing so you are more likely to remember the incredible truth that you carry within you the presence of the living God.

242

Don't forget!

'Be careful that you do not forget the Lord your God'

Deuteronomy 8.11

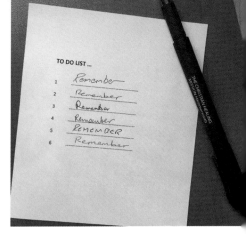

We all have moments when we feel close to God; precious times of intimacy that we want to hold on to and take with us into the days ahead. At the time, we think we will never forget how we felt and what he said to us. However, before long the events of the day overwhelm us and our moment of intimacy with God has retreated to the back of our mind.

This verse from Deuteronomy recognises this tendency in us, and the preceding verse gives us wise advice: it encourages us to give thanks by praising the Lord. It makes the point that if we are not thankful, we are likely to forget God and lose our intimacy with him.

One practical step to help with this is to spend a little time each morning or evening looking back over the past day or hours, giving thanks for as much as possible. As well as giving thanks for events, also give thanks for the people who have impacted you during the day and given you joy. When you do this, you will begin to see God as the source of blessings, both large and small, in your life.

It is not that God needs to be thanked, but rather that he knows that if you fill your mind and heart with thankfulness, you will be changed and grow in intimacy with him – and that is a huge blessing to both you and God.

God's eyes – not yours

'The Lord will do what is good in his sight.'

2 Samuel 10.12

The leader of King David's army, Joab, was about to go into battle against a large enemy. He drew up his battle plan and entrusted the outcome to God.

The situations you face, or the prayers you pray, may not be battle situations, but Joab's confidence in the Lord is a wonderful mindset to follow. When you find yourself in a tough situation, it does not necessarily mean this is God's plan for you; and by taking the problem to him in prayer, you are deliberately opening the door for him to act. At this point you may well start to sense a new confidence that, 'The Lord will do what is good in his sight.'

It is worth remembering that God's vision is infinitely greater than yours, and he holds all things in his hands. God may not do what seems good to you, because your vision is usually tied into the immediate situation, whereas he sees the much bigger picture. At times like this, faith becomes so vital. What sometimes appear to be disappointments in prayer for you may not be for God.

He is the Lord, and as you bring your situations to him, allow him to exercise his lordship according to his vision, and not yours.

244

Chilling out with God

'I have sought your face with all my heart; be gracious to me according to your promise.'

Psalm 119.58

There is something very special about seeking the face of God. It is about longing to be in his presence and to know him more; a longing beyond any specific desire for him to act on your behalf. Of course, there may well be things God has laid upon your heart that he wants you to carry to him in prayer, but to seek his face is to come to him with no other agenda than wanting to be with him.

The second part of this verse picks up on this theme: it asks God to be gracious according to his promise. In other words, it is knowing that he is gracious, and recognising that since this is his character and what he promises, he cannot be otherwise. Believing this enables you to trust implicitly that the grace of God will flow.

So on a practical level, how can you hope to focus on this? Begin by making time for prayer. If you only have a brief time, the likelihood is that you will jump straight into your requests. Instead, try to allow time to enjoy the graceful love of the Father, trusting that he loves your attentive presence even more than your prayers.

Your commitment to God's commitment

'. . . he struck the rock, and water gushed out, streams flowed abundantly, but can he also give us bread? Can he supply meat for his people?'

Psalm 78.20

Psalm 78 outlines the story of the Israelites wandering in the desert, living in a cycle of rebellion and repentance towards God – a situation not unfamiliar to many of us! Then at this point an underlying grievance came to light. God may have done some wonderful things for the Israelites in the past, but was he able to do the specific thing they wanted? The sentiment behind their question was probably not so much whether God was *able* to do it, but was he *likely* to do it?

The psalmist's comment about their attitude was that they did not 'trust in his deliverance' (verse 22). In other words, it was not the actions of God they doubted,

but rather his character; they knew that he could do mighty deeds, but would he choose to meet their desires?

You may well be able to look back on wonderful things God has done in your life, but still feel unsure that he wants to do them again. As you focus on your needs, there are two questions to consider:

- What can Jesus do in this situation?

- How can I open the door for him to act?

Jesus' commitment to you has been proved by his action on the cross; the question is, what is your commitment to his promises for you?

Listen carefully or you might miss something

'Some time later God tested Abraham.'

Genesis 22.1

Many a sermon has been preached on the story that follows these words – the account of Abraham being asked to sacrifice his son, Isaac – with many ending with a challenge to consider whether we would be prepared to give up what is most precious to us. However, one of the most astonishing things about this account is Abraham's ability to hear the voice of God and to distinguish it from all the other distractions around him. It is something that we would all love to be able to do better, and the good news is that we can practise this every day.

When you have important decisions to make, you would probably prefer the voice of God to be loud and booming, with his directions written in large letters in the sky! However, we all need to learn to listen for his gentle voice that is so easy to

miss. Many people find it easier to do this with a paper and pen.

Take a moment to focus on the truth of God's love for you, and to recognise the presence of Jesus with you. Where would you say he is? Can you pinpoint him in the room, or do you sense him somewhere in your mind? Now speak to him, and then pause to let him reply. Write down whatever comes into your mind, however random, without thinking too hard about it. So often we have an immediate desire to analyse everything, and it's easy to dismiss God's voice before really taking it on board.

Now look at what you have written. Does it seem like the sort of thing God might say? Is it what you thought he would say? What are you going to do with it and how will it affect your day?

Think about your words | 1

"Be still, and know that I am God"

Psalm 46.10

These words, tucked away in the body of this psalm, have become familiar and significant for many people, almost like a rock to which we can return time after time. Yet it's interesting to consider whether the psalmist had any idea of just how much these words would affect millions of people in generations to come.

Do you have any sense of the importance of some of your own words? James wrote about the power of the tongue in his New Testament letter. We really do have an immense ability to build people up or knock them down with what we say.

What comments about you have really been a blessing, or perhaps you are only too aware of words that have damaged and hurt you? Quite possibly they were spoken without much thought or consideration, yet they still had a significant effect upon you.

Today, set out to bless at least one person with your conversation; to notice something about them and offer genuine encouragement and praise in a way that will bless and lift them up.

248

Finding the quiet | 2

"Be still, and know that I am God"

Psalm 46.10

The reason these words appeal so strongly to many of us is that they point to quietness and peace, qualities that seem so attractive in comparison to the busy striving of our daily routines.

However, rather surprisingly the context of this verse is a psalm about war and struggle! It isn't a psalm that calls us out of the storm and into the quiet, but instead to the stillness within the storm, often called 'the eye of the storm', while it's still raging. All too often we hear a call to quietness and inwardly think, 'I wish!' Even if we appear calm to others, there can still be a storm within. Yet presumably the encouragement of this psalm is that finding an inner peace is possible.

When we are told to 'Be still', the sentiment behind the command is to disengage from the storm howling around, not by walking away from it but by finding a different focus within it. This different focus is the presence of God. Even to pause and say the name of 'Jesus' can be enough to remind us of a different reality – God with us.

Wherever you are right now, whatever is demanding your attention, speak the name of Jesus quietly and with expectation. In doing this, you are stepping into the quiet and finding his stillness.

Look for the positive, not the negative

"For in the same way as you judge others, you will be judged, and with the measure you use, it will be measured to you."

Matthew 7.2

Could there be any greater incentive to thinking and speaking kindly of other people than this? Our internal attitude to others may well rebound on us. It is not that God's love for us changes or that we are punished for what goes on in our minds, but there is another factor at work.

When we choose not to judge someone, we experience a new level of freedom ourselves. This works in a very simple way. If we are constantly finding fault – even when we do not express it verbally – this becomes the filter through which we view life. As this continues, we become accustomed to looking for the less than perfect and soon find it all around us, and certainly within ourselves.

If, on the other hand, we do not spend our time finding fault with others, we are unlikely to be pre-occupied with our own faults. Instead of looking for the negative, we will find ourselves looking for the good and the positive in ourselves and in others.

Whenever you catch yourself judging someone, let it be an alarm bell to alert you to look for something positive in them instead.

Being loved just as you are

"And even the very hairs of your head are all numbered."

Matthew 10.30

It is extraordinary that God knows us to such an extent that the hairs of our head are numbered! It is something that is echoed in Psalm 139 – he knows when we sit or rise, he perceives our thoughts from afar (verse 2). Initially, the thought that God knows every single thing about us and nothing escapes him can feel quite alarming. However, it is also extremely releasing. When you sit before God, there is absolutely nothing you can hide from him, even if you try, so you might as well relax in his presence and be completely honest with him without attempting to put on any masks at all.

The astounding thing about sitting before God with no masks and pretensions is that he loves us to be totally open with him. This is always a difficult truth for us to grasp; something inside us assumes that God will somehow love us more if we can appear to be holier than we really feel, or speak in more religious language. This simply is not true. No amount of pretending is going to make any difference to the amount that God loves us.

So sit before him just as you are, and find the peace that comes from knowing that he loves you just as you are – and nothing you can do will ever change this.

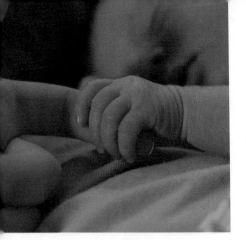

Hanging out with Jesus

'When they saw the courage of Peter and John and realised that they were unschooled, ordinary men, they were astonished and they took note that these men had been with Jesus.'

Acts 4.13

With a little imagination and a touch of dreaming, you can probably summon up some sense of what God could achieve through you. It may be something to do with your influence on your family, a longing to introduce friends to Jesus, or some other work you could undertake on God's behalf to achieve glorious things.

The trouble is that most of our dreams stay on the level of dreams, as things we could achieve but probably will not. This comment about the disciples in Acts 4 gives us a clue about how dreams can be translated into reality. It starts with us being with Jesus and spending time with him.

Your intimacy with Jesus is the clue to achieving so much: hearing his whisper, sensing your heart beating in time with his, seeing things around you becoming alive and having a faith that doesn't become legalistic.

There is no short cut to intimacy – it involves spending time with Jesus. It doesn't really matter what you do in his presence as long as you do something! What's more, it can start today, and as you begin to spend time with him you can be certain that he has been there waiting for you all along.

What will you look at?

'But you, Lord, are a shield around me, my glory, the One who lifts my head high.'

Psalm 3.3

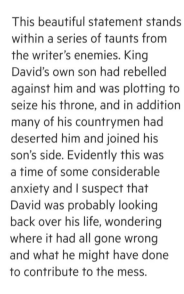

This beautiful statement stands within a series of taunts from the writer's enemies. King David's own son had rebelled against him and was plotting to seize his throne, and in addition many of his countrymen had deserted him and joined his son's side. Evidently this was a time of some considerable anxiety and I suspect that David was probably looking back over his life, wondering where it had all gone wrong and what he might have done to contribute to the mess.

In the midst of all this, and against the backdrop of the taunts of his enemies, David chose to focus on God as his shield and the one who lifts up his head. It would have been so easy to look at the negative, but David chose to look at who God is and what he could do for him.

We all face battles of different kinds; ill health, difficult and challenging situations in life or the darkness of our fears and inner thoughts. You may not feel that your battles are of the same nature as those faced by David, but you certainly have the same choice he had; what are you going to look at?

Are you going to focus on what is on your mind, or will you lift your vision and look at the wonder of God and what he can do for you?

How wealthy are you?

'One person pretends to be rich, yet has nothing; another pretends to be poor, yet has great wealth.'

Proverbs 13.7

What do you really have and how do you take stock of it? There are any number of ways in which you can try to assess your worth: looking at your bank balance, the possessions you have accumulated, your achievements, the number of friends you have, your education and the knowledge you have acquired. An inventory of each of these might come up with a different scale by which to assess your wealth.

However, one aspect of wealth that is often overlooked is spiritual wealth, which is all about what you have through your relationship with God – or perhaps a better way to put it is what you have through his relationship with you.

The riches that can never be taken away from you stem from the fact that your Father longs for you. He sent Jesus, who willingly gave himself so that nothing can separate you from your heavenly Father. You carry within you the constant companionship, presence and power of the Holy Spirit. God is for you! He is on your side today, and because of this, whatever else you may possess or lack, you have wealth beyond measure.

Incredibly good news

'Christ Jesus came into the world to save sinners'

1 Timothy 1.15

There are four key words in this verse that warrant our attention and we are going to look at them in reverse order.

Sinners – This is us, and so often we don't need reminding of it! However good our intentions and resolve might be, there are plenty of days when we look back over the past hours and are only too aware of our failures. This may well be the case, but it is good news because this verse applies directly to us.

Save – Jesus certainly did not come to heap on the guilt, or to punish us for our failings. His purpose was to save us, set us free and let us know freedom from sin. Jesus came to give us the joy of forgiveness.

Came – Jesus did not utter a decree from heaven and suddenly everything on earth changed. Instead, he came to this world and grappled with the same temptations and sufferings that are so real to us. Jesus came so that he could look each of us in the eye and say, 'I know!'

Jesus – There is nothing mechanical about forgiveness; it is based on the actions and personal love of the Son of God for each one of us. Whenever we feel we have failed or sinned, it is wrong to hide until we feel a bit better. Instead, the invitation is for us to go straight back to Jesus and find the presence of the one who came to rescue us.

Imitating God

'Make sure that nobody pays back wrong for wrong, but always strive to do what is good for each other and for everyone else.'

1 Thessalonians 5.15

This verse sounds very challenging – or at least putting it into practice certainly does! We can all happily read about not paying people back with what they deserve, but it gets a lot more challenging when we are called to do it!

It's worth remembering that God is not sitting in heaven dreaming up impossible commands for us to follow simply because he loves to give us a challenge! Instead his calling is for us to be like him, or as Paul puts it: 'Be imitators of God' (Ephesians 5.1).

This suggests that the commands he gives us are pointers to what God is like, and that if we can fulfil these commands we will indeed be like God. This particular verse tells us two amazing things about God: first, he does not repay us wrong for wrong; and secondly, he strives to do good for us.

All too often we live with a secret anxiety that God is storing up trouble for us because of our sins, but how could he command us to do what he is not prepared to do himself? He does not repay our sins with punishment; instead Jesus took the punishment for our sins upon himself. Yet rather than treat us with disdain, Jesus now strives to do good for us – just as he commands us to do for others.

Our problem is accepting this. A possible starting point is to sit before God letting these words go through your mind: 'Father, you strive to do what is good for me.' Capture this sense of his heartfelt desire to bless you.

Spreading the kingdom

"You will hear of wars and rumours of wars, but see to it that you are not alarmed."

Matthew 24.6

Matthew 24 is not exactly a 'pink and fluffy' passage! It speaks about events leading up to the end of the world, and touches on subjects such as war and persecution. We all know only too well that at times we look at the news and events around us and are reminded of these words spoken by Jesus.

One of the reasons it seems a depressing chapter is that there doesn't seem to be much we can do about it – but actually there is! In these tough times, we are told, "this gospel of the kingdom will be preached in the whole world" (verse 14). It is not angels who are going to do this 'preaching', nor is it just the work of evangelists – it is something for all of us to engage in as best we can.

Preaching the gospel of the kingdom is about proclaiming the good news of God's kingdom and revealing his heart. All too often, we can be put off from doing anything because we don't think we can do enough, but all of us can do something to bring good news to the people we meet and the situations we face.

Spreading the good news can take many forms: doing small acts of service for people, encouraging a friend to go to church with you, offering to pray for someone (either in person or at home on your own) or mentioning that you find prayer helpful next time someone shares their anxieties with you.

You carry the kingdom of God within you – so where are you going to take it?

The impossible is possible after all!

"What is impossible with man is possible with God."

Luke 18.27

The context for this statement is money! A rich man had just been told that if he really wanted to follow Jesus he needed to sell all he had and give to the poor. Jesus then told his followers how hard it was for those who were rich to enter God's kingdom. Hearing this, the disciples wondered how some folk could ever change, and in reply Jesus spoke these words: "What is impossible with man is possible with God." He was saying that even though greed and attachment to money can be driving forces, God can still break into these attitudes and bring heartfelt change.

Being financially too rich may not be your greatest problem! However, you may be aware of an attitude, circumstance or feeling that seems to have a grip upon you, and try as you might you cannot seem to get free of it. If this applies to you, then the amazing good news is that even if change seems impossible to you, it is certainly possible with God.

Perhaps the change begins with honesty. Begin by bringing your situation into the light of God's love; he knows all about you and what is going on in the deepest part of your heart anyway. So tell him how helpless you feel and wait with expectation to see what he does.

258

Jesus is there

"I AM"

Exodus 3.14

When God revealed himself to Moses, he explained that he wanted to be known as "I am". As far as names go, it is hardly the catchiest he could have chosen, but it is probably the most powerful!

For a moment, call to mind any situation facing you that may be causing you some concern. There may be any number of reasons why you are anxious about it: fear of a person, plans that haven't worked out well or a general sense that circumstances beyond your control are piling up against you.

However, instead of focusing on your concerns, try to picture Jesus there. He is the exact representation of God's being, and as he stands in the midst of the situation facing you, hear him speak his name – "I am".

Ephesians 1.21 speaks of Jesus being seated far above all other powers. He is not above them because he is detached from them, far from it, he is over them because he is greater than them all. Whatever situation may be causing you anxiety, Jesus is present and speaking the words, "I am". He is there, all-powerful, concerned for you and on your side.

Be prepared

'... be prepared in season and out of season'

2 Timothy 4.2

This verse is interesting because it speaks about seasons, but not the four seasons that make up our calendar year. Instead it suggests that there are times when we seem more spiritually alive, and other times when we feel a bit duller; seasons when our Christian life seems to bear fruit as opposed to other times, when it is harder to spot any.

A real encouragement from this verse is that feeling 'out of season' is not our fault. There are some aspects of our spiritual life over which we have control, such as how much energy we put into it, but other things over which we have little control, and often our feelings come into this bracket.

Yet as well as giving reassurance, this verse also provides us with a challenge. However you are feeling, and whatever spiritual season you feel you are going through, you are still called to 'be prepared'. In Romans 13.14, Paul tells us to clothe ourselves with the Lord Jesus. In other words, to consciously remember that Jesus is present with you, whatever you are feeling, and to call to mind that you have access to everything through him. This means that when you feel weak, he is strong; when you are anxious, he is peace; and when you feel empty, he has everything you need.

Think before you speak!

"Be my . . . priest"

Judges 17.10

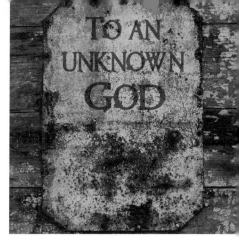

Judges 17 and 18 tell a strange story about a man, and later a tribe, who establish their own pattern of worship. What is odd is that they have a strong desire to do this, so go to extraordinary lengths to find something they can worship without any real sense of what they are doing or why. It's very easy to read such stories and find them faintly ridiculous, but perhaps they contain a lesson for all of us: true worship cannot take place outside relationship.

This is what Paul shared with the Athenians in Acts 17.23. He said, "For as I walked around and looked carefully at your objects of worship, I even found an altar with this inscription: TO AN UNKNOWN GOD. So you are ignorant of the very thing you worship. . ." This discovery gave Paul a perfect reason to proclaim to the people the nature of the God that he knew personally.

It can be so easy to begin to pray or worship, either corporately in church or on our own, by launching straight into it without first remembering the relationship into which we are called. Before opening our mouths in word or song, let's recognise who we are – children of Abba Father, loved and cherished by him. Let's focus first on the truth of this, and then begin to proclaim it.

Your approachable Father

'Grace and peace from God the Father and Christ Jesus our Saviour.'

Titus 1.4

Some people feel there is something rather stern about the image of God the Father. They would rather turn to Jesus with their problems, because somehow he seems kinder and more approachable. However, this verse cuts right through such thinking by presenting us with an image of the Father from whom grace and peace flow.

If you hold to the view of a Father God who seems distant, absent or somehow unapproachable, remember that when Jesus was asked what the Father was like, he said: "Anyone who has seen me has seen the Father." (John 14.9). In other words, if you have a sense that Jesus is approachable, it is because he is reflecting the very approachability of God the Father.

God the Father did not give us Jesus as a 'softer' version of himself, but rather as an exact image of what he himself is like. Take a moment to gently whisper the word, 'Abba'. It is the same word Jesus used when he talked to his Father (Mark 14.36) and it reflects God's longing to be known as Father; the one who knows everything about you and loves you completely. As your Father, he longs to bring you grace and peace.

Seeing and hearing more

"For truly I tell you, many prophets and righteous people longed to see what you see but did not see it, and to hear what you hear but did not hear it."

Matthew 13.17

These words are amazing! Jesus was telling his disciples that they were experiencing things that their forebears throughout the Old Testament longed to have seen and heard. What's more, this doesn't simply apply to the disciples. Thanks to the Bible and all it reveals about the Father, Jesus and the Holy Spirit, we, too, have access to a vision and understanding of God that people before the time of Jesus did not have. The question is, what are we doing about it?

There seems little point in living with the amazing revelation that Jesus is present with us if we do not take it seriously and call upon his presence whenever we can. What is the point of Jesus revealing the Father's love to us if we do not recognise and enjoy living in it? The Christian faith is so glorious, but the full weight of it only touches us if we let the truths revealed in the pages of the Bible touch us personally.

Why not let the truth impact you more deeply today? Jesus said he would always be with you, so choose to believe him. He is with you right now, so take a moment to close your eyes and focus on the significance of these three simple words: 'You are here.'

Flattering God!

'They came to him and said, "Teacher, we know that you are a man of integrity."'

Mark 12.14

God does not seem to take kindly to flattery! Those who sought to trick Jesus by asking whether or not it was right to pay taxes soon discovered that somehow he could see right into their hearts and was well aware of their motives. It is a sobering thought that when we come to God in worship it is not simply the words coming out of our lips that he hears, but also the thoughts of our hearts.

We are often told that it is good to begin a time of prayer with worship and somewhere at the back of our minds we may have a vague idea that God might be more inclined to hear our prayers if we worship him first – so we dutifully do so! However, God can probably see through this, just as he could see through the false flattery of those who sought to trick Jesus!

Worship is not about buttering God up so he is more kindly disposed to our requests, but is the response of our hearts to who he is and opening ourselves up to his wonder, whether or not we feel like it. Even if we feel wretched, worship is turning to God in absolute honesty and saying, 'Here I am. You are everything the Bible says of you, and I need you.'

Take a moment to come before him now. However you feel, choose to be there before him and worship him.

264

Too good to be true

'Such knowledge is too wonderful for me'

Psalm 139.6

In this beautiful psalm, David is seeking to remind himself of the wonder of God. He recounts the truth of God's hand upon him and reminds himself that the presence of God is always with him. At this point we can almost sense him shaking his head in wonder and declaring that these things are almost too good to be true!

For much of the time, our vision of God's presence and his goodness to us is woefully small. All too often we limit our sense of God to what we can discern using five senses, but God is not limited to those senses. If we can begin to grasp this and believe that his presence is absolutely everywhere and his hand is upon us – even right now – we would probably share David's sense of wonder that this is almost too good to be true.

We sometimes hear the expression 'living by faith', usually when referring to people who live without regular income, trusting in what God will provide for them. Actually, living by faith is something that we are all called to do, but in a much wider sense. It is about holding fast to our belief in his constant presence and his hand upon us, and applying this to our daily lives. Such knowledge is wonderful and almost too good to be true – but it is true!

Keep looking up

"Queen Vashti has done wrong, not only against the king but also against all the nobles and the peoples of all the provinces of King Xerxes."

Esther 1.16

The story of Esther is set in a time when customs and laws were very different from our own and the whole story is strange in many ways. It begins with the king summoning his wife, who refused to come to him. As a result she was deposed and a search for a new queen began. Queen Vashti seemed to take a stand against being regarded as a mere possession of the King, and yet she lost everything.

This episode was actually the start of a chain of events that ended with God moving in incredible power to save his people from the scheming in the king's court. At the heart of this story is God's ability to use what might seem to us to be unfair and wrong situations to bring about his purposes. It still seems unfair that Vashti was treated as she was – and it may seem unfair that you are treated in the way that you often are – but what this story teaches us is to keep looking up.

God was at work in this situation and he used it to save his people. When things turn against you, even if it seems unfair, why not lift your eyes from your present circumstances and instead invite God to reveal his glory in them? If it's hard knowing quite what to pray, just saying the name 'Jesus' brings him right into the heart of it. Keep looking up!

Doing the work with perseverance

"My food," said Jesus, "is to do the will of him who sent me and to finish his work."

John 4.34

These words occurred in what must have been a frustrating conversation for the disciples. They were talking about something entirely practical, but Jesus was speaking on a different level. The subject under discussion was about what sustained them. The disciples were talking about literal food and Jesus about the will of God. He told them that what fed him was doing God's will and finishing his work.

Perhaps the biggest challenge for us is not the notion of doing God's will, but rather of finishing it. If God were to reveal to us that he wanted us to do something, we would be rather foolish not to do it. In fact, we would probably set about it with great joy and enthusiasm. The challenge, however, is to keep at it and see the work through to completion, even when it becomes a slog and when we might not sense the continual whisper of God in our ears or his prodding at our heart.

A challenging question is this: what are the things that you were once called to do, but have let slip? It may be that God has called you to new things, but could it be that due to discouragement or lack of perseverance you have let some of his work go unfinished?

Your God who saves

'Our God is a God who saves'

Psalm 68.20

This statement about God reveals that it is his very nature to bring about salvation and help in every situation.

Throughout the Bible, the term 'salvation' has many different meanings. It is not just about the forgiveness of our sins and our destiny in heaven, it encompasses all God's actions in rescuing his people from the things that afflict them. It is his very nature to bring this rescue to us.

We might worry that what God really wants is to allow us to suffer, but if you are tempted to think like this you are building an image of God that is contrary to what the Bible actually reveals

about him. He is not the 'God who likes to make us suffer', but the 'God who saves'.

The implication of this fact is that you don't need to ask whether God is willing to help you; since his very nature is to help, the answer is always 'yes'. You may not know how his help comes, but it is always his heart to help you in some way.

Perhaps you are facing a situation right now that is beyond any resources you have to find a way through. As you hold this situation before God, do so with these words on your lips: 'You are the God who saves'.

The tenderness of Jesus

'... we have one who speaks to the Father in our defence – Jesus Christ, the Righteous One.'

1 John 2.1

Whenever you think you have done something wrong, remember that you always have Jesus speaking for you, not in judgment or condemnation, but in your defence – speaking on your behalf.

Does Jesus need to do this? Would we really be in trouble if it wasn't for Jesus? Actually, this message about Jesus speaking to his Father on our behalf is written for our benefit, as it enlarges our perception of the love and understanding God has for us. Out of his love for us God listens to Jesus' profound understanding of the situations we are going through.

When Jesus speaks in our defence, it is from the perspective of someone who knows exactly what's going on. He was tempted in every way that we are tempted; nothing we experience is unknown to him. When he speaks to his Father, it is because he understands what we are going through and remembers the feelings and temptations; he knows how hard it is.

Jesus does not look at you with a pained expression telling you 'to get on with it'. Rather he sees you and whispers words in your defence to the Father: 'I know what they are going through. It is hard for them – have mercy on them.'

For a moment catch a sense of Jesus' gentleness as he sees your life and speaks to the Father about you.

Forgiveness is not just about you

'He is the atoning sacrifice for our sins, and not only for ours but also for the sins of the whole world.'

1 John 2.2

This reassuring verse has a slight sting in its tail! It is with great joy that we proclaim that Jesus has taken away our sins so we are innocent before God. It is not that we have been let off, but rather that he has paid the price and taken the punishment for us. The 'sting in the tail' is this: he did not just die for our sins, but for the sins of the whole world. This includes the sins of the people who have hurt us and caused us pain.

It is so easy to long for God's mercy for us, but at the same time want God's punishment (or at least a deep conviction of sin) for those who have hurt us. Part of fully accepting the mercy of God in our lives is also to accept his mercy on those who have caused us pain. We all belong to the same Father and he has no favourites; the mercy he longs to show to one of us is the mercy he longs to show to all of us.

Have you the courage to pray for those who have hurt you, and ask that God will show them the same mercy and love you long to receive yourself?

Away with fear!

'There is no fear in love. But perfect love drives out fear, because fear has to do with punishment. The one who fears is not made perfect in love.'

1 John 4.18

The writer, John, may seem a little harsh in saying that those who fear have not been made perfect in love. After all, we all feel fear and anxiety at times. However, what John says is actually very encouraging – there is always more of God's love to discover.

John stresses that if we really know God's love we won't be scared, and the very fact we feel fearful means that we have not yet tapped into the full depths of God's love. It must certainly be the Father's desire that we really know his love, so where do we begin?

When fear began to descend on Jesus in the Garden of Gethsemane (Mark 14.33-36) he did not dwell on it or seek to banish the darkness, but concentrated on God's love for him and cried out, "Abba, Father." What a wonderful way to refocus on the truth. Allow these two words to go through your mind, slowly repeating them. Let something of God's love and tenderness reach you as you speak to the Father with the same words that Jesus used when he prayed.

There is more!

". . . they exchanged their glorious God for something disgraceful."

Hosea 4.7

When God spoke these words to the priests of the land, he gave them a glimpse of his vision for their lives. He could see their potential, but also their indifference to his plans for them.

There is probably an element of truth in this for all of us. I don't think Jesus would want to call us disgraceful, but perhaps he does look at our lives and see that there could be more. We could have more awareness of our Father's love, more yielding to his grace and more times of turning to him to find his presence.

What we do have in common with the priests who were being addressed in this verse is that the decision is ours.

There is always more. The words of Jesus, 'Come to me', are a continual refrain urging us to turn and find the 'more' that he offers. How much more is there? In any situation you face today, if Jesus was standing in your shoes what could happen? This is how much more there is.

Asking for healing

"Very truly I tell you, my Father will give you whatever you ask in my name."

John 16.23

So many people have probably read this verse and thought something along the lines of 'I wish!' It seems so simple, yet in reality we have to ask whether it really works? We do what we can to pray in the name of Jesus, but if we are honest it doesn't always seem to make any real difference to what happens.

However, Jesus was not talking about a formula for success here. There is something about this verse that can be all too easily overlooked: prayer is always in the context of a relationship. There is a deep prayerful relationship between Jesus and his Father, and it is this relationship we need to explore more in order to learn to have increased confidence in our own prayers. Jesus' desire is that we discover the extent of his Father's love for us and have a sense of just how loved we are – just as he experienced it. When we are captivated by his love, we can capture his heart and will for those things we pray about.

You can begin right now! Before you bring anything to God in prayer, spend a little time reflecting on the love that the Father has for you. This is not just something to soften his heart towards you, it is because knowing more of his love will affect your prayers for healing – and for anything else – as well as being something that will change your life for ever.

Be honest!

"I counsel you to buy from me gold refined in the fire, so that you can become rich; and white clothes to wear, so that you can cover your shameful nakedness; and salve to put on your eyes, so that you can see."

Revelation 3.18

It can be hard to be honest about our spiritual lives. It is never easy for us to admit that our lives with God are not as good as we think they should be, but honesty is a sign of humility. Today's verse contains some words spoken by Jesus to the church in Laodicea, to people who thought they were doing fine, but in reality were not. The good news he shared was that despite their failings there was more; a closer relationship with Jesus, a richer experience of God and a new sense of purity and vision.

So how do we access all this? Jesus shared a picture of him standing at the door knocking, eager to come in when the door was opened. Our starting point is the image of Jesus wanting to come in: he wants more! He is longing for us to let him come in and share a deeper intimacy and friendship with us. Unless we believe that he wants more, perhaps we will not hear him knocking – and even if we do we may not recognise that it is him at the door.

It may be a humbling thought that Jesus is seeking a deeper relationship with you simply because he loves you. How does this make you feel and what are you going to do about it?

Past, present and future

'Grace and peace to you from him who is, and who was, and who is to come'

Revelation 1.4

This powerful phrase gives us a picture of Jesus in his entirety, not as a king currently enthroned on high, but as one who spans all of time – present, past and future. Even more is added to this image: grace and peace flow from Jesus, who stands throughout all time. Let's make this reality more relevant for us!

You may be going through anxieties or difficulties at the moment, and perhaps there are things you haven't told even those closest to you. The hope for you is that grace and peace can flow from Jesus into your present situation.

You also have a past, some of which might bring happiness as you recall memories, but some

that brings hurt – and perhaps there are even recollections that you simply do not want to revisit. The invitation from Jesus is that grace and peace can flow into your past.

The future is unknown, but sometimes fears about what might lie around the corner can cause anxiety. Again, the hope that you can cling to is that the grace and peace of Jesus will be there.

So grace and peace for your present, past and future will flow from Jesus. He is the source of so much and to find him is to find what flows from him. Take a moment to hold your present, past and future before him and whisper his name over them.

Good news in troubling times

"In this world you will have trouble. But take heart! I have overcome the world."

John 16.33

Are these words of Jesus good or bad news? No-one likes to be told that there is going to be trouble and we would much rather be told that from now on life is going to be wonderful! However, Jesus is no deceiver and he told us the truth when he said that there would be trouble in this life.

The first reassurance is that when trouble does come to us, we need not go down the road of wondering what we have done wrong to deserve it – it just happens. Jesus said it would and he certainly does not judge us for going through hard times.

The second lesson is that whatever trouble we are going through, it is not as big as the person of Jesus. This can sound like a well-meaning cliché, but Jesus was pointing out the truth when he said that he had overcome the world by rising from the dead – a vision that we are invited to hold onto in every trouble that we experience. God is able to pour power into every situation we face – a power that is beyond our wildest comprehension.

Whatever you may be going through right now, in your mind place them in one hand, and in the other hand hold on to the power that God released through the resurrection of Jesus. As you bring your two hands together, remind yourself of Jesus' promise that the power of God will be at work in your life in some glorious way.

God's mercy and not your goodness

"We do not make requests of you because we are righteous, but because of your great mercy."

Daniel 9.18

In this moving prayer, Daniel touches on a lovely truth about God: we approach him because of who he is and not because of what we have done. Suppose you are seeking God for healing – and have been doing so for a while – it is tempting to assume that for God's mercy to flow unimpeded there must be more that you can do: more Bible reading, longer times of prayer, more repentance and a fresh resolve to lead a godly life.

However, to think like this undermines one of the greatest truths about our faith – that we are saved, helped and healed by grace and not by our works. Of course, no Christian deliberately plans to live an ungodly lifestyle, but the basis of turning to God is that he is a God of such great mercy.

It takes a little courage and honesty to come before him and say: 'Father, I come to you today, not because of anything I have done but simply because you are a God of mercy.'

Your ever-present Father

"Yet I am not alone, for my Father is with me."

John 16.32

It can be easy to look at some of the things Jesus says about his relationship with his Father and think that it's all very well for Jesus to say them, but he was different from us! It's true, of course, that in so many ways Jesus was different from us, but there are also ways in which he was desperate to reveal ways in which we, too, can share in what he experienced. His relationship with God was one of them.

At the end of John 17, Jesus states something wonderful: that the relationship he wants us to have with God is exactly the same as his relationship with God (John 17.26). If this is what he really wants, it must also be true that we share in what today's verse reveals, and which Jesus knew so well: that the Father is always present.

We often think of Jesus being with us, or of the indwelling of the Holy Spirit, but we may not have such an awareness of the Father's presence with us. Yet he is here. At any time of the day or night you can whisper these words, 'Abba, Father', knowing that the source of all love and power is intimately present with you. Wherever you are, you are never alone – the Father is with you.

God is thrilled with your faith

"Because you have seen me, you have believed; blessed are those who have not seen and yet have believed."

John 20.29

Jesus spoke these words to Thomas just after he had shown him the physical scars of the crucifixion on his risen body, but his words are also so affirming to us. If we ever stopped to consider what God thinks about our faith, we would probably imagine he would say something along the lines of – 'could do better!'

However, the truth is far from this. Thomas believed once he saw with his own eyes and touched with his own fingers, but actually what Jesus said to him is along the lines of, 'Big deal! The ones who really impress me are those who believe without having actually seen me with their own eyes or physically touched me.' That's us – that's you! In Jesus' eyes, the faith you have is beautiful to him. Jesus calls you blessed; he is delighted with your faith. Of course, there could always be more, but he rejoices in what he sees within you.

If you can accept this, you will begin to sense something of his delight in you. It's not that Jesus simply tolerates you, but that he really delights in you. Spend some time getting your head around this incredible message!

God has seen everything | 1

'In the beginning God . . . '

Genesis 1.1

We are going to spend the next week or so looking at some verses from the first few chapters of the book of Genesis. Whatever stance we take on how creation happened and the timing of it, one thing that unites all believers is this simple fact: God was there at the beginning. There is something humbling and releasing about this; God has seen the lives of every person who has ever lived. He has been watching, calling and whispering to every single person – and he still does it to us.

We may think that we are the only people to experience some of the things we go through, that our temptations are unique and our situations unlike any other. Yet the truth is that God has literally seen it all before. This does not mean he lumps us all together in categories, but he has seen folk come through the struggles facing them. He has seen the effect of his grace upon people and there is a proven power in the words, 'I can do all this through him who gives me strength.' (Philippians 4.13)

God's presence within you gives you power, and because he has seen its effect upon countless people through the ages, he knows what it can do, what you can achieve and that it is trustworthy. How does this make you feel?

The power of God's word | 2

'And God said, "Let there be light," and there was light.'

Genesis 1.3

The truth behind this simple sentence is this: God spoke and what he said came into being. There is an incredible power in his words – creative power. Sometimes we read about Jesus speaking and amazing things happening as a result. The question this raises for us is this: how seriously do we take God's words?

Every time we read the Bible, we are reading and interacting with the voice of God. Each time we sense his voice in prayer, even if it is something as gentle as the assurance of his love, we are hearing the voice of God. So what is the effect of his words upon us?

Perhaps creation was compelled to listen and to take his word seriously, but we have a choice. Sadly, all too often we choose to take his voice lightly, disregarding it because it seems too good to be true so we simply don't believe it is for us.

As you read the Bible today, what is the one phrase that seems to be underlined for you or lingers on in your mind? Recognise this as God's word for you today and let these words do what he desires them to do.

Bringing life to others | 3

'Then the LORD God formed a man from the dust of the ground and breathed into his nostrils the breath of life, and the man became a living being.'

Genesis 2.7

Many people share the desire to know that they have a purpose, a significance and that they matter. Actually, the simple act of breathing can remind us of our worth to God. God breathed into the first Adam and his breath caused life to fill Adam's body. From that moment on, every breath he took was a reminder of that first breath that God blew into him; a reminder that God created him and put him on earth for a purpose – and so it is with us.

You have been chosen by God, set in the place and time that he has determined for you, and into you he has breathed his life. Let every breath you take remind you of the first breath that God breathed into you. He chose you to live and placed within you his life-giving Spirit, not just to give you life but so that you might be a source of life to others.

It is a challenging thought that you can be a source of life to every person you meet today, whether by a kind word, a small act of kindness or a prayer for them. The life God has given you is a life that brings life to others.

Being who you were created to be | 4

'. . . and the man became a living being.'

Genesis 2.7

It has been said that a tree gives glory to God by being a tree. In other words, it is content being what it was created to be. In a similar way we give glory to God when we are ourselves; not trying to be someone else but finding a contentment in being the person God created us to be.

We can also look at this more generally. What is it that we, as humans, were created to be? If each of us can find the truth for ourselves, our personal contentment grows.

As we read about Adam, we discover he had a number of tasks or callings and in each we can glimpse something of what it means to be fully alive. A good question to ask yourself is how much these callings are a part of your own life and how you can take hold of them in a deeper way so you can become more of the person you were created to be.

Before we embark on this journey over the following days, take to heart this truth and revel in it: you give God glory simply by being yourself and not imitating anyone else. After all, he created your inmost being, the part of you that makes you wonderfully unique.

It's all about relationship | 5

'Now the Lord God had planted a garden in the east, in Eden; and there he put the man he had formed.'

Genesis 2.8

The story of Adam and the beginning of his life speaks about a dependency and fellowship with God that he would lose later on. It is this fellowship that Jesus came to restore to us, and because of him we can rediscover and enjoy it. Saint Augustine put it much more strongly when he said, "Our hearts are restless until they rest in you." He was saying that until we find this dependency and fellowship, we are incomplete.

I wonder if there are times in your life when you wonder if you will ever become a better person? If you have ever felt

like this, rejoice! It is a sure sign that you need God – his grace, strength and forgiveness. You simply could not cope without him – and you are not meant to! In fact, if you ever get to the stage of being tempted to think you could manage without God and act in your own strength, you have lost what he longs for – your dependency and fellowship with him.

Take a few moments to repeat these words and address them to your Father who loves having a relationship with you: 'My heart is restless until it rests in you.'

Listening to God through creation | 6

'The Lord God made all kinds of trees grow out of the ground – trees that were pleasing to the eye and good for food.'

Genesis 2.9

It is a lovely thought that God creates things that are pleasing to the eye. No wonder creation can so often lead us to him, whether it be the splendour of a glorious sunset or something much smaller. Julian of Norwich contemplated God by looking at a hazelnut!

When you next find your attention turning to God's creation, whether big or small, you may find it helpful to reflect on some of the following thoughts:

- Why did this particular view or object attract my attention?

- What does it tell me about God?

- What does it say to me about his character?

- Does this say anything about my relationship with God?

- What can I take into my day from this?

You may think you are not very good at hearing God speak to you. This may be true, but it says more about your ability to listen than God's to communicate. He may speak frequently, but perhaps you are not attuned to hearing his voice.

Let your reflections about creation encourage you to hear God communicating with you in a different way, and draw you closer to him.

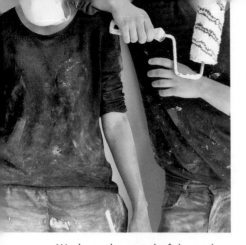

God's co-worker | 7

'The Lord God took the man and put him in the Garden of Eden to work it and take care of it.'

Genesis 2.15

Work can be wonderful – and a curse! It depends on what your job is, or even whether you have one. When we are stuck in a period of grinding humdrum activity, the thought of getting away from it all can seem very attractive.

However, God has called us to be his co-workers. You might think this only applies to those whose work can be categorised as 'Christian ministry', but today's words from Genesis are general, speaking to everyone rather than just ministers. You may not see the work you do as having much to do with God and the extension of his kingdom, but it is worth bearing

Paul's words from Colossians 3.17 in mind: 'And whatever you do, whether in word or deed, do it all in the name of the Lord Jesus, giving thanks to God the Father through him.'

You are God's co-worker and once you start to believe it you will begin to see him involved in your day-to-day activity and recognise the opportunities it presents through his eyes.

As you set about your work today – whether it be in paid employment, voluntary work or being there for others – dare to see yourself as God sees you, his co-worker where he has put you.

From the Father's heart to you | 8

"... but you must not ..."

Genesis 2.17

Commandments can be like a red rag to a bull! The very fact that we are told not to do something often makes us want to do it even more! None of us like being given long lists of rules, but sometimes the Bible seems to be just that. However, are rules necessarily bad? Let's consider two points.

The first is that rules form the boundaries within which life can be lived safely and enjoyed. If there was no highway code it would lead to mayhem, and a lack of rules in any sport would lead to it being unidentifiable and probably grossly unfair. It is rules that allow safety, fairness and fun.

This leads on to the second reason why rules can be good – they point to the heart behind them. God gave rules because in his love he knew the best way for us to live, and some were even given because they encompass principles that are there for our protection and well-being. All the Father's commandments show he loves us and wants us to live life in all its fullness.

Ask yourself what each commandment shows you about the Father's heart for you and for the world? The more you seek for his heart, the more you will find it.

It's OK to think! | 9

'So the man gave names to all the livestock, the birds in the sky and all the wild animals.'

Genesis 2.20

Adam choosing names for all the animals must have been an entertaining part of creation! Presumably he looked at each one and used his reason and imagination to name what he saw in front of him. It wasn't the case that God told him what to name each creature, but that Adam was encouraged to choose the names himself.

There are many different aspects to worship and one of them is using our minds. As we think and wrestle with difficult issues, or study our Bibles, we are worshipping God just as we do when we praise him for all he has done, surrender to his will and listen to his voice. There may be times when we are baffled by challenges in the world that seem daunting and by some very confusing passages in the Bible, but instead of throwing up our hands in despair and deciding that it is all too much for us, it is worth thinking things through and pondering them as part of our worship to God. We may still end up as confused as when we started, but we will have worshipped him with our minds.

288

Bringing God pleasure | 10

'But the Lord God called to the man, "Where are you?"'

Genesis 3.9

There is a real sense of sadness in this question. The picture we have is of God walking in the garden looking for Adam as he loved to walk with him – but he was not there. He felt ashamed to be with his God because of what he had done.

The implications of this story are incredible. It gives God pleasure to walk with us. We often think of our walk with God in terms of our obedience to him – and, of course, this is a part of it – but suppose it is more? What if God actually enjoys walking with us, taking pleasure in our company and missing us when we are not with him?

Perhaps you are tempted to react with a certain cynicism: why would he be that bothered with you when he has plenty of other holier people? Why would he miss you?

God would miss you because you are individually created by him. You bear a unique touch of him that no-one else has, and there is something about you that is unlike anyone else. This is what God misses when you do not walk with him. Take a moment to turn to him and give him that pleasure.

You have choices | 11

". . . sin is crouching at your door; it desires to have you, but you must rule over it."

Genesis 4.7

This portrayal of sin crouching at our door is very graphic. It gives us an image of sin waiting to spring upon us, but also – very encouragingly – the knowledge that it is something we can resist. It may seek to have control over us, but the reality is that we can have control over it.

The word 'sin' covers a wealth of actions and thoughts, perhaps all of them summed up by the implications of walking a path that is not God's path. Something specific may come to mind as you read this, but for now let's take as an example the way we see ourselves before God.

Throughout the Bible God has revealed his heart of love, and the path he has laid out for us is that we remain in his love. Therefore, it makes sense that by not doing so we sin – but it is a sin over which we have control. We can make a choice to live in the knowledge of God's love throughout this day, irrespective of whether we feel it. Certainly, the temptation is there to believe the opposite – it's waiting at the door, crouching – so whether we welcome this crouching figure or kick it off the path God has laid out for us is our choice.

What choice will you make today?

Knowing that God hears

'This is the confidence we have in approaching God: that if we ask anything according to his will, he hears us. And if we know that he hears us – whatever we ask – we know that we have what we asked of him.'

1 John 5.14-15

Do you ever find yourself seeking a missing ingredient to prayer, wondering if there is something you can do to help get your prayers answered?

Prayer is a living conversation with Father God. All of us will relate to him slightly differently, just as different children within one family all have a unique relationship with their parents. There is no missing ingredient! However, this verse does tell us something about prayer that we often forget: it speaks of the knowledge and certainty that our prayers have been heard. Logically we know that this is true, but from time to time, in our hearts, we probably wonder – did he hear me?

It is an amazing thought that every prayer you have ever prayed has been heard by God. Giving thanks for this is natural and it is also an important act of faith – not just for God's benefit but also for your heart. When you give thanks that he has heard your prayers, and really believe that this is true, it can give you great peace to know that the one who loves you more than you could know has heard the cry of your heart – and being God, he won't forget it!

Being at peace without knowing why!

"It is not for you to know the times or dates the Father has set by his own authority."

Acts 1.7

There are some things we know and some things we don't know! These words that Jesus spoke to his followers just before his Ascension to heaven imply that there are some things we are simply not meant to know, so any quest to find answers will be fruitless.

When we are seeking healing, either for ourselves or someone else, one question that is unlikely to receive a clear answer is, "Why?" Possible reasons may be suggested, but deep down they may not be completely satisfactory and perhaps we need to learn to be at peace with this. Yet there are some things that we do know, and are called to rely on.

One is God's love for us. Despite confusion and things beyond our understanding, his love is always a reality. In our limited understanding, we might be tempted to look at our situation and ask: 'If he loves me, then why . . .?' However, our calling is to take a different attitude and say: 'Because God loves me, then . . .'

Don't allow your situation and suffering to cause you to doubt the love of God, but instead try to apply God's immense love for you to the issues in your life so they can be touched and transformed.

Is anything too hard for God?

"Is anything too hard for the Lord?"

Genesis 18.14

The answer to this question is bound to be 'No'. If anything was too hard for him, he would not be God! However, God was not asking a philosophical question here; he was asking for trust.

The context for this passage is Sarah being told that she would bear a son within the next year and laughing at the thought, because as the Bible simply puts it, she 'was past the age of childbearing'. It is at this point she was asked this simple question: "Is anything too hard for the Lord?" What is most encouraging about this question is that it is not purely random, but is based on the promise that God had already given to Abraham (Genesis 15.4: "This man will not be your heir,

but a son who is your own flesh and blood will be your heir."). This was not something new that Sarah was called to believe, but a promise of old to which she could attach her faith.

Similarly, when we are asked to trust in God, it is not a random call that comes to us from nowhere, it is in the light of his unending love for us. Our ability to trust is based on God's promise that he will always be with us, and in the knowledge of Jesus' promise that he came to give us abundant life.

It is when we hold on to these truths that we find a new confidence to answer that same question that was put to Sarah – "Is anything too hard for the Lord?"

Living in two worlds

'I, John . . . was on the island of Patmos . . . On the Lord's Day I was in the Spirit.'

Revelation 1.9-10

This phrase highlights a real truth for all of us: we dwell in two places at once!

On the one hand, we are born into, and live in, the physical world. This is what our natural senses – our sight, hearing and touch relate to. It is also the world to which we react emotionally, and with which we interact on a daily basis. Since Jesus lives in us through the Holy Spirit, he interacts with this physical world through us.

However, the indwelling of Jesus has another implication for us. In John 17.21, Jesus talks to his Father about his followers and says, "May they also be in us. . . " Christ dwells within us, but we are also within him. In other words, Jesus dwells with us in our physical world, but we also dwell with him in his heavenly environment. The implications of this are incredible. It means that we, too, are seated 'far above all rule and authority', where everything is beneath the feet of Jesus and where the wonder of God's love is a tangible reality. It is so easy to look at the challenges and difficulties around us and forget that we actually live in Christ, for whom nothing is impossible and who reigns over absolutely everything.

You may feel that this natural world around you is the 'real' world, but the truth is that you belong to two worlds, both of them equally real. Remembering your dual-citizenship can really change the way you view each day.

294

Love reflects God's nature

"But I tell you, love your enemies and pray for those who persecute you, that you may be children of your Father in heaven. He causes his sun to rise on the evil and the good, and sends rain on the righteous and the unrighteous."

Matthew 5.44-45

Of all the commands that Jesus gave us, this is one of the hardest! It is much easier to think of all the bad things that we would like to happen to those who stand against us! The truth is that this command reveals something incredible about the nature of God.

We are commanded to love our enemies, and in doing so we will be children of our Father in heaven. In other words, by doing this we will reflect the very nature of God who loves his enemies and whose heart is to do good to them. All too often we beat ourselves up over whether we are good enough to receive blessings from God, for in our minds we can easily associate them with what we deserve. This verse teaches us that God blesses anyway. Of course he wants us to be involved in what is good, but not because such goodness will open the door to his blessings.

Our actions cannot change God's nature: he is good, he loves everyone, and his heart is to bless. Why not take a moment to sit in his presence now and enjoy his love, no matter how you feel? Nothing you have done can ever change his love for you.

The Father who sees you

"But when you pray . . . pray to your Father, who is unseen. Then your Father, who sees what is done in secret, will reward you."

Matthew 6.6

Jesus encouraged us that however we may feel about our prayers, and whether or not we sense that they are getting anywhere, the truth is that the Father sees us at prayer and it will make a difference. Jesus is not talking about the quality of our prayers, whether they are good and eloquent, but simply this: the Father sees what we are doing.

If this is true, then the fact that we are praying is more important than getting the words right. It will certainly bless us to catch this truth as we pray and to know that we are indeed being listened to and watched.

As you pray, it might help to visualise yourself praying. See yourself as if you were an observer and then let your vision change, so that rather than simply seeing yourself sitting in a chair or wherever you are, visualise yourself kneeling before the very throne of God. The truth is that you are just as visible to God sitting in your room at home as you would be if you were the only person kneeling before his throne.

Just do it!

'Then Ananias went to the house and entered it. Placing his hands on Saul, he said, "Brother Saul, the Lord – Jesus, who appeared to you on the road as you were coming here – has sent me so that you may see again and be filled with the Holy Spirit."'

Acts 9.17

If we think about the details of Saul's conversion and how it happened, it is clear that it was God's plan but also that there was a level of human involvement. God does some things sovereignly but at other times he uses people. On the Damascus Road, Jesus spoke directly to Saul – but then it seems that a human being, Ananias, was needed, to lay hands on Saul so his sight would be restored. It is pointless asking why God did one thing without human intervention and not the other – he just did!

The lesson this teaches us is that it is entirely possible that God may ask us to do something and we might think what's the point of that? The answer is likely to be, 'Just because'! When we think about God asking us to do something, we may have the impression that he will speak loudly or give us a real compulsion to do something. However, his voice might simply be a nudge, a whisper or a thought that comes to us, often prompting us to do something that seems quite trivial and small for someone – just because!

So just do it! You will probably never know the real significance of your actions and small acts of kindness, but the one who nudges you does know.

Setting God before you

'I have set the Lord always before me. Because he is at my right hand, I shall not be shaken.'

Psalm 16.8

This verse is a powerful help to us in difficult times, and it is particularly helpful if we work backwards through the phrases. The very fact that the author wrote about being shaken meant he was experiencing some difficulty, and many of us can identify with this; it may be that you really need God's divine touch in some aspect of your life. Sometimes our need can cause us to doubt his love, and yet we desperately do not want to lose sight of this – we want to stand firm. So how can we stand firm and not be shaken?

Our ability to do this is based on the knowledge that God is with us; he is at our 'right hand'. Whatever we are going through – whether it be sickness, hardship or worry – knowing that he is actually with us changes our outlook and expectation. It is when we cannot find him that helplessness can set in. So how do we find God? David's answer is quite clear: set him before you!

It is not that David is 'making up' a sense of God's presence, but rather that he is so convinced of his presence with him that he can, with great ease, imagine God there – because he is. This was not David doing some imaginative exercise, but rather tuning into the reality of God being right there with him.

Take a moment to set the Lord before you. Where is he for you? How would you describe his presence with you? Enjoy him!

298

Let panic lead to prayer!

'... so when the disciples heard that Peter was in Lydda, they sent two men to him and urged him, "Please come at once!"'

Acts 9.38

This urgent request was because a wonderful Christian named Tabitha had become sick and died. Distraught at her death, the disciples heard that Peter was near and sent for him in haste. We are not told what was going through Peter's mind at this point – did he know that he was expected to raise someone from the dead? Did he have any idea of the situation to which he had been summoned?

What we do know is that Peter responded, and as soon as he got there we are told that he prayed. It is a simple detail, but it says so much to us. We are often caught off guard; either presented with unexpected circumstances or situations that are beyond our human experience, strength or capability. We would like to think that the first thing we would do is to pray, but often our first reaction is to panic or to doubt. We need do neither.

It is likely that as Peter prayed, he caught a vision of what he should do, and this is what he did – and God was glorified. It is OK to panic if panic leads to prayer, but it is through prayer that wisdom about what to do next will come.

Co-operating with God

"See, I have delivered Jericho into your hands, along with its king and its fighting men. March round the city"

Joshua 6.2-3

God gave the Israelites the city of Jericho, but he didn't just open the gates and cause all the people inside to surrender. The Israelites had to co-operate by being obedient and marching around the city for seven days.

The Bible says that God has given us so much – so where is it? Paul says that God has 'blessed us in the heavenly realms with every spiritual blessing in Christ' (Ephesians 1.3). So how do we get these blessings? Like the Israelites, we must co-operate with the process.

We need to stick close to Jesus. He said: "Neither can you bear fruit unless you remain in me" (John 15.4). Fruit is not something that the branch decides to grow, any more than the Israelites could draw up their own plan to take Jericho. Fruit is the natural consequence of a branch staying attached to a healthy tree; the energy is not in bearing the fruit, but in staying attached.

Sit quietly for a few moments, and say the name 'Jesus' slowly and deliberately. Do this a few times now and whenever you remember throughout the day, and through this simple action find yourself dwelling in him.

God chose you – get over it!

'For he chose us in him before the creation of the world to be holy and blameless in his sight.'

Ephesians 1.4

Jacob was a man chosen by God, yet if you read the account of his life and his actions he was far from perfect. In fact, since he seemed to make an art out of deception he was certainly not chosen for his uprightness! It was simply that God chose him. If we were invited to select someone to occupy his place in history, we would almost certainly have selected someone else, perhaps even his brother who was to show grace and forgiveness when they were reunited after Jacob's deception had driven them apart.

Similarly, you too are chosen by God – Ephesians 1.4 states this clearly. You can probably think of many reasons why he should not choose you – but he has. You need to be at peace with this because God evidently is! He wants you to be attentive to your lifestyle and walk closely with him, of course, but these aren't things you have to do in order to qualify for his favour. You have his favour already; he chose you before the very foundation of the world – so rejoice in it.

Seeking help

'. . . a synagogue leader came and knelt before him'

Matthew 9.18

This synagogue leader was also a desperate father and his action was to lead to two beautiful miracles in the New Testament. Jairus came to Jesus on behalf of his sick daughter (who actually died as the story enfolds) and during the course of the narrative a woman from the crowd touched Jesus' cloak and was healed. It all started with two desperate people coming to Jesus, rather than with him looking for people in need.

The point is clear – it all begins with coming to Jesus. However, this is a step that can be hard for us to take. Doesn't he already know about our suffering and what we are going through? Of course he does – and he cares about it – but the encouragement of scripture is that we actively cast our burdens upon him (1 Peter 5.7) and don't assume he will automatically do everything for us.

Another step for us to take, which might seem even more difficult, is to ask for God's help through other people; to ask someone to pray for us. It means admitting that all is not well and we need the help of others. Yet, as in the case of the synagogue leader who knelt before Jesus, it is these acts of humility that so often open the door for God to do things in our lives that he otherwise may not do.

Seeing yourself through God's eyes

'Do not remember the sins of my youth and my rebellious ways; according to your love remember me, for you, Lord, are good.'

Psalm 25.7

When David prayed these words to God, it was not as if God was wondering what to do – should he remember David's sins or shouldn't he? God didn't need persuading to see him in a different light, but rather David was attempting to see himself through God's eyes.

David presents us with a completely different way of understanding how God sees us, and remembers us according to his love. What does this mean? Paul revealed a beautiful insight when he wrote about love in 1 Corinthians 13.5, that love 'keeps no record of wrongs'. If God really is the perfect definition of love, then for God to remember us according to his love is for him to look at us and keep no record of wrongs.

When you look at your image in a mirror, you may be confronted by thoughts and even recall the past as it looms large over your shoulders, but God does not. He sees you as the beautiful, adopted and forgiven person he created. The next time you see yourself in the mirror, give thanks for his vision of you.

The right perspective

"'. . . will it seem marvellous to me?" declares the LORD Almighty.'

Zechariah 8.6

The Living Bible puts these words of God in a wonderful way: "This seems unbelievable to you, but it is no great thing for me." This verse calls us to regard our lives, our relationship with God, and the resources of heaven from God's perspective rather than our own.

Often, when people ask for prayer, they are quick to point out that God can do amazing things but the implication is that he probably won't! Thinking like this puts us in danger of losing our sense of the wonder of God and replacing it with the routine of what has always been.

Even the most stunning touch of God – whether it be healing or answered prayer – is nothing compared to all the resources he has at his disposal. Yet we consider it highly unlikely that he would ever do such a thing for us. Why? Do we consider the task too hard for him? This verse from Zechariah confronts us with just how ludicrous such thinking is – can anything possibly be too marvellous for God? Seeing more of his wonders in our lives may well begin by us being open to the very real possibility that such things could actually happen to us. This doesn't mean acknowledging they could but probably won't, but rather that nothing is too marvellous for God.

As you ponder your own needs in prayer, speak these words over them: 'Is there anything too marvellous for God?'

Difficult people!

'A bruised reed he will not break, and a smouldering wick he will not snuff out'

Matthew 12.20

In his gospel, there came a point when Matthew paused to reflect on the nature of the person about whom he was writing, and he chose these words from Isaiah which seem to perfectly sum up Jesus. This phrase overflows with the gentleness and kindness of God to those who are in need. Matthew tells us that what Jesus sees so clearly is that hurting people are like bruised reeds, and if this is true the last thing they need is to be broken.

Not only does this describe the way Jesus longs to treat us, but also how he longs to treat others. It is so often true that those who need the most love are those we find most unlovable! Whereas we can be quick to condemn and judge because we see the exterior of people, Jesus sees the bruised reed within; just as he longs to bring the full nature of his gentleness to us, so he longs to bring it to those whom we could so easily dismiss.

If there is someone you are finding very difficult at the moment remember that God is not looking at their exterior, which is so trying for you, but at the bruised reed within.

Aligning yourself with God's will

"A bruised reed he will not break, and a smouldering wick he will not snuff out, till he has brought justice through to victory."

Matthew 12.20

It is very easy to look at the gentleness and kindness of Jesus and confuse these qualities with softness. As we look at today's verse in which Matthew applies Isaiah's words to Jesus, the gentleness of Jesus goes hand in hand with his mission – a mission that is nothing short of justice and victory. Not only does Jesus have a deep love for those who are suffering, he also feels the injustice of it.

This is so powerful for us to grasp because it presents us with a picture of Jesus who is not simply holding our wounded selves with a 'there, there' attitude. Instead he holds us tenderly, but with an anger that we should be suffering and a determination that injustice shall not prevail.

This is where prayer comes in. Prayer is not simply expressing your wish to God, but is about aligning yourself with his vision for the wholeness of his people – including yourself and those you know. So, as you sit quietly, why not say 'yes' to God's vision and invite him to intervene in your life and in the lives of those for whom you pray?

306

What do you expect today? | 1

"Who among the gods is like you, Lord? Who is like you – majestic in holiness, awesome in glory, working wonders?"

Exodus 15.11

What is your image of God? As a Christian, you would probably want to say that it reflects the description of God in the Bible. However this needs keeping alive and fresh, as too often we find ourselves reducing the God of the Bible to a smaller picture that fits into our own experience of him, or a God that behaves as we expect him to behave.

This verse keeps the wonder of God alive for us and the more we dwell on it, the larger our image of God becomes. Over the next few days we will be looking at the three glorious phrases expressed within it, and through them seeking to enlarge our vision of God.

However, as a starting point it might be worth taking a moment to reflect on what your expectation of God today is. This is not a trick question and there are no right or wrong answers, so give it some thought – what do you expect to experience of God today? How do you expect to interact with him? In what ways do you expect to see his hand at work? How do you expect to grow?

Majestic holiness | 2

"Who is like you – majestic in holiness"

Exodus 15.11b

We give holiness a bad name! We tend to think of it in terms of what we shouldn't do or what we ought to give up. The Bible portrays holiness quite differently – as something majestic.

This only makes sense if we see holiness in terms of what we gain rather than lose. If we are commanded to be holy as God is holy (1 Peter 1.16), then surely we can expect to reflect something of this majestic holiness? It has to be more than us looking miserable because of the harsh demands we feel God puts upon us. Holiness is more to do with having something than giving it up; it is about the presence of God within us.

The Bible commands us to be holy – not to act in a particular way – and this begins by us taking seriously the truth that the presence of our glorious God dwells within us. Whatever you feel, the majestic presence of God is with you wherever you go.

Rooted to
the spot! | 3

"Who is like you . . .
awesome in glory?"

Exodus 15.11b

The word 'awesome' has taken on a new meaning in recent years and many understand it to mean 'amazing'. However, at its root the original word contains the concept of 'fear'. It conveys something of the feeling that can root us to the spot and over which we have little control. When God is described as 'awesome in glory', this is what is being conveyed. It is not just that it would be an amazing sight to see God, but that it would root us to the spot and render us helpless.

When we think of the presence of God within us, we might imagine a sense of peace or the ability to do something we are otherwise unable to do. Sometimes we may not feel anything at all. God is probably being very good to us in this, for if we could sense the 'awesomeness' of his glory and presence within us, we would probably be unable to move or do anything at all.

When the Bible calls on us to 'fear' the Lord, it is this sense that we are being encouraged to capture. It is not about any fear or anxiety in approaching him, but is about the truth of what we do not necessarily experience – how awesome he really is, whether or not we feel it.

Capturing the wonder of how awesome God is – the fear of the Lord – will help to feed your worship, guide your path and give focus to your prayers.

Praying to the God who works wonders | 4

"Who is like you . . . working wonders?"

Exodus 15.11b

We probably all believe that God works wonders; this must be within his capability or he would not be God. What we are less certain about is the faith that God works wonders on our behalf. Of course God sustains us and we are surrounded by his wonders – but could there be more?

Jesus foresaw the wonders of his ministry carrying on after him, and it is this continuation of his work that many of us are not so certain about: we may not feel worthy recipients of such wonders, or we are aware of plenty of people in far greater need than us. However, by thinking like this we are putting the focus on ourselves rather than on him. He is the God who works wonders; it is about him and not us.

There is a moment when two blind men went to Jesus and the question he had for them was not about their blindness or why they were suffering in this way, but rather, "Do you believe that I am able to do this?" (Matthew 9.28) His question seems designed to lift their eyes away from their condition and on to him – the one who works wonders and who wonderfully met their needs.

In the end it comes down to attitude. Too often we approach God with an unspoken attitude of, 'I don't suppose you're interested in this but I'll mention it anyway!' God is not ashamed to be known as the one who works wonders. This is who he is, so let's recognise it and turn to him.

Be my shepherd

'Save your people and bless your inheritance; be their shepherd and carry them for ever.'

Psalm 28.9

This beautiful prayer of trust and surrender asks the God who loves you to 'be my shepherd'.

Shepherds lead their flocks, but they don't always consult them about where they are going to be led. It might be interesting to ask yourself, 'Where did my Shepherd lead me yesterday?' If you are in a challenging situation, you may wish you weren't facing it – but what if the Shepherd led you there? Perhaps he wanted you to learn something or to be there for someone else?

If this is the case, are there situations that are causing you some anxiety? If so, what does this picture of a shepherd leading an anxious sheep say to you? Surely if the shepherd is doing the leading he will protect, guide and bless – and his task is so much easier if the sheep is not constantly trying to turn back and head in the opposite direction!

Surrender more

'When the hour came, Jesus and his apostles reclined at the table.'

Luke 22.14

At the point in the communion service when the bread and wine are about to be consecrated as a memorial of what Jesus did at the Last Supper, the words usually begin with this powerful phrase: 'On the night that he was betrayed. . . ' On that particular night – when his friends would leave him, another friend would hand him over to the authorities and when he was to feel a desperate sense of darkness – we are told that he gave thanks to his Father and entrusted his life entirely to him.

The point is this: we all have times when we feel let down and betrayed by other people – sometimes we might even feel betrayed by God. The question is what do we do at these times? Our temptation is often to withdraw and hide away, either physically or emotionally. Yet in Jesus we see something totally different.

His reaction was to surrender even more, to see beyond what was happening to him and keep alive a belief that, despite his present circumstances, the pit was not the end.

There is a lovely detail in one of the healing stories in Mark 7 when we are told that Jesus raised his eyes 'to heaven'. It may be that he simply looked up, but perhaps he was looking to a different place or a different reality – taking his eyes off the situation that was immediately in front of him. We need to learn that ability.

Right now, turn your gaze away from whatever is causing you heaviness or anxiety. Instead look to the reality that you are loved by 'Abba, Father', that Jesus gave his life for you and that living within you is the powerful presence of the Holy Spirit.

Do you act forgiven?

'Blessed is the one whose sin the Lord does not count against them and in whose spirit is no deceit.'

Psalm 32.2

Being forgiven deeply affects our standing before God; there is nothing that comes between us and him. Yet there are other implications, including the way we treat other people.

There is a powerful story in Matthew 18 about a man who owed a fortune, and as an act of mercy his debt was wiped clean and he was allowed to go free. So what did he do with his freedom? He promptly went out, found a man who owed him the merest fraction of his own debt that had just been cancelled, and started to demand the small amount that he was owed.

Why he would act in this way is a mystery – even though it is probably a fictional story that Jesus told. Perhaps one reason behind his inability to forgive was that it hadn't yet sunk in just how much mercy he had been shown. So often we do not appreciate the extent of our own forgiveness, and the extent of God's love for us, and so act harshly towards others.

The death of Jesus stands as the ultimate illustration of how forgiven you are and also of your amazing value to God, in that Jesus was prepared to give his life for you. Allow this knowledge to impact how you relate to others.

Making connections

'They told him, "Jesus of Nazareth is passing by." He called out, "Jesus, Son of David, have mercy on me!"'

Luke 18.37-38

The story of the healing of a blind man (named Bartimaeus in Mark's gospel) is so powerful that it's tempting to think of looking for clues to help us in our own longing for healing. Of course, the story is not about us finding the correct 'way to be healed', but it does reveal a lovely attitude on the part of the blind man.

How much Bartimaeus already knew about Jesus we don't know, but it seems that he made a wonderful connection: having been told that Jesus of Nazareth was walking past, he recognised that this same Jesus was none other than the Messiah, the Son of David. We have no idea whether he worked this out himself or was told by others, but the fact that he made

that connection seemed to be enough to get Jesus' attention. The challenge to us is also to make a connection with Jesus.

As beautiful as the stories about Jesus in the pages of the New Testament are, it is all too easy for them to remain as stories in a book about a great person living in a different time. Our calling is to recognise that the person of Jesus revealed in the Bible is also our Saviour now – today.

Is there some area of your life in which you are in need? Come to the one who is not just the Jesus of the pages of the Bible, but also the Saviour of your life today. Talk to him, encounter him and be open to his touch upon your life.

Don't miss the small shoots

"Who dares despise the day of small things . . ."

Zechariah 4.10

In the fourth chapter of Mark's gospel, Jesus told a parable in which he likened the kingdom of God (and presumably the things of the kingdom) to a seed that grows. First it grows unseen by anyone beneath the soil, then a small shoot appears and finally it grows into something magnificent.

It is a parable that we would do well to remember as we look for God in our lives. It is so easy to get disappointed because God does not answer all our prayers in a sudden and dramatic way. It is this that Zechariah is warning us about when he speaks about not despising the day of small things.

When we pray, it is good and right to hold before us the vision of what Jesus came to do for us – to bring us abundant life (John 10.10) – but it is also good to recognise that the growing seed, small though it may be, can contain the means by which great visions come about.

Are you praying for something particular at the moment? If so, look for the small things that God is doing to encourage you – the barely perceptible shoots. Rather than complaining that a bush has not grown overnight, rejoice in the shoots, give thanks for them and be encouraged.

Come out of the pit

'. . . and a man with a shrivelled hand was there. Looking for a reason to bring charges against Jesus, they asked him, "Is it lawful to heal on the Sabbath?" He said to them, "If any of you has a sheep and it falls into a pit on the Sabbath, will you not take hold of it and lift it out? How much more valuable is a person than a sheep! Therefore it is lawful to do good on the Sabbath."'

Matthew 12.10-12

'Would Jesus ever want to heal me?' This is often the underlying question that niggles at us as we begin to think about praying for healing; could it ever happen to me? At it's heart is a suspicion that healing is reserved for special people who have a key place in God's heart. However, this story cuts right through such thinking and gives us Jesus' view of healing – and it is quite simple. Healing is about lifting people out of a pit, just as we would an animal that had fallen into a hole.

If you think about it, people fall into pits for any number of reasons: accidents, misadventures or even being pushed. The reason doesn't matter – healing is all about lifting them out. Nor is there any suggestion that some sheep are worth rescuing and some are not. If they are in the pit, they need to come out!

If you feel as if you are in a pit, perhaps one of the first things you need to know is that Jesus wants you out of it. He takes no pleasure in you being there, so this should give you confidence to pray. Today's story reveals his will – he wants you out of the pit.

316

Seek guidance

'I will instruct you and teach you in the way you should go; I will counsel you with my loving eye on you.'

Psalm 32.8

We all want God's guidance! At times life can be very hard and we are not always sure what we should be doing. Sometimes we have important choices to make and don't know which route to take, or perhaps we simply want to be in a different place – whether it be geographical, emotional or spiritual. We really want God to speak to us.

The trouble is that many people find that the times when they most want God to speak are when they hear him the least! This verse is so helpful on occasions like this. It is not just a matter of God speaking to us, but also of his 'loving eye' being upon us. We tend to want him to shout loudly to us and tell us what to do, whereas perhaps first we need to be aware of his loving eye – his presence with us and his love for us. Then, we are in a better place to hear his counsel.

It comes down to the way we pray. Do you often find that the first thing you do is to tell God about your needs? Instead, even before you worship him, it may be helpful to take time to be still and focus on his love for you; being open to it and enjoying it with no other agenda on your part. Once you sense the reality of his loving eye upon you, listen for the whisper of his guidance.

This is personal! | 1

'This poor man called, and the Lord heard him; he saved him out of all his troubles.'

Psalm 34.6

This lovely psalm warrants several days of study. It contains many wonderful promises, and at this point David made it all very personal – he had discovered from his own experience that they were all true.

This is the challenge of the Bible for us. Instead of reading it as simply God's promises for the whole world, we would do well to recognise that it includes his promises for us personally. Can we rely on these promises? There

is only one way to find out – to try. This is what David did when he knew he was in trouble; he called out to God and found him to be true.

Of course, God is not just there in our times of need, but it is particularly in our times of need that we can begin to directly experience his love and presence. As you read the Bible, which promise speaks most to your need today? Dare to take it as God's invitation to you to trust him and find more of his goodness and love.

Beginning to fear the Lord | 2

'Come, my children, listen to me; I will teach you the fear of the Lord. . . keep your tongue from evil and your lips from telling lies.'

Psalm 34.11-13

One practical aspect of fearing the Lord concerns what we say. There are several ways in which we might be challenged about telling lies.

One such area is gossip. We may not equate gossiping with lying, but it is an incomplete truth passed on about someone else. Gossip never reveals the whole story, only a detail. Another way in which we are prone to lie is in how we speak of ourselves, repeating lies along the lines of: 'I am useless', 'I can never be used by God' and 'I am unloved'. To use such phrases is to disregard the heart of God for us. If to fear God is to take him seriously, then to speak the opposite of what he says about us is to belittle his deep love for us..

A key step in this journey towards fearing God is to honour others by speaking well of them, as well as honouring yourself.

Turn away from evil | 3

'I will teach you the fear of the Lord ... turn from evil and do good'

Psalm 34.11-14

The next step on our journey of how to fear the Lord concerns our actions. We need to change the way we live – turn from evil and do good. The slight issue here is whether we really are evil. We probably wouldn't say that we are perfect, but is it really appropriate to call us, or our actions, evil? If we are not directly involved in evil, from what are we meant to turn?

The word 'evil' translates as calamity or badness. What we are called to do is adopt God's attitude to evil. This means not regarding it as the dominant force around us, refusing to believe there is not much we can do about it and not giving in to the helplessness that so often accompanies distress.

There is always something you can do to combat evil and bring about good. To do good is not to wait until an opportunity lands in your lap, but to walk around with open eyes seeking to say something, pray for someone, intercede for them and help them. You are called to be a blessing in as many situations as you can.

320

Be guided by peace | 4

'I will teach you the fear of the Lord . . . seek peace and pursue it.'

Psalm 34.11-14

Paul encouraged the Colossians to let the peace of Christ rule in their hearts (Colossians 3.15); Christ's peace would exist as a guide, pointing them to the course they ought to take. Both Paul, and David in this psalm, seem to be saying that in all our thinking about the future and decisions that need to be made, there is a path of peace to be discovered.

Do you have a decision to make? Take a moment to write down all the options and consequences of the different paths open to you. Think through these consequences in your mind and see yourself walking down the different paths available to you. Which of the paths gives you peace as you think about it? This is not the same as deciding which you would prefer, nor is it asking which is the most comfortable, but rather which of these paths is the way of peace?

If you are facing a major decision, it is always worth sharing your feelings with someone you trust – but also trust the presence of Jesus with you. After all, when the prophet Isaiah looked into the future, he described Jesus as the 'Prince of Peace'. If Jesus is the one beckoning you down a certain path, you will catch a sense of his peace as you follow him.

God is there – whatever you feel! | 5

'The Lord is close to the broken-hearted and saves those who are crushed in spirit.'

Psalm 34.18

This verse states the opposite of what we often feel to be true! When we identify with the term 'broken-hearted' – whether because of hurt, disappointment, despair or some other setback – we would probably say that we feel the Lord is far from us. We often feel rejected, abandoned and left with a sense that God has deserted us.

Too often we equate blessings with God's approval. If things are going well, then God is near and happy with us; if things are going badly then he is distant. This is why the truth conveyed in this verse goes beyond our feelings and is so powerful: when times are hard, God is especially near.

There may be all manner of reasons why you are unable to sense his presence. Perhaps your emotions are firmly focused on what you feel you have lost so you are unaware of what is unseen and yet so close – the saving presence of God.

Faith is a wonderful gift from God, given because at times we need it. When you feel hurt and cannot find God, he is there; you are not being punished or at fault for not being able to find him. Just hold on!

Looking backwards and forwards

'Continue your love to those who know you, your righteousness to the upright in heart.'

Psalm 36.10

The way in which these words are expressed is very comforting. They convey the sense that the love of God continues or carries on; it was there yesterday, it will be there for us today and it will be there tomorrow. Sometimes it is only by reflecting on yesterday and spotting instances of God's love for us that we can have any real sense of where his presence has been. It is by seeing his love yesterday that we can trust in the presence of his love today and tomorrow.

Take a moment to jot down examples of God's love in the past day. These may be occasions when you directly sensed his presence with you or when his love was expressed through the kindness and encouragement of others.

It may be that before you started this exercise you didn't think there would be much to record, but as you began to focus on God's love, your awareness of it increased. When you have compiled your list, give some thought to how it will help you be aware of what you can expect to see of God today. He will be with you so look out for him as the day progresses.

Keep going!

"Even the dogs eat the crumbs that fall from their master's table."

Matthew 15.27

The gospels reveal that Jesus was so willing to heal the sick he went out of his way to bring an end to the suffering of individuals who came across his path. Yet the account of Jesus meeting the Canaanite woman does not fit comfortably with this image. Here we see Jesus apparently unwilling to do what he is asked and even appearing to make life difficult for this lady who approached him for help. Sadly some people today feel only too able to identify with her!

However, the story is still encouraging for us as we seek his touch on our lives. We see a woman who was desperate for Jesus' help and who was not going to take 'no' for an answer. If you look at her responses to Jesus, she did everything she could to persuade him to touch her – and her tenacity won through! So what can we learn from this?

It is very easy to give up in prayer if the answer we seek does not come quickly or in the way we expect. There is a tendency to assume that 'no' today means 'no' forever. However, Jesus valued persistence and faith – so keep lifting your needs to him in the confidence that he values your tenacity and wants to bring his transformation to you.

Being salty

"You are the salt of the earth."

Matthew 5.13

today
you carry his presence

There is something very powerful in this verse – notwithstanding the health risks associated with eating too much salt! Salt changes the taste of every ingredient. When salt is sprinkled over a plate of food, it's not just some of the dish that tastes different, but everything. Salt changes everything.

So it follows that when Jesus calls us to be the salt of the earth, he says that we have the potential to change every situation in which we find ourselves – not just some situations, but all of them. This is quite simply because we carry the very presence of God within us.

Really knowing this and being aware of carrying God's presence within you is what makes all the difference. It does not mean trying hard to say the right words or doing something spectacular whenever possible, but simply remembering the truth that God is in you. He will seep out of you quite naturally and make a difference.

A good practice is to try to get into the habit of bringing your mind back to the name, 'Jesus'. This serves as a perfect reminder of who it is within you and what he could do in any of the situations in which you find yourself today.

Bring your needs to him

'All my longings lie open before you, Lord: my sighing is not hidden from you.'

Psalm 38.9

The fact that God knows our every longing and sighing can affect our attitude in two ways.

The first is that if he knows everything, it is not necessary for us to bombard him with our needs as soon as we begin to pray. So often our attitude is that there isn't much time so we had better say the important bits first – and then we can draw breath. However, if God knows it all anyway there really isn't a rush! Instead we can take time to sit with him and enjoy his love and favour.

The second outcome of God knowing everything about us is that we have an invitation to be utterly honest with him. Nothing we express is going to shock or surprise him; he has seen everything there is to see about us – every action, motive and inner desire. When we do share our deepest thoughts and longings with him, rather than recoiling in horror he is probably thinking, 'At last!'

So if there is something particular on your mind today, try spending a few minutes savouring God's love and nearness to you before moving on to speak honestly to him about your concerns.

Confident expectation

'Lord, I wait for you; you will answer, Lord my God.'

Psalm 38.15

This verse expresses a wonderful confidence in the certainty of God answering prayer. Of course, all prayers are answered – as someone rather jokingly once said: "God, I know you answer all my prayers, but couldn't you sometimes say yes?"

However, the writer of this psalm has something different in mind and there is a confidence about his prayers that is reflected in the statement 'I wait for you'. It is one thing to pray and articulate our needs to God, but it is quite another to wait in expectation for the answer – whatever it may be. Waiting in expectation expresses a real confidence that our prayer has been heard. It involves holding on by faith and trusting that what we say really is heard by God. It also carries with it a sense of trust; in whatever ways our prayers are answered, we trust he will bring about his glory and that his love to us will be demonstrated.

There is a responsibility in prayer. It is not simply about us handing whatever issues we choose to God and then bringing another list of things the next day. It is also about us holding these things in confident expectation of his answer.

Despite it all, God is exalted

'For troubles without number surround me; my sins have overtaken me, and I cannot see. They are more than the hairs of my head, and my heart fails within me.'

Psalm 40.12

At times it may be that you feel just like this! It's not just that something is wrong with your life, but that there seem to be so many things piling up against you. These probably tend to dominate so you can't really see past them and they make it difficult for you to find God.

A little later in this psalm, David writes: 'May all who seek you rejoice and be glad in you.' The significance of this is that the same person who spoke about all his troubles also spoke about the reality of seeking God and being glad. In other words, whatever is going on, God is present. It may well be hard to find him, but he is there.

It might be helpful to look to his throne, as God is seated above all the things that crowd you. He is not 'dethroned' by them, but is longing for you to look up – as David did in the psalm – and, despite everything that you might be going through, to say along with David, 'The Lord is great!' (verse 16)

When you are weak

'Blessed are those who have regard for the weak'

Psalm 41.1

There are many similar phrases in the Bible that encourage us to reach out and help those in need, and when we do this we are called blessed. Perhaps the reason we are blessed when we care for others is that we find that our hearts are acting in tune with God's heart.

This simple truth is lovely in the way that it reveals that God himself has a heart for those who are weak – and so often that includes us. At times when we are feeling less strong than we would like – maybe when our prayer times seem a little lacking, the words of the Bible wash over us, we feel spiritually dull or have given into temptation – we rather assume that God has moved away or that he is waiting for us to pick ourselves up and get going again. This is simply untrue. If we are to have regard for the weak, it is because God himself has regard for the weak, which means that in our times of weakness, he has regard for us.

If you are feeling a lack of strength in some way, talk to God about it. Be reassured that he is not disappointed in you but is always there for you, even when you feel weak.

The awesome presence of God

'The Lord said to Moses: "Tell your brother Aaron that he is not to come whenever he chooses into the Most Holy Place behind the curtain in front of the atonement cover on the ark, or else he will die."'

Leviticus 16.2

This is amazing! Aaron could not come directly into God's presence whenever he wished, as to do so would have killed him. He was kept away for his own protection. This gives us some indication of just how powerful and real God's presence is. Yet we are invited to stand in his presence whenever we choose. How lightly we take it!

If Aaron had been afforded the same privilege as us he would probably have treated it with huge awe and respect, probably gasping at the honour afforded to him. There is an old saying that 'familiarity breeds contempt', and the very availability of God's presence can cause us to be quite casual towards him. We can so easily become accustomed to hearing the great truths – such as Jesus' promise to be with us always and the assurance that we are living temples of his Holy Spirit who dwells within us – yet lose our sense of amazement and wonder at the enormity of what has been given to us.

If God chose to live in you for only one day a year, you would probably take that day very seriously. How much more seriously should you take the fact that he chooses to dwell within you every day of the year? Take a moment to reflect on the wonder of his presence within you; give thanks for it and embrace it.

You are beautiful

'Let the king be enthralled by your beauty; honour him, for he is your lord.'

Psalm 45.11

This is a very challenging verse because it requires us to have an awareness of our own beauty as we stand before God, whereas most of the time we are more aware of our unworthiness, sin and failings. None of us is perfect; we all do things that we know are wrong and assume they must be pretty unattractive to him. However, we are missing the fact that God is looking at more than this.

First, he is looking at someone whom he loves; the Bible tells us that he loves us so much that he gave Jesus for us. He didn't only start to love us once Jesus had taken away our sins, he loved us when we were at our most sinful – even then there was something about us that attracted him. There is more! The second thing about us that he finds attractive is his own presence that he has placed within us. If he loved us before he touched us, we are astoundingly beautiful now that we shine with him.

Take a moment to sit before God. Don't bow your face, lift it to him as if he were right in front of you. Have the courage to let him gaze upon your beauty.

God shines forth

'. . . God shines forth.'

Psalm 50.2

There are occasions when we need to know this is true! Our lives can waver between times when we sense we are walking in step with Jesus and it's easy to rejoice in his love and presence, and other times when he seems utterly distant and our experience of him is minimal. These three simple words tell us that whatever our feelings might be, God is shining forth; light is coming from him and change is happening because of him. How can we put this faith into practice?

In one sense, we don't have to put anything into practice: if God is indeed shining, he will do so whether or not we are conscious of it. Increasing our awareness of him shining forth continually is for our own benefit, as it will bring peace and increase our confidence when life might seem quite bleak.

One of the simplest ways to increase your awareness of God's presence is to whisper the name 'Jesus' – in other words, to acknowledge his presence. He is with you in all his gentleness, but also as the light of the world, and to be able to hold onto his light in the darkness is everything.

God sees everything

"I know every bird in the mountains, and the insects in the fields are mine."

Psalm 50.11

This is quite some statement and the implications are incredible. God did not simply begin a process of creation whereby life would automatically reproduce for thousands and thousands of years. Instead, he has observed the whole of creation throughout all time and he has an intimate knowledge of every aspect and part of it.

Where this gets personal is that we are all included! If God knows every bird in the mountains, then he knows you and sees every part of you. If he can look under rocks and see insects there, he can certainly see through any masks that you may put on, and he sees every detail of your life. The question is whether this is really good news? How happy are you that God sees such detail?

Your response to this needs to take on board the value that God places upon you. Jesus said, "Look at the birds of the air . . . Are you not much more valuable than they?" (Matthew 6.26) Such is your value to him that he loves you enough to give Jesus to die for you; he wants you to be in eternity with him.

God's intimate knowledge of you is definitely good news! He sees every part of your life and knows exactly what you are going through – and he loves you.

Two types of shepherd

"You have not strengthened the weak or healed those who are ill or bound up the injured. You have not brought back the strays or searched for the lost."

Ezekiel 34.4

When Jesus spoke about himself as the good shepherd, one of the Bible passages he probably had in mind was Ezekiel 34, in which God spoke through Ezekiel about two sorts of shepherds. The first was self-seeking and cared little for the flock entrusted to him, whereas the other delighted in his sheep, tended to the flock's every need and searched for every lost animal that went astray.

By speaking of himself as the good shepherd, Jesus committed himself to a ministry of caring deeply about every part of us. The implication is that, whatever your needs, you should never be tempted to wonder, does he care? If you think like this, you are questioning which type of shepherd he really is.

It doesn't mean that at times you will not be confused by his actions or even his apparent silence, but it does mean that Jesus has told you he is looking out for you and is utterly committed to you, even if it is only in retrospect that you can look back and see his guiding, healing hand at work in your life.

334

Call to mind the character of God

"The Lord is slow to anger, abounding in love and forgiving sin and rebellion."

Numbers 14.18

This description of God occurs in the middle of one of Moses' prayers. The people were grumbling, even to the extent that they considered killing Moses and Aaron, and then God appeared. He seemed to be about to strike the people with a plague, but Moses spoke up for them and in the middle of his prayer he reminded God of his loving nature. God seemed to change his mind.

This story presents us with many questions: does God need to be persuaded to calm down on occasions? Can we change God's mind even when he seems set on a particular course of action? It is Moses' utter conviction of the goodness of God that shines through here, however. Even when he sensed that God was about to do something terrible, Moses was still utterly convinced of God's love and goodness. How convinced are we of this, or is there part of us that feels that at times God is mean and harsh? If so, this may be because we simply cannot understand why some things have happened.

Instead, let's choose to learn from Moses and recognise that the nature of God is unchanging; he is abounding in love – all the time. He probably does not need reminding of this, but we do! Take these words, "The Lord is . . . abounding in love", and turn them into worship. Call to mind the events of the day ahead, both positive and any you may be anxious about or dreading, and over each event say these words: 'Lord, you are abounding in love.'

Would you be **more** surprised if God answered your prayers or if he didn't?

Prayer: his power and your faith

'Some men came carrying a man on a mat ... When Jesus saw their faith ...'

Romans 5.2

Jesus evidently saw something on the faces of those four men who brought their paralysed friend to Jesus. I wonder what it was? We are not told, but perhaps it was a real expectation that something was going to happen. Certainly their action in breaking through the roof was some indication of the seriousness with which they took their request!

It is so easy to pray without any real expectation that God is going to do anything. It is not that we don't have expectation, but we probably don't think much about it. We pray about things – and then sometimes completely forget that we have prayed.

Next time you pray for someone or for something in particular, give some thought to what you are expecting to happen, not what you would like to see, but what you actually expect to take place. Ask yourself whether you would be more surprised if God did something or if he didn't!

Your response may well reveal something about the state of your faith, and you may find yourself challenged as you continue to pray for God's healing touch in your life and in the lives of those around you.

336

Growing through suffering

'. . . we also glory in our sufferings, because we know that suffering produces perseverance'

Romans 5.3

It must be said that this verse does not reflect our usual attitude to suffering! Usually we fight it, pray against it and avoid it like the plague! How on earth are we meant to glory in our sufferings, especially when we believe in the God who heals?

There are a couple of points to make here. The first is that suffering does not necessarily mean sickness; never once did Jesus encourage a sick person to patiently endure their sickness. His reaction to it was always to set the person free from the effects of it. The second thing to bear in mind is that Jesus did encourage perseverance in prayer. By doing this, he intimated that prayer will sometimes not be answered as quickly as we would like. It does not mean that God is unwilling to act, but that his timescale might be different to ours.

The first step is to identify the hard things in your life; they may not seem like terrible sufferings compared to others, but they may cause you hurt and anxiety. The next step is to consider what effect they are having upon you. Are they wearing you out or are you able to recognise that the waiting is producing godly and patient endurance, or something else positive? Whichever option you select, it's worth talking to Jesus about it!

Reigning in life

'For if, by the trespass of the one man, death reigned through that one man, how much more will those who receive God's abundant provision of grace and of the gift of righteousness reign in life through the one man, Jesus Christ!'

Romans 5.17

What a fabulous verse – the more we receive, the more we reign! Yet too often, any sense of reigning in life is a distant dream. We may feel as though we stagger through life, stumbling around pot-holes and occasionally crawling out from under a rock. In an attempt to improve our quality of life we may redouble our efforts for a while, only to sink back exhausted into a sense of failure – it's hardly a picture of reigning in life!

The clear message that Paul gives is inspiring: it's not what we put into life or achieve that makes the difference and determines our quality of life, but rather what we receive – God's abundant grace. His 'abundant provision of grace' means there is plenty available to us for any situation we might be facing. Along with this we also receive God's gift of righteousness – the effect of Jesus dying for us.

The more you open your heart to what Jesus has done and what he can give you, the more you will not be pushed under by all that life brings your way. Take a moment to call to mind some of the things God has done for you, and the ways in which the death of Jesus has benefited you, and begin to reign in life.

God's care

'You have kept count of my tossings; put my tears in your bottle.'

Psalm 56.8 (English Standard Version)

If we are ever tempted to think that God does not care about us and what we are going through, this verse brings us up short. This picture of our tears being stored up in a bottle is an image of tenderness and care that is beyond comprehension.

However, it might lead us to question why God doesn't do something to help us if he cares so much? There are many ways of approaching this honest question and one is connected to the way we regard prayer.

Rather than questioning God's apparent lack of action, we would do well to catch his tenderness – and indeed his pain – at our suffering.

The image of God storing up your tears implies they are valuable to him, something precious that he does not take lightly. Before you begin to pray about some of the issues that are hurting you, try to catch his heart for you at this time. This insight may well change the way you pray.

Knowing God's love

'This I know, that God is for me.'

Psalm 56.9 (English Standard Version)

All manner of thoughts tend to pass through our minds at any one time: uplifting occasions, lists of things we need to do, less pleasant memories from the past, random observations about other people and sometimes thoughts we would not want anyone else to know! For this reason, there is a value in taking a verse from the Bible and training ourselves to come back to it through the day.

This is one such verse. Spend a few minutes right now letting the richness of the words soak in. As you breathe in, say to yourself, 'This I know', and as you breathe out, say, 'God is for me'. Repeat the process for a few minutes.

You should find this amazing verse resonating within you and focusing your mind on the wonder of God's love for you during the day.

340

Tapping into God's strength | 1

'You are my strength'

Psalm 59.9

Sometimes we come across striking verses about God that we would do well to explore and consider how they really apply to our lives. This verse is a great example.

There are so many ways in which we need the strength of God but don't call upon it. Perhaps you need his strength to cope with certain situations that are causing you anxiety, or maybe people are a cause of concern for you? You need more than your own strength – and God's promise is that he is there for you. It follows, then, that if he is there for you, so is his strength.

There is a key issue here. Many of us probably call out something like, 'God, please give me strength', but it isn't about us waiting until he has breathed some of his divine strength into us. Rather, it is God himself who is our strength.

When you feel weak and in need of strength, whisper the name, 'Jesus'. This isn't an idle word, it's a reminder that God has come to you already and is with you in Jesus. To whisper his name is to remember his presence and draw on his strength.

What do you expect to happen? | 2

'You are my strength, I watch for you'

Psalm 59.9

It is very easy to be quite passive in the way you think about God answering your prayers, and you may even have a list of prayer requests that you tick off when God has done his bit! This phrase, 'I watch for you', raises two challenges.

The first is that it addresses the question of your expectation. Sometimes you might pray about something and then take the attitude that it is up to God whether or not he wants to answer it. To 'watch' for him implies an expectation that he is going to answer in some way. Psalm 5.3 makes a similar point: '. . . in the morning I lay my requests before you and wait expectantly.'

Supposing God dealt with your intercessions according to how seriously you took them!

The second point about prayer is linked to this. Not only should you expect God to answer, resolve to look for early signs that's he is at work – shoots appearing from the ground to encourage you that something else is going to follow. You may well miss the wonderful things God does because you are not looking for them, and in missing them you can easily lose heart and become discouraged.

Bring your needs to God now, and then 'watch' in expectation for the first signs of his response.

God's standards

". . . when a man makes a vow to the Lord or takes an oath to bind himself by a pledge, he must not break his word but must do everything he said."

Numbers 30.2

From time to time, most of us say things we don't mean. We may say them simply out of enthusiasm or exaggeration, or perhaps promise things to others and to God that we can't actually deliver. Since we have this tendency, we imagine that others do as well, and now and again might wonder if even God is prone to a bit of exaggeration!

This verse encourages us to take our words very seriously and to think carefully about our promises. The implication that these are important to God is challenging. It follows that if he tells us not to take our promises lightly, neither does he. When we read the Bible, we sometimes come across promises that seem to offer so much we can't believe God really means it. What an incredible thought that he takes his promises so seriously – perhaps far more seriously than we do.

As you read the Bible and come across one of God's promises, recognise that it comes from the one who has told you not to break your word and who lives by a far greater standard than we do.

Being at home with God

'I long to dwell in your tent for ever and take refuge in the shelter of your wings.'

Psalm 61.4

There is something about today's verse that prompts us to ask, how? How can we dwell with God in a more permanent way? The answer involves a simple realisation, that all we have to do is to step into what already exists.

In John 14.23, Jesus says this: "Anyone who loves me will obey my teaching. My Father will love them, and we will come to them and make our home with them." He is saying that because we have turned to him, both he and the Father have already made their home within us.

Sometimes we can find ourselves seeking an experience we don't require, because what we are seeking is already ours. We long to experience unity and be closer to God, when in this world we could not be any closer than we are already. How much closer can we get than having the Father and the Son making their home within us? Take a few moments to rejoice in this truth and worship God for the reality that he has made his home within you.

What is trust?

'Trust in him at all times, you people; pour out your hearts to him, for God is our refuge.'

Psalm 62.8

It is easy to tell people who are in need to trust in God. In saying this, we are often encouraging them to take an extra leap of faith or find a deeper level of trust, to do slightly more than they are already doing.

However, when this psalm encourages us to trust in God it is more than a simple cliché, for we are also encouraged to pour out our hearts to him. The writer was saying that to trust God was not just about having confidence that everything would turn out fine, but also trusting him with all our emotions and feelings – especially if we fear that things are not going to turn out well.

One of the most wonderful privileges about worshipping Father God is that, because he knows everything, we do not have to put on a mask or pretend to be or feel anything other than what is really going on within us. Why not pour out your heart and speak honestly to him right now?

God's driving force

'The Lord did not set his affection on you and choose you because you were more numerous than other peoples, for you were the fewest of all peoples. But it was because the Lord loved you and kept the oath he swore to your ancestors that he brought you out with a mighty hand'

Deuteronomy 7.7

When we sense that we are not good or doing well, it can be hard to believe that God loves us.

Yet this encouraging verse is right there in the first few books of the Bible, reminding us that God's activity on our behalf is all down to the fact that he loves us. His motive and the driving force behind all his actions is the profound depth of his love towards us.

When we are in need it is tempting to bargain with God: if he shows love towards us, we promise in return to do something sacrificial for him. However, we need to remember the certainty of his unconditional love for us. The new covenant that Jesus made with us was not an agreement that we could bargain with God for his goodness, rather that he would give himself totally for us and do everything needed to release God's blessing to us. Once again it comes back to his love for us, and not our goodness or whether we deserve it.

As you pray, let these words from 1 John 4.16 run through your mind: '. . . we know and rely on the love God has for us.'

346

Life's potential

'All things were created by him, and all things exist through him and for him. To God be the glory for ever!'

Romans 11.36 (Good News Bible)

This is one of those statements in the Bible that is so easy to gloss over without really taking in what it says. There is one phrase that really seems to stand out – that all things exist for him. What could this mean?

Supposing every situation in which you find yourself has the potential to lead you closer to God? You probably have no difficulty in recognising that some situations are in God's hands, because there have been moments in your life when you could clearly see his hand at work. However, it can be harder to see the potential for God to work in every situation in which you find yourself.

What makes all the difference and can transform every situation into an opportunity for God to act is your attitude. Are you able to turn to him in every situation and offer it to him for his glory? One uncomplicated way to begin practising this is to let the name 'Jesus' be on your lips in every idle moment, and then you will naturally find him there in times of crisis.

Why not begin now? Spend the next few minutes simply whispering the name 'Jesus', and then try to keep his name close to you throughout the day so he is brought right into the centre of every situation you face.

Using your fear

'I was ashamed to ask the king for soldiers and horsemen to protect us from enemies on the road, because we had told the king, "The gracious hand of our God is on everyone who looks to him, but his great anger is against all who forsake him."'

Ezra 8.22

This verse is so honest: Ezra was forced to confront what he really believed about God and whether he was willing to act upon his conviction. He seemed to be in a position where he could understandably ask for human protection, but given what he really believed should he do this? Eventually he concluded that he should put his trust in God alone.

Perhaps one area we all have in common that causes us to face this challenge is fear. Different things cause us anxiety, but given our faith – that we are loved by God and that he has promised to be with us wherever we go – why is it that we let anxiety and fear grip us so often? Their existence is actually like a ringing bell asking us what we really believe; are we certain that our loving God is actively with us?

When you next feel fearful, instead of giving in to it or pretending it doesn't exist, try letting it draw you to a deeper truth and make a decision to focus on this instead. What is it that brings you fear and anxiety? What is the truth that stands against these fears? Rejoice in these truths, celebrate them, and walk into this day with God's presence with you.

You are unique

'Jesus answered, "If I want him to remain alive until I return, what is that to you? You must follow me."'

John 21.22

Most of us are experts at comparing ourselves to other people! It was evidently something to which Peter was prone. In this passage, he has just been told about his death – a death, the author adds, that would glorify God (verses 18-19). I'm not sure what your response would be if you were told something like this, but Peter's first reaction was to point to another disciple and ask why not him. Jesus' reply is very releasing; it is along the lines of, 'Don't worry about them, I want you to follow me'.

When you are tempted to compare yourself to others, recall these words and hear them for yourself – 'Don't worry about them, I want you to follow me.'

If you sometimes wish you were someone else, or more like someone else, you are actually doing a great dis-service to God, who took such care to knit you together and create your inmost being. You can be inspired by others, but the last thing God wants for you is to be anything other than the person he took such trouble to create.

God's command to you personally is to follow him, and certainly not try to be someone else.

Keep the birds out of your hair!

'Blessed is the one who does not walk in step with the wicked or stand in the way that sinners take or sit in the company of mockers'

Psalm 1.1

The first of the psalms describes the way to find joy. In the opening verse the psalmist tells us what not to do: we should avoid the company of the wicked, sinners and mockers. Now, it may be that you think you do this quite well and you aren't particularly tempted in this way.

However, this psalm provides a challenge if we think about the company we keep with our own thoughts. It is possible that at times you find yourself wallowing in resentment, thinking unkindly of others or approaching things with cynicism. The good news in this psalm is that we have choices

and if you find yourself thinking any of these thoughts, you don't have to. You can choose to make a decision to take a different stance. In fact, the nature of temptation is such that it is probably inevitable that we will have such thoughts, but it is what we do with them that is within our control.

There is an old saying along these lines: 'You can't stop birds from flying over your head, but you can stop them nesting in your hair.' Don't feel condemned by the thoughts that go through your mind, but don't give them a place to reside either!

God wants to use you

'Father, use me'

"This is to my Father's glory, that you bear much fruit, showing yourselves to be my disciples."

John 15.8

A question many of us often ponder is why would God use us? No doubt he has big plans and dreams and as we look back through history he has raised up great people to bring them about. Could we ever be included in what he wants to do?

By asking such questions, we are putting the emphasis on ourselves; looking at our own lives and situations. In this verse from John 15, Jesus puts it quite another way – within the context of the glory of God.

Today God wants to use you to bring glory to him. This is not a matter of you being good enough for this to happen, but rather of you being open. A simple prayer before you do anything is, 'Father, use me.' It might be before you go to see someone or just as you leave your front door. What God does with you might not seem very dramatic to you, but a simple act of kindness to someone else brings glory to him.

Your friend and your God

'Thomas said to him, "My Lord and my God!"'

John 20.28

Finding the friendship of God, and knowing that the Father of our Lord Jesus Christ is also our 'Abba, Father', is so incredibly meaningful. However, if there is one danger of this friendship, it is perhaps that we are apt to forget the sheer majesty and wonder of God.

No doubt Thomas had shared many intimate moments with Jesus as they walked down dusty roads, sharing personal conversations. Yet after he had witnessed for himself the wonder of the risen Jesus, he made this profound statement: "My Lord and my God!" In other words, this Jesus whom he counted as one of his closest friends was also his Lord and his God.

Wherever you go today, you take Jesus with you. He is your friend to bring you comfort and encouragement, but he is also your Lord and God, with you in every situation in which you find yourself. It is not just that you are accompanied by your friend, but also by the wonder and power of God who is active and reigning.

Take a moment to think through the day ahead. In every situation, the Lord God of heaven and earth will be there with you. Just think what could happen!

Worship

"You are worthy, our Lord and God, to receive glory"

Revelation 4.11

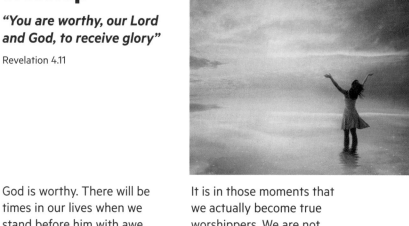

God is worthy. There will be times in our lives when we stand before him with awe and praise at who he is and what he has done. We can see just how worthy he is, so it comes very naturally to respond to him in this way at such times.

However, this is not always the case. God's ways are not our ways and he does not always act like a human being. When we are faced with times of confusion, doubt, disappointment and questioning, it can be a real challenge to admit that this statement is still true – that God is worthy to receive glory.

It is in those moments that we actually become true worshippers. We are not worshipping according to our feelings or comfortable circumstances, but instead are worshipping in truth despite what is going on around us. The way we worship can be a dividing issue in some churches, but perhaps the preference God has is not based on the age of the songs but on the heart of the worshipper.

Turn to God and choose to worship him right now, especially if life seems hard. Despite your circumstances, worship him because he utterly loves you.

Go up and never stop

Being persistent | 1

'For some time he refused. But finally he said to himself, "Even though I don't fear God or care what people think, yet because this widow keeps bothering me, I will see that she gets justice, so that she won't eventually come and attack me!"'

Luke 18.4-5

In many ways this is a strange parable! God seems to be compared to an unjust judge who doesn't really care about others and only dispenses justice to get some peace in his own life. However, Jesus is not saying that God is like this, rather that there is a real power in persistence. If it can even move an unjust judge, then how much more will it touch the heart of the Father who loves us?

There is something about Christmas that moves us to pray. Perhaps it is a heightened focus on the needs of others, or maybe the sheer possibility of what could happen if this story about God coming to earth is really true. What difference could it really make to us, our families and those whose plight touches us?

Our call is to persist in prayer. Hold on to the truth of the Christmas story that you will hear over the coming days. God did not come to earth for one day only, but for every day; for those days you are happy and excited, as well as when you feel barren and overwhelmed. Jesus came, he is still here, and he is with you right now.

Tapping into God | 2

"And will not God bring about justice for his chosen ones, who cry out to him day and night? Will he keep putting them off?"

Luke 18.7

As we return to the well-known story of Christmas, it is easy to be drawn into a 'sanitised' version of the story: smiling people bathed in light, surrounding a spotless manger which houses an incredibly content and happy-looking baby! It is highly unlikely that this describes the scene of the first Christmas, yet all too often this Christmas card picture is where we stop; we don't think beyond our modern visual imagery.

In the approach to Christmas, as we continue to think about the story of the unjust judge, a whole new concept of justice arises. In the context of this parable, justice is what God thinks of a situation and is doing about it. In the context of Christmas, justice is about what God thinks of the way the world is, and what he has done about it.

The Bible tells us clearly that God loves the world (John 3.16), and this well-known verse tells us what he has done about it – he has given us Jesus because we need him. This is still God's heart for the world, and it is God's heart for you.

When you pray, you are not bothering God and wearying him with your prayers! Rather, you are tapping into his heart and receiving the very thing he gave you and wants you to use – the gift of Jesus.

Being shaped by Christmas | 3

"I tell you, he will see that they get justice, and quickly. However, when the Son of Man comes, will he find faith on the earth?"

Luke 18.8

In this parable about prayer, Jesus commends perseverance because he wants us to catch his heart to bring justice to the world. Justice is about us being able to live the life he wants for us. In the final words of the parable, Jesus introduces the concept of faith, which it seems is something for which he is looking.

As you begin to celebrate Christmas, it is good to catch the eternal message that it is about the Saviour giving himself to you so you can live the life he desires for you – but he is still looking for your faith. At this time of year, most people familiarize themselves with the story of baby Jesus

again, but as a believer you are called to do more than recognise the story – you are called to take its application for you seriously and personally.

- Why did Jesus have to come for you?

- What have you done with this astounding message?

- What more does he want from you?

- What can you do with this message?

The coming of Jesus is good news; he was given because of God's amazing love for you. The faith he is looking for is the faith that says 'yes' to his glorious Christmas message.

Do you want God's gift?

'For to us a child is born,
to us a son is given'

Isaiah 9.6

God has given us Jesus! This is the most wonderful truth about Christmas. Let's take a moment to reflect on it. God gave us the gift of Jesus precisely because he loves us. Jesus was not given so we could see what perfection looked like and recognise our own guilt and failings more than we do already; he was given because of the depth of God's extraordinary love for us.

You have probably been busy buying and wrapping gifts, some decorative and others practical; each gift is chosen with a specific person in mind and needs to be received, opened and enjoyed. Yet while few of us would refuse to accept a Christmas present, we are prone to turning down God's perfect gift for us, given in love and designed to bring change. Every time we neglect Jesus' offer of love or forgiveness, God's gift is returned unopened.

Jesus is God's gift to you this Christmas, and always. Accept him with gratitude and enjoy his presence in your life.

You have a Saviour

'"The virgin will conceive and give birth to a son, and they will call him Immanuel" (which means 'God with us').'

Matthew 1.23

Today you will probably hear Christmas carols – in church or piped out over loudspeakers in shopping centres, lifts and even car parks! People are being exposed to the amazing message of Christmas.

Carols may be extremely familiar to us, but we would do well to take to heart the central message being proclaimed – that God has sent us a Saviour, Jesus.

Many of us are beset by difficulties of one sort or another, such as illness, anxiety, fear or a host of other things, and wonder whether we have the capacity to deal with them. This is where the Christmas message becomes very real: God has sent us a Saviour – Jesus can help us.

It really is OK to acknowledge your difficulties and concerns and admit that you don't have what it takes to deal with them yourself. The good news is that you don't have to! Jesus is closer to you now than you can even imagine. Talk to him and share your heart with him.

God trusts you

'God sent the angel Gabriel to . . . Mary.'

Luke 1.26-27

We live in a different culture to that of Bible times, but it can still bring us up short to realise that God trusted a teenage girl with the salvation of the world! Of course, God was watching over Mary, but any number of things could have gone wrong. After all, she still had her free will – but God trusted her.

He trusts us as well. Our task may not have the same eternal significance as Mary's, but nevertheless God places a responsibility upon us all – the responsibility to be a temple of his Holy Spirit and to be people who bear his presence in whatever places and parts of the world we find ourselves. The nature and extent of our influence will vary from person to person and for some it may seem quite lowly, but the truth remains the same – we are those who carry God's presence into the special days ahead of us.

Take a moment to ponder this responsibility. Where will you be going today? Whose life will you touch? What will you bring to them? Take this calling seriously because God trusts you with it.

Christmas is about you!

"Today in the town of David a Saviour has been born to you; he is the Messiah, the Lord."

Luke 2.11

Who really benefits from Christmas? You may have heard comments such as, 'Christmas is for the children', 'Christmas is so important for the retail trade', 'Christmas is a wonderful time to show people that you love them'. These statements are only a part of the truth; Christmas is really about you!

God did not *require* Christmas, he has no need of a Saviour – but you do. God did not have to be born among us to discover the way – but you desperately need to know the way. As God looked at the circumstances of the whole world, and the demands upon your life, he saw that each of us really need Jesus.

Throughout this special day, amongst all the trappings that will characterise your Christmas, try to focus briefly every so often on these words: 'To me a Saviour is given' – not someone to judge you or spy on you, but someone to rescue you.

You can bring healing

'Fools show their annoyance at once, but the prudent overlook an insult . . . The words of the reckless pierce like swords, but the tongue of the wise brings healing.'

Proverbs 12.16, 18

We can all be involved in healing this Christmas! During this festive season, many of us are in the company of others, either at church or with family and friends, and this verse says that whenever we are with other people we have the opportunity to 'pierce' them or to bring healing.

It seems to come down to attitude. Do you tend to react quickly to what is said, perhaps finding yourself frustrated by people's comments and responding a little sharply? Or would you say you are generally able to hold your tongue, speak a soothing word, encourage others and build them up?

When Matthew reflected on the ministry of Jesus, he said: 'A bruised reed he will not break' (Matthew 12.20). In other words, Jesus seemed able to recognise that all people are hurting in some way, and maybe this is why we are all hesitant, weak and difficult at times. He seldom criticised people for being who they were, but loved them and sought to bring something of God to them.

This Boxing Day, if you are mingling with others, you will come up against some bruised and hurting people, and it is your attitude to them that will make all the difference. Try to use your tongue to bring comfort and encouragement, just like Jesus was with people.

God has come

"I would not have told the people of Israel to seek me if I could not be found."

Isaiah 45.19 (New Living Translation)

One of the most striking aspects of the Christmas story is the extent to which God has reached out to us. The simple truth of Christmas is this: out of his love, and out of his desperation to reach out to you so that you might take his hand, God came to you in the person of Jesus.

This is the key: Jesus has come. He is here already so you do not need to go looking for him, or travel to Bethlehem, or search for a stable to find him! He also promised that having come, he will be with you forever.

Spend a few moments now reminding yourself that Jesus is with you, waiting for you to acknowledge him, so pause before him and be still in his presence.

What's your response?

'Jesus knew that the Father had put all things under his power . . . so he got up from the meal, took off his outer clothing, and wrapped a towel round his waist.'

John 13.3-4

At this time of year, we focus on the very beginning of Jesus' life – yet the readings today and tomorrow occur towards the end of his life just before he washed the feet of his disciples.

It is highly likely that all of us believe that God has ultimate power – after all, being God must surely mean that he is all-powerful. However, the Christmas story reminds us of the second part of today's verse, that the all-powerful God came to earth, not as a ruler but as a servant.

The image of a baby in a manger is so vulnerable; a less likely picture of an omnipotent God we could not find! Yet it is this vulnerable image that is at the heart of our faith. In coming as a servant, Jesus made himself open to the risk of his service being rejected and people misunderstanding both him and his mission. We might be tempted to think that he could have been more effective if he had come in all his glory – at least then his message would not have been overlooked – but perhaps what he really wanted was for us to catch it out of choice, not out of force.

As you spend some time with Jesus now, he is with you as one who came to serve both his Father and you. What is your response to him?

Being part of God's story

"Unless I wash you, you have no part with me."

John 13.8

There is a lot of glitter and gloss around the season of Christmas, some of it wonderful, but some distracting. In the midst of it all, it can be easy to miss the central message that Jesus, our Saviour, has come into the world. It is also true that we can lose the personal impact of this message – that Jesus has come for us individually.

It was deeply personal for each of the disciples when Jesus washed their feet. It was not simply a demonstration for them to observe or a beneficial action. It was an incredibly meaningful moment for each of them. However, unless they chose to apply it personally they were going to miss out on so much – a relationship with Jesus.

This is a challenge for you at this special time of year: to find once again the relevance of the Saviour coming for you. Jesus wants you to reflect on this, to make it personal and to discover the joy of being part of his story.

364

Continue in what you have learned

'But as for you, continue in what you have learned and have become convinced of, because you know those from whom you learned it . . . '

2 Timothy 3.14

It can be very easy to assume that Christmas is over now: the decorations and the mood may continue, but the actual story has been heard. However, Paul's words to Timothy have a real relevance for us: 'continue in what you have learned'.

The message of Christmas is not for one day only; it has a relevance for every day. God sent Jesus out of his love for you and me, not to judge us but to rescue us. It can be easy to focus on this when we look at an image of the baby Jesus in a manger, but once we come back to real life – perhaps facing our struggles or sicknesses again – then the magical bits of Christmas can seem to fade away and we are faced with the harsher realities of life. This is why Paul encouraged Timothy to continue in his faith.

There are always times when we experience 'highs'. Things seem to go well, we sense a closeness to Jesus and it is easy to continue in what we have learned. Sadly there are also times when things are not so good; God may not seem so close and life does not seem to be working out quite as well. It is in these times that our tenacity and faith are called to the fore, and I suspect that it is when we are holding on to Jesus through gritted teeth that we move him so much.

God has been there

'Surely God is my help; the Lord is the one who sustains me.'

Psalm 54.4

This is a day when we can look back at the months and year that have passed and look forwards to the days and year ahead. As we do this, let's have these words from Psalm 54 undergirding us.

The first word, 'surely', conveys the sense that whatever else might be going on, the following words are certainly true: 'God is my help.'

This year may have been good, difficult or a bit of a mixture, but regardless of how it has been, there is one thing that has not changed: God has been there with you throughout. Not only has he been there but he has been at work, helping, sustaining and seeing you through – even if you couldn't really sense it at the time.

If you can look back and recognise this, it will give you confidence to look forwards to the year ahead, knowing that God – faithful, ever-present and sustaining – will be there as well. It is likely that the more you can see him in the past, the more you will be able to see him in the future.

Spend some time reflecting on the past year and turning as many memories as you can into praise and thanksgiving that Father God has been your help and your sustainer.

Index

Esther

22 September Esther 1.16

Job

27 August   Job 16.19
28 August   Job 16.19

Psalms (87)

15 December Psalm 1.1
22 August   Psalm 1.1-2
9 September Psalm 3.3
24 October   Psalm 16.8
10 May   Psalm 18.3
29 October   Psalm 25.7
1 June   Psalm 26.8
14 June   Psalm 27.1
6 November   Psalm 28.9
19 August   Psalm 31.19
8 November   Psalm 32.2
12 November Psalm 32.8
13 November Psalm 34.6
14 November Psalm 34.11-13
15 November Psalm 34.11-14
16 November Psalm 34.11-14
17 November Psalm 34.18
18 November Psalm 36.10
21 November Psalm 38.9
22 November Psalm 38.15
23 November Psalm 40.12
24 November Psalm 41.1
25 June   Psalm 42.1
26 November Psalm 45.11
4 September Psalm 46.10
5 September Psalm 46.10
6 August   Psalm 48. 4-5
27 November Psalm 50.2
28 November Psalm 50.11
31 December Psalm 54.4
4 December   Psalm 56.8
5 December   Psalm 56.9
6 December   Psalm 59.9
7 December   Psalm 59.9
9 December   Psalm 61.4
10 December Psalm 62.8

24 September Psalm 68.20
2 September   Psalm 78.20
5 January   Psalm 88.1
24 March   Psalm 88.6
8 January   Psalm 89.15
12 January   Psalm 90.8
13 January   Psalm 90.17
14 January   Psalm 91.1
15 January   Psalm 91.2
16 January   Psalm 92.2
19 January   Psalm 93.1
3 January   Psalm 93.2
16 June   Psalm 94.18-19
2 January   Psalm 97.1
31 January   Psalm 98.1
3 February   Psalm 100.2
4 February   Psalm 100.4
8 February   Psalm 103.14
10 February Psalm 104.34
13 February Psalm 105.4
18 February Psalm 113.4
25 February Psalm 119.24
1 September   Psalm 119.58
2 March   Psalm 119.64
3 March   Psalm 119.81
5 March   Psalm 119.91
6 March   Psalm 119.91
17 March   Psalm 119.126
21 March   Psalm 119.173
10 April   Psalm 130.2
27 March   Psalm 130.6
11 April   Psalm 131.2
12 April   Psalm 136.26
20 April   Psalm 137.4
27 April   Psalm 137.7
29 April   Psalm 138.1
17 May   Psalm 138.6
23 April   Psalm 139.1
21 September Psalm 139.6
19 March   Psalm 139.7
12 May   Psalm 139.12
15 May   Psalm 140.12
18 May   Psalm 141.2
19 May   Psalm 141.2

24 May	Psalm 142.3
27 May	Psalm 143.1
2 June	Psalm 144.3-4
6 June	Psalm 146.5
8 June	Psalm 147.3-5
9 June	Psalm 147.11

Proverbs
18 June	Proverbs 3.3
20 June	Proverbs 4.23
24 June	Proverbs 5.1
11 July	Proverbs 9.1-2
13 July	Proverbs 10.12
21 July	Proverbs 11.1
26 December	Proverbs 12.16, 18
10 September	Proverbs 13.7

Song of Solomon
| 12 August | Song of Songs 2.4 |

Isaiah
22 December	Isaiah 9.6
27 December	Isaiah 45.19
16 August	Isaiah 48.17
13 August	Isaiah 63.16

Lamentations
| 1 January | Lam 3.22-23 |

Ezekiel
| 29 November | Ezekiel 34.4 |
| 1 April | Ezekiel 36.22 |

Daniel
| 3 October | Daniel 9.18 |

Hosea
| 28 September | Hosea 4.7 |

Haggai
| 26 August | Haggai 2.19 |

Zechariah
15 June	Zechariah 4.6
10 November	Zechariah 4.10
30 October	Zechariah 8.6

Matthew
23 December	Matthew 1.23
6 January	Matthew 2.2
20 November	Matthew 5.13
21 October	Matthew 5.44-45
22 October	Matthew 6.6
10 July	Matthew 7.1
6 September	Matthew 7.2
28 October	Matthew 9.18
7 September	Matthew 10.30
11 February	Matthew 11.27
11 November	Matthew 12.10-12
31 October	Matthew 12.20
1 November	Matthew 12.20
19 September	Matthew 13.17
19 November	Matthew 15.27
11 May	Matthew 15.38
13 September	Matthew 24.6

Mark
7 April	Mark 1.29-31
8 April	Mark 1.29-31
9 April	Mark 1.29-31
5 May	Mark 1.40
6 May	Mark 1.44
7 May	Mark 1.40-41
8 May	Mark 1.41
9 May	Mark 1.44
29 March	Mark 4.8
13 June	Mark 5.36
4 January	Mark 6.52
11 January	Mark 8.11
17 January	Mark 8.34
25 January	Mark 10.27
26 January	Mark 10.29-30
1 February	Mark 10.45
20 September	Mark 12.14
15 February	Mark 14.6

Luke

24 December	Like 1.26-27
28 February	Luke 2.11
25 December	Luke 2.11
18 March	Luke 5.17
28 March	Luke 5.24-25
22 March	Luke 6.35
23 March	Luke 6.35
25 April	Luke 9.48
26 April	Luke 9.48
28 April	Luke 10.5
21 April	Luke 10.13
16 February	Luke 10.19
13 May	Luke 10.33
14 May	Luke 10.36-37
20 May	Luke 11.2
21 May	Luke 11.5
28 May	Luke 11.34
7 June	Luke 12.6-7
17 June	Luke 13.18
19 June	Luke 14.1
22 June	Luke 14.17-18
27 June	Luke 14.33
5 August	Luke 15.1
15 July	Luke 15.12
16 July	Luke 15.14
17 July	Luke 15.22
12 July	Luke 16.10
14 July	Luke 16.31
19 July	Luke 17.7-10
23 July	Luke 17.14
24 July	Luke 17.16
25 July	Luke 17.19
19 December	Luke 18.4-5
20 December	Luke 18.7
21 December	Luke 18.8
28 July	Luke 18.13
14 September	Luke 18.27
9 November	Luke 18.37-38
2 February	Luke 19.5
7 November	Luke 22.14

John

23 September	John 4.34
10 January	John 5.24
30 April	John 5.42
9 August	John 6.26
27 February	John 9.5
30 March	John 10.10
31 March	John 10.10
2 April	John 11.21-22
28 December	John 13.3-4
29 December	John 13.8
16 December	John 15.8
29 September	John 16.23
4 October	John 16.32
2 October	John 16.33
14 February	John 17.26
4 May	John 20.21
17 December	John 20.28
5 October	John 20.29
14 December	John 21.22

Acts

18 October	Acts 1.7
29 August	Acts 3.6
8 September	Acts 4.13
23 October	Acts 9.17
25 October	Acts 9.38
14 August	Acts 20.23

Romans

7 August	Romans 1.16
1 December	Luke 5.2
2 December	Romans 5.3
3 December	Romans 5.17
12 December	Romans 11.36
3 April	Romans 15.30

1 Corinthians

25 March	1 Corinthians 11.23
26 March	1 Corinthians 11.24
7 January	1 Corinthians 12.11
9 January	1 Corinthians 12.15
29 February	1 Corinthians 15.10

2 Corinthians

21 January	2 Corinthians 1.3
22 January	2 Corinthians 1.4
24 January	2 Corinthians 1.20
27 January	2 Corinthians 2.14
28 January	2 Corinthians 2.15
8 March	2 Corinthians 3.6
5 February	2 Corinthians 6.1
6 February	2 Corinthians 6.2
9 February	2 Corinthians 8.16
12 February	2 Corinthians 9.8
29 January	2 Corinthians 10.4

Galatians

2 May	Galatians 2.20
19 February	Galatians 3.26
20 February	Galatians 5.1

Ephesians

27 October	Ephesians 1.4
24 February	Ephesians 1.11
26 February	Ephesians 2.4
11 August	Ephesians 2.10
25 August	Ephesians 4.31
15 August	Ephesians 4.32-5.1
9 March	Ephesians 6.13
10 March	Ephesians 6.14
11 March	Ephesians 6.14
12 March	Ephesians 6.15
13 March	Ephesians 6.16
14 March	Ephesians 6.17
15 March	Ephesians 6.17
16 March	Ephesians 6.18

Philippians

20 March	Philippians 2.21
1 March	Philippians 4.4

Colossians

22 May	Colossians 1.22
23 May	Colossians 1.22-23
4 April	Colossians 1.29
5 April	Colossians 2.10
18 January	Colossians 2.13
6 April	Colossians 3.12

1 Thessalonians

19 April	1 Thessalonians 2.4
10 August	1 Thessalonians 2.13
24 April	1 Thessalonians 2.19
30 January	1 Thessalonians 5.9
12 September	1 Thessalonians 5.15
25 May	1 Thessalonians 5.18
26 May	1 Thessalonians 5.23

2 Thessalonians

3 June	2 Thessalonians 1.1
29 May	2 Thessalonians 1.4

1 Timothy

4 June	1 Timothy 1.1
11 September	1 Timothy 1.15
17 August	1 Timothy 2.6
23 June	1 Timothy 3.13
21 August	1 Timothy 4.7
29 July	1 Timothy 6.11
30 July	1 Timothy 6.11
31 July	1 Timothy 6.11
1 August	1 Timothy 6.11
2 August	1 Timothy 6.11
3 August	1 Timothy 6.11
4 August	1 Timothy 6.11

2 Timothy

20 July	2 Timothy 1.8
7 July	2 Timothy 2.1
8 July	2 Timothy 2.9
9 July	2 Timothy 2.13
30 December	2 Timothy 3.14
16 September	2 Timothy 4.2

Titus

18 September	Titus 1.4
8 August	Titus 3.1

Philemon

22 April	Philemon 6

James

| 18 August | James 4.1 |

1 Peter

| 12 June | 1 Peter 1.6-7 |
| 24 August | 1 Peter 2.11 |

2 Peter

28 June	2 Peter 1.3
29 June	2 Peter 1.5
30 June	2 Peter 1.5
1 July	2 Peter 1.5-6
2 July	2 Peter 1.6
3 July	2 Peter 1.6
4 July	2 Peter 1.5-7
5 July	2 Peter 1.5-7
23 August	2 Peter 3.18

1 John

25 September	1 John 2.1
26 September	1 John 2.2
20 August	1 John 4.4
27 September	1 John 4.18
17 October	1 John 5.14-15

Revelation

1 October	Revelation 1.4
20 October	Revelation 1.9-10
30 September	Revelation 3.18
18 December	Revelation 4.11